CONTEMPORARY
Black
Biography

CONTEMPORARY

*B*lack

*B*iography

Profiles from the International Black Community

Volume 63

THOMSON

GALE

Detroit • New York • San Francisco • New Haven, Conn. • Waterville, Maine • London

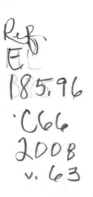

Contemporary Black Biography, Volume 63
Sara and Tom Pendergast

Project Editors
Pamela M. Kalte, Margaret Mazurkiewicz

Image Research and Acquisitions
Leitha Etheridge-Sims

Editorial Support Services
Nataliya Mikheyeva

Rights and Permissions
Mollika Basu, Aja Perales, Jhanay Williams

Manufacturing
Dorothy Maki, Cynde Bishop

Composition and Prepress
Mary Beth Trimper, Tracey L. Matthews

Imaging
Lezlie Light

ISBN 13: 978-0-7876-7935-4
ISBN 10: 0-7876-7935-6
ISSN 1058-1316

This title is also available as an e-book.
eISBN 13: 978-1-4144-3282-3
eISBN-10: 1-4144-3282-8
Please contact your Gale sales representative
for ordering information.

Printed in the United States of America
10 9 8 7 6 5 4 3 2 1

Advisory Board

Contents

Introduction

Contemporary Black Biography provides informative biographical profiles of the important and influential persons of African heritage who form the international black community: men and women who have changed today's world and are shaping tomorrow's. *Contemporary Black Biography* covers persons of various nationalities in a wide variety of fields, including architecture, art, business, dance, education, fashion, film, industry, journalism, law, literature, medicine, music, politics and government, publishing, religion, science and technology, social issues, sports, television, theater, and others. In addition to in-depth coverage of names found in today's headlines, *Contemporary Black Biography* provides coverage of selected individuals from earlier in this century whose influence continues to impact on contemporary life. *Contemporary Black Biography* also provides coverage of important and influential persons who are not yet household names and are therefore likely to be ignored by other biographical reference series. Each volume also includes listee updates on names previously appearing in *CBB*.

Designed for Quick Research and Interesting Reading

- **Attractive page design** incorporates textual subheads, making it easy to find the information you're looking for.
- **Easy-to-locate data sections** provide quick access to vital personal statistics, career information, major awards, and mailing addresses, when available.
- **Informative biographical essays** trace the subject's personal and professional life with the kind of in-depth analysis you need.
- **To further enhance your appreciation** of the subject, most entries include photographic portraits.
- **Sources for additional information** direct the user to selected books, magazines, and newspapers where more information on the individuals can be obtained.

Helpful Indexes Make It Easy to Find the Information You Need

Contemporary Black Biography includes cumulative Nationality, Occupation, Subject, and Name indexes that make it easy to locate entries in a variety of useful ways.

Available in Electronic Formats

Diskette/Magnetic Tape. Contemporary Black Biography is available for licensing on magnetic tape or diskette in a fielded format. Either the complete database or a custom selection of entries may be ordered. The database is available for internal data processing and nonpublishing purposes only. For more information, call (800) 877-GALE.

On-line. Contemporary Black Biography is available on-line through Mead Data Central's NEXIS Service in the NEXIS, PEOPLE and SPORTS Libraries in the GALBIO file and Gale's Biography Resource Center.

Disclaimer

Contemporary Black Biography uses and lists websites as sources and these websites may become obsolete.

We Welcome Your Suggestions

The editors welcome your comments and suggestions for enhancing and improving *Contemporary Black Biography*. If you would like to suggest persons for inclusion in the series, please submit these names to the editors. Mail comments or suggestions to:

The Editor

Contemporary Black Biography

The Gale Group

27500 Drake Rd.

Farmington Hills, MI 48331-3535

Phone: (800) 347-4253

Laila Ali

1977—

Boxer

From the shadow of her famous father, Muhammad Ali, Laila "She Bee Stingin'" Ali emerged as a pioneer in boxing in her own rite. Ali refused to rely on name-recognition alone; she took the boxing world by storm, using grace, athleticism, and determination to pave the way not only for herself, but for female fighters worldwide. From her first world title in 2002, Ali added two more by 2004, and became the first woman to win a World Boxing Council super middleweight title in 2005.

Ali, Laila, photograph. Frederick M. Brown/Getty Images.

came restless and rebellious. She disliked high school and was caught stealing her mother's car on more than one occasion. In 1995, she was arrested for shoplifting and spent three months in juvenile hall. Prior to that, Ali was spending considerable time in the seedy areas of Los Angeles. "Everyone else was trying to get out of the ghetto," Laila told writers Alex Tresniowski and Kelly Carter of People. com. "I was trying to get in."

Captivated by Women's Boxing

Troubled Youth

Born on December 30, 1977, in Miami Beach, California, Laila Ali was one of two daughters her former heavyweight champion father had with Veronica Anderson, the third of his four different wives. Her parents divorced when she was eight years old. She grew up in Los Angeles' Hancock Park area with her mother and sister, Hana.

It was Ali's sister, Hana, who was the aggressor, typically roughhousing with her little sister. Ali was described as quiet, usually keeping to herself and playing with dolls. During her teenage years, Ali be-

Ali started working at a beauty salon in Marina Del Ray. By 1996, she had her own nail salon. It was at that time when Ali saw women's boxing champ Christy Martin on television. Ali recalled to Aldore Collier of *Ebony* that the women's bout took her by surprise. "I remember thinking, 'Oh, my God! Oh, my God! Women are about to fight.' I had the popcorn and was getting ready to watch Mike Tyson. I was looking around like, 'What's going on? Women fighting?' I was so excited I couldn't wait to see it. I was like, 'I can do that.'" Inspired, Ali began a rigorous training regimen, including daily two-mile runs and two-hour gym workouts. That summer, she spent a couple months at her

At a Glance . . .

Born on December 30, 1977, in Miami Beach, California; daughter of Veronica Anderson and Muhammad Ali; married Johnny "Yahya" McClain (her manager), 2000 (divorced 2005); married Curtis Conway (former NFL wide receiver), 2007. *Education:* Attended Santa Monica College, business management, AA, late 1990s.

Career: Nail salon, owner, 1990s; professional boxer, 1999–.

Awards: International Boxing Association super middleweight championship, 2002; Women's International Boxing Association and International Women's Boxing Federation championships, 2002; International Women's Boxing Federation light heavyweight title, 2004; World Boxing Council super middleweight title, 2005.

Addresses: *Web*—www.lailaali.us.

father's 81-acre spread in Berrien Springs, Michigan, training and getting tips from the former champ.

After two years of working with her father, Ali would be ready to break into the ranks of female boxing. She had her debut match on October 15, 1999 against April Fowler in the casino ballroom of an upstate New York Indian reservation. Ali needed only 31 seconds to dispose of her opponent. "After a left-right to the jaw knocked April clear back to last February, the 21-year-old Ali cocked her fists and glowered over her opponent, screaming 'Get up! Get up!' just as her old man hollered over Sonny Liston 34 years ago," *Sports Illustrated's* Franz Lidz wrote.

Lidz observed that in the ring, Laila Ali has the similar characteristics of her father, while incorporating her own personality. Under the nickname "Madame Butterfly," Ali impressed many with her boxing debut. "Madame Butterfly is brash, brazen and almost as pretty as her pop," Lidz wrote. "At 5'10" and 168 pounds, she can mimic the Greatest's routines—biting her lips as if seething in anger, feigning outrage with widened unblinking eyes—and she certainly shares his playfulness. Asked if she feared being punched on the nose, Laila said 'I have a cute nose already. If it's moved a little to the left or a little to the right, it will still be cute.'"

Ali made her transition to mainstream women's boxing shortly thereafter. She won her second bout on November 10, 1999 at the Mountaineer Race Track in Chester, West Virginia, scoring a technical knockout against Shadina Pennybaker with just three seconds left in the fight.

Exactly one month later, at Cobo Riverfront Ballroom in Detroit, more than 2,200 people watched as Ali ran her record to 3-0. Ali knocked Nicolyn Armstrong down late in the first round with a jab, and followed up with three hard rights. In the second round, according to geocities.com, "Ali battered Armstrong in a corner then knocked her flat on her back." The referee stopped the fight at that point and Ali walked away with the winner's purse of $25,000.

On March 7, 2000, Ali went to a record of 4-0 at the Casino Windsor in Windsor, Ontario. She knocked out countrywoman Crystal Arcand after one minute and ten seconds in the first round. Her opponent started the bout swinging wildly while Ali circled and landed an uppercut combination that sent Arcand to the mat. Ali continued the attack and sent her to the canvas again, this time with a straight right to the head. "I underestimated her," Arcand told geocities.com. "She's got the power and she can back it up. I've never experienced a woman with the amount of power she has."

Emerged as a Powerhouse

With four professional wins and all of them knockouts, Ali appeared unstoppable. But when she stepped in the ring at Detroit's Joe Louis Arena on April 8, 2000 against Karen Bill, Ali was brought down to the earth. Bill knocked Ali down in the second round with an uppercut. Even thought she quickly got up and began fighting again, Bill kept tagging Ali with sharp jabs to end the second round. Ali opened a cut above Bill's eye in the third before the referee ended the fight in Ali's favor.

Two weeks later, Ali would defend her unbeaten record against 166-pound Kristina King on April 22nd at Tian He Stadium in Guangzhou, People's Republic of China. Ali battered King in the second round and bloodied her in the third, a round where a booming right from Ali knocked out King's mouthpiece. King came out for the fourth round, but the fight was stopped. *Jet* magazine highlighted the fight, which was Ali's hometown boxing debut: "Ali needed just 68 seconds to put down the 48-year-old Jones as Ali's famous father Muhammad Ali and his former heavyweight rivals sat ringside. The 22-year-old Ali knocked down Jones three times, the last time with a right to the head. The referee didn't bother to count."

About 3,500 fans where in the audience to see the fight, which was on the Oba Carr-Juan Soberanes undercard (an undercard is a boxing match that takes place before the main event). After the fight, Ali told *Jet* she was a little disappointed that the bout didn't go into later rounds. "I feel good, but of course, I would have liked it to last longer," Ali said. "I told the referee to let me knock her out."

Ali's winning streak continued on June 15th at the Universal Amphitheater in Los Angeles when she knocked out 173-pound Marjorie Jones. Her trainer, Deb Huntly, told geocities.com that Ali's intense work regimen and focus on the sport is the foundation to her success. Huntly added that Ali's best punch is a right hand into a left hook. Ali is said to train three hours a day, six days a week. She runs three to four miles daily, jumps rope, spars, and works on punching bags in order to keep up with the super-middleweights.

That work paid off again for Ali on October 13th in Auburn Hills, Michigan. On the undercard of the Mike Tyson-Andrew Golota fight, Ali won a decision against Kendra Lenhart, going the distance for six rounds. *Detroit Free Press* sports writer Steve Crowe wrote that the first three rounds of the fight had Lenhart clearly ahead of Ali. "For the first three rounds of Ali's six-round survival victory by decision, Lenhart, 34, pressed most of the early action and landed the harder shots," Crowe wrote. "But stamina and punching flurries, especially to Lenhart's body, served Ali well in the later stages." The win moved Ali's record to 8-0, with seven knockouts.

Boosted Women's Boxing

In these first years of Ali's boxing career, women's boxing was a fledgling sport. Ali used her famous name to increase the popularity and legitimacy of the sport with the much-hyped bout between her and Jacqui Frazier-Lyde, the daughter of Joe Frazier in 2001. Touted as a "grudge match" because of three historic fights between their fathers in the 1970s, the "Ali vs. Frazier IV" bout attracted a crowd of 6,500 to the Turning Stone Casino resort on the Oneida Indian Nation Reservation near Syracuse, New York. While the two put on a good show, slugging each other toe-to-toe with impressive intensity, no one suggested that the daughters fought with the skill or power of their fathers. "The two women proved to have more game and more heart than many might have expected," *Washington Post* reporter Jennifer Frey wrote, adding that they finished the last round "with a burst of punches that had the crowd on its feet." "We're not the most skilled fighters," Ali admitted to Lynn Snowden Pickett in an interview for *Vogue.* "I would never disrespect my dad and Joe Frazier by saying this is the same type of fight. Those are two gold-medal winners from the Olympics, great fighters who have proved themselves, and we're just beginners." Both were undefeated, but Ali had only fought nine times and Frazier only seven. After the eight scheduled rounds, Ali was declared the winner by majority decision. Frazier declared after the fight that "we made our contribution to elevate the sport," according to *Jet.* Indeed, Collier called it "biggest shot in the arm that women's boxing has received to date." Ali acknowl-

edged the benefit of public attention that the bout brought women's boxing, but announced her intention to now go after championship belts.

Ali quickly realized her goal. In September 2002, she won her first world title. She nabbed the International Boxing Association super middleweight championship belt after a second round technical knockout of Suzy Taylor. After the fight, Ali declared her title quest continued: her targets, according to *Jet,* "the girls that have belts."

By November of that year, Ali added the Women's International Boxing Association and International Women's Boxing Federation championships her title list with a win over Valerie Mahfood in the first women's boxing match to be an ESPN main event. Ali held onto her titles when she defeated Mahfood with a technical knockout in a rematch in July of 2003.

As Ali racked up titles, women's boxing continued to grow in popularity. For Ali's bout to defend her IBA super middleweight championship against former *Sports Illustrated* model Christy Martin in August of 2003 a crowd of more than 9,000 filled the Mississippi Coast Coliseum in Biloxi and was available on pay-per-view. The two were the most popular women boxers at the time, and their fight garnered the most media attention for women's boxing since the Ali-Frazier bout in 2001. Ali, who had predicted that the fight would not last more than four rounds in her taunts before the match, proved her dominance in the sport after flattening Martin with a knockout within the first minute of the fourth round.

Her famous name, good looks, and successful defense of her titles kept Ali in the limelight. "From the standpoint of public image and anything that might be described as public appeal, Laila Ali is women's boxing," boxing commentator Jim Lampley told Jake Schaller of the *Washington Post.* Businesses took notice. Adidas signed Ali to a multi-year endorsement deal in 2003. "Laila is an inspiration to women and all athletes that aspire to break new ground," said Erich Stamminger, Adidas-Salomon executive board member responsible for global marketing, according to *Sporting Goods Business.* Ali agreed, saying, according to Schaller, "My presence in the game has made so much of a difference that people probably don't even recognize. The growth takes a long time, but since I've been boxing, I've seen women boxing on music videos, in ads for anti-perspirant. It's not so much thought of to be for gay women or rough women or ugly women, it's more of an empowerment thing. People see it differently all together." Ali did more to promote herself and her sport, signing more endorsement deals with such companies as Dr. Pepper and Ford. She even published an inspirational autobiography entitled *Reach! Finding Strength, Spirit, and Personal Power* in 2003.

The media buzz continued when Ali racked up more wins. She won the International Women's Boxing

Federation light heavyweight title after a third round knockout of Guyana's Gwendolyn O'Neil in Atlanta in October 2004. And in 2005, she became the first woman to win a World Boxing Council super middleweight title. The title fight against her opponent Erin Toughill ended with Ali delivering a technical knockout in the last second of the third round. Ali, who left Toughill bloodied, noted her own ferocity during the fight, telling Dan Steinberg of the *Washington Post* that "people are not used to seeing me hit my opponent like that." But her father, who drew the attention of the crowd even more than his victorious daughter, approved, saying simply, "She's bad," according to Steinberg. Ali fought her first bout in Madison Square Garden in 2006, with her famous father ringside. In a historic first, HBO televised a short clip of her fourth round technical knockout of Shelley Burton. The following year, Ali headlined with Gwendolyn O'Neil in the first women's professional boxing match in South Africa.

Sought Other Challenges

With a 24-0 career record with 21 knockouts, Ali found little competition in boxing. She decided to seek out a completely different type of competition in 2007, when she joined the reality television show *Dancing with the Stars*. Ali moved with a polished grace that belied her massive, muscled frame and she charmed audiences. She and professional dance partner Maksim Chmerkovskiy earned a perfect score for their rumba, yet finished the competition in third place. For the finale, Ali dedicated her last dance to her father, who sat admiringly in the audience. About her experience on the show, Ali admitted to syndicated columnist Kam Williams in the *Tennessee Tribune* that "it was a nice change for me, to do something glamorous, but challenging."

Competition seemed to be a driving force for Ali. She explained to Williams in 2007 that in her boxing career she had "definitely reached my goals." "Unfortunately," she added, "it's left a void in how I feel about my career, because it wasn't as challenging as I would have liked it to have been on the way up." She concluded "I'm pretty much where I thought I'd be right now, undefeated and a world champion." With her retirement on the horizon, Ali began seeking various other business opportunities, making a documentary *Daddy's Girl* for PBS and workout videos with boxing great Sugar Ray Leonard. She also hinted at starting a

family with her husband Curtis Conway, whom she wed in 2007. Whatever Ali's next step might be, she will certainly take it with the same confidence and vigor that enabled her come out from behind the shadow of her father's greatness to create her own.

Selected works

Books

Reach! Finding Strength, Spirit, and Personal Power, Hyperion, 2003.

Films

Daddy's Girl (documentary).

Television

Dancing with the Stars, 2007.

Sources

Periodicals

Ebony, October 2001, p. 164.
Jet, July 3, 2000, pg. 52; June 25, 2001, p. 51; September 2, 2002, p. 51; October 18, 2004, p. 51; September 12, 2005, p. 54; July 9, 2007, p. 54.
Los Angeles Times, October 26, 2005, p. D1.
New York Times, November 9, 2002, p. D4.
People, May 7, 2007, p. 124.
Savoy, April-May 2005, p. 76.
Sentinel (Los Angeles), August 28, 2003, p. B3.
Spokesman Review, August 23, 2003, p. C1.
Sporting Goods Business, October 2003, p. 18.
Sports Illustrated, Oct. 18, 1999, pg. R1.
Sports Illustrated Women, December 2002-January 2003, p. 112.
Tennessee Tribune, June 14-20, 2007, p. 33.
Time Magazine, May 1, 2007, pg. 66.
Vogue, April 2002, p. 292.
Washington Post, June 9, 2001, p. C1; July 16, 2004, p. D1; June 12, 2005, p. E17.

On-line

Laila Ali, www.lailaali.us (September 5, 2007).

—Sara Pendergast

Norman Carey Amaker

1935-2000

Law professor, civil rights activist

Norman C. Amaker had several things in common with Dr. Martin Luther King, Jr. For one, they shared a birthday. More importantly, they shared a passion for and a commitment to social justice and a burning desire to make the legal structures of the United States pay attention to matters of race and discrimination. During some of the civil rights movement's key moments, Amaker served as King's attorney. As a leading legal scholar on civil rights matters, it could be argued that Amaker represented an entire nation.

Norman Carey Amaker was born on January 15, 1935, in New York, New York, and grew up in the predominantly black Harlem section of the city. He was raised in a politically engaged household. His parents, Gladys and Carey Amaker, were social activists who worked on various issues through their church. As a teen, Amaker often worked with his father on these projects, passing out leaflets and helping with other tasks. During his youth, Amaker was strongly influenced by the work of Adam Clayton Powell, Jr., the noted Harlem minister, community activities, and, eventually, Congressman.

Worked under Marshall at NAACP

After finishing high school, Amaker went to Amherst College in Massachusetts, where he graduated with honors in 1956. He then moved back to New York and enrolled in law school at Columbia University. He received his law degree from Columbia in 1959, at a time when the civil rights movement was in high gear. He immediately immersed himself in the movement.

Fresh out of law school, Amaker was hired by Thurgood Marshall—who went on to become the first black U.S. Supreme Court Justice—as a staff attorney for the NAACP Legal Defense and Educational Fund.

At the NAACP Legal Defense and Educational Fund, Amaker played a role in many important civil rights cases during the early 1960s. He served as counsel for the plaintiffs in cases challenging racial discrimination in every corner of society, including public schools, housing, jury selection, elections, and employment. He represented thousands of civil rights protesters in the South, arguing cases at every level of the judicial system, all the way up to the U.S. Supreme Court. Amaker's highest-profile client was Dr. Martin Luther King, Jr., whom he represented in both Birmingham and Selma, Alabama. When King wrote his famous essay on law and justice, "Letter from a Birmingham Jail," in 1963, it was Amaker who delivered the document from the jailhouse to the printer to be disseminated to the public. As busy as he was standing up for the civil rights of black Americans in the South, Amaker found time for a social life. In 1962 he married Mattie Jeannette Owens. The couple eventually had three children: Alicia, Alana, and Arthur.

In 1967 Amaker published his first book on civil rights, titled *Civil Rights and Civil Liberties*. The following year, he was promoted to first assistant counsel at the NAACP Legal Defense and Educational Fund, a position he held for three years. He left the organization in 1971 to become executive director of the Neighborhood Legal Services Program in Washington, DC. He switched jobs again in 1973, when he accepted a

At a Glance . . .

Born Norman Carey Amaker on January 15, 1935, in New York, NY; died on June 7, 2000; married Mattie Jeannette Owens, 1962; children: Alicia, Alana, Arthur. *Education:* Amherst College, BA, 1956; Columbia University, JD, 1959.

Career: NAACP Legal Defense and Educational Fund, New York, NY, staff attorney, 1960-68, first assistant counsel, 1968-71; Neighborhood Legal Services Program, Washington, DC, executive director, 1971-73; National Committee Against Discrimination in Housing, Washington, DC, general counsel, 1973; Rutgers University, New Jersey, professor of law, 1973-76; Loyola University, Chicago, IL, professor of law, 1976-2000.

Memberships: Society of American Law Teachers, board of directors, 1979-86.

Awards: IBPOE of W (Elks Club) award, 1965; BALSA award, 1973; Faculty Member of the Year, Loyola University, 1995.

position as general counsel for the National Committee Against Discrimination in Housing. After just a short time there, however, Amaker felt the pull of the field he would work in for the rest of his career, education. In the fall of 1973, he was hired as a professor of law at Rutgers University in New Jersey. Amaker taught at Rutgers until 1976, when he accepted a professorship at Loyola University in Chicago, where he would remain for the duration of his career and his life.

Established Himself as Leading Legal Scholar

At Loyola, Amaker further established himself as a leading authority on civil rights law and federal civil procedures. He taught courses in civil rights law, civil procedure, federal jurisdiction, and constitution law. He was also a prolific writer, publishing articles on his areas of expertise in leading law journals and other periodicals. In 1986, the same year Martin Luther King, Jr., Day became a national holiday, Amaker was instrumental in establishing an annual Dr. Martin Luther King, Jr., Lecture Series at Loyola. Amaker himself delivered the first lecture in the series. He delivered another in 1993. While he was solidifying his national reputation, Amaker was also involved in local

and professional politics. He served on his local school board from 1980 to 1987, and on the board of governors of the Society of American Law Teachers from 1979 to 1987.

Amaker gained national attention with the 1988 publication of his book *Civil Rights and the Reagan Administration*, a highly critical analysis of the federal government's record in enforcing civil rights laws during the Reagan presidency. He followed that up with a paper, initially delivered at a 1990 conference and later published by the American Law Institute, called "The Faithfulness of the Carter Administration in Enforcing Civil Rights."

In 1990 Amaker worked with Linda Greene, a law professor at the University of Wisconsin, to co-found the Midwestern People of Color Legal Scholarship Conference, an annual meeting at which scholars gather to discuss the work of professors of color teaching and researching at law schools across the Midwest. The success of the conference led others to develop similar events in other parts of the country.

Untimely Death Sparked Honors

By the 1990s, Amaker was regularly receiving honors for his long career as both an expert on and activist in civil rights. In 1995 he was named Faculty Member of the Year by Loyola. The following year, he was a Distinguished Visiting Professor at William Mitchell Law School in St. Paul, Minnesota.

Amaker died unexpected at his Skokie, Illinois, home on June 7, 2000. After his death, Amaker's memory was honored in a number of ways by a variety of individuals and institutions. On November 29, 2000, the Illinois House of Representatives passed a resolution officially mourning his death. The Midwestern People of Color Legal Scholarship Conference, which he had co-founded a decade earlier, named an award after Amaker. And the Society of American Law Teachers named its annual Midwest Public Interest Law Retreat after him. Chicago Mayor Richard M. Daley proclaimed January 15, 2001 to be Norman C. Amaker Day. That day—which also happened to be the Martin Luther King, Jr., holiday—Loyola held a memorial celebration of Amaker's life. The people of Chicago had two important civil rights leaders to honor that day.

Selected writings

Books

Civil Liberties & Civil Rights, Oceana, 1967.
Civil Rights and the Reagan Administration, Urban Institute, 1988.

Sources

Periodicals

Chicago Tribune, June 10, 2000, p. 23.
Los Angeles Times, January 20, 1989, p. 1.

On-line

"House Journal, House of Representatives, Ninety-First General Assembly, 130th Legislative Day, Wednesday, November 29, 2000—House Resolution 940," *Illinois General Assembly,* www.ilga.gov/house/journals/hdailyjrnls91/hjd91130_r.html (August 10, 2007).

"In Memoriam: Norman C. Amaker (1935-2000)," *Loyola University School of Law,* www.luc.edu/law/faculty/amaker.html (August 10, 2007).

"News Release: Loyola School of Law to Honor Amaker during Martin Luther King, Jr., Celebration," *Loyola University Chicago,* www.luc.edu/news/releases/2001/january/amaker.html (July 5, 2007).

"Who Is Norman Amaker?" *6th Annual Norman Amaker Public Interest Law and Social Justice Retreat,* http://indylaw.indiana.edu/clinics/amaker/whois.htm (August 10, 2007).

—Bob Jacobson

Emma Amos

1938—

Artist

In her acclaimed paintings and prints, artist Emma Amos explores themes of feminism, race, and culture. Beginning her career in the early 1960s, Amos developed a style that was influenced by the abstract expressionist movement and by the civil rights movement. Many of her works deal with overtly political content, including the exclusion of women from full participation in society, the enduring negative stereotypes of racism, and the legacy of colonialism. Hailed for its feeling, intellect, and vibrancy, her work has been exhibited across the country and is held in the collections of several leading museums.

Born in Atlanta, Georgia, where her father was a pharmacist, Amos grew up in a middle-class home with parents who encouraged her artistic aspirations. From her earliest childhood she loved to draw, and her talent was apparent to her grade school classmates and teachers, who asked her to copy pictures for them. As Amos explained in an interview with Al Murray in *Smithsonian Archives of American Art,* she taught herself by looking at pictures in magazines. It wasn't until she enrolled as an art student at Antioch College that she began to realize that "I wasn't the best thing in the world, that there were people who didn't learn how to draw from [copying] Vargas girls [in magazines], who knew what drawing really was and that it wasn't just a technical thing, that there was something to it."

Turned to Printmaking, Design

Though Amos loved Antioch, she became truly inspired when she took art courses in England at the London Central School of Art. She studied there during her senior year at Antioch, and returned for two more years of training. "I was surrounded by real painters and it was wonderful," she commented to Murray. She also became fascinated by printmaking. "I really think I found and stopped worrying about myself as an artist my second year in England," she observed. "Etching and the whole idea of printmaking and having a handsome, a well-thought-out and finished work that satisfies you. Well, I sort of discovered color then too. I think the main thing about my painting now stems from then and it was the discovery of color."

On returning to the United States, Amos moved to New York City, where she got a job teaching at the Dalton School. Not able to produce much art during this time, she left Dalton after a few years to try her hand at designing. Having taken a few weaving courses at Antioch, Amos landed work as a rug designer and textile weaver. Many of the resulting works, Amos told Murray, "were counted as art...They're very modern real life paintings."

In the early 1960s Amos was asked to join Spiral, an organization of African-American artists formed by Romare Bearden. Its goals were to affirm black artistic identity in a white-dominated art world and to provide a forum for members to discuss issues relating to art, politics, and culture. Amos was the only female member of this group, with which she began exhibiting lithographs and silkscreen prints. Amos was also back in school during this period, studying lithography at New York University, where she earned a master's degree in 1966.

Born on March 16, 1938, in Atlanta, GA. *Education:* Antioch College, BA, 1958; London Central School of Art, diploma, 1960; New York University, MA, 1965.

Career: WGBH-TV, Boston, MA, *Show of Hands*, creator, writer, and co-host, 1977-1978; Mason Gross School of the Arts, Rutgers University, New Brunswick, NJ, professor of art, 1980–, undergraduate director, 1994–.

Memberships: Skowhegan [ME] School of Painting and Sculpture, board of governors; Richard Florsheim Art Fund, trustee.

Awards: National Endowment for the Arts fellowship, 1983; New York Foundation for the Arts fellowship, 1989; Rockefeller Foundation fellowship, 1993; Catalog Publication Award, Richard Florsheim Art Fund, 1993; Art Matters fellowship, 1994.

Addresses: *Office*—21 Bond Street, New York, NY 10012.

Incorporated Textiles and Photographs in Paintings

When Amos turned back to painting in the late 1970s, she began incorporating other materials into her canvases, which often dealt thematically with race, feminism, folklore, and family history. Her work was noted for its elements of collage, with many critics pointing out its similarities to the narrative quilts of fabric artist Faith Ringgold. Onto her painted canvases Amos added photographs, bits of fabric she wove herself, embroidery, and strips of different kinds of African cloth. *Art in America* writer Anastasia Aukeman described Amos's works from the 1980s, including "Out in Front" (1982), "Runners with Cheetah" (1983) and "Black Dog Blues" (1983), as "banner-sized, celebratory fabric collages of athletic African-Americans, mostly women, dancing, running and diving."

In 1991 Amos completed her *Woman Artists* series, which included portraits of such mentors and friends as Elizabeth Catlett, Camille Billops, Faith Ringgold, and a group of Amos's mother's friends, as well as a self-portrait in which Amos wears a T-shirt with the word "artist" on the front. The series also includes a reference to one of Amos's students, Giza Daniels Endesha, who died of AIDS.

Amos's 1994 solo exhibition in New York City, *Changing the Subject*, brought the artist considerable critical respect. The show demonstrated the mature expression of Amos's political awareness and artistic skill. Among the most notable works from this exhibit is "Tightrope" (1994), which depicts the artist on a tightrope high above the ground, wearing a leotard made from the American flag and from the Wonder Woman costume. The image suggests the woman artist as both warrior and temptress. At the same time, the painting—which includes pictorial references to the artist Paul Gauguin's life in Tahiti—also questions attitudes about colonialism. As Amos put it in remarks quoted in the Antioch College introduction to the exhibition *Emma Amos: Paintings and Prints, 1983-2003*, "I became concerned with the issue of freedom of expression in figurative imagery, particularly the symbolic use of dark bodies. Researching the impact of race, I found that white male artists are free to incorporate any image.... They found that their work which included nonwhite figures was seen as more exciting, more provocative, more sexually charged and more noteworthy." Citing the work of such noted white artists as Picasso and Gauguin, Amos added that though such work continues to be admired for its willingness to cross boundaries, "when African-American artists cross boundaries, we are often stopped at the border."

Though Amos is a passionate critic of Western appropriation of African art, she has also spoken out, through her work, about other kinds of racism in the art world. She particularly objects to collectors focusing only on works by African-American artists that include images of black figures. In response, she has chosen to include human images in her work that represent a broad range of skin tones. "By calling attention to problems of self-censorship and the compartmentalization of artists by race and gender," she observed, as quoted in the introduction to *Emma Amos: Thinking Paint* at Kenyon College, "I was, and still am, rebelling against the expectation that a black woman does paintings only of and about black people."

A professor of art at Rutgers University since 1980, Amos has participated in numerous group exhibitions and has shown her work in solo exhibitions across the country. Her work is included in the permanent collections of several museums, including the Museum of Modern Art and the Studio Museum of Harlem in New York; the Library of Congress in Washington, D.C.; the Minnesota Museum of Art in Minneapolis; Spelman College in Atlanta, Georgia; and Williams College in Williamstown, Massachusetts.

Selected works

Solo exhibitions

Alexander Gallery, Atlanta, GA, 1960.
Davis Fine Arts Gallery, West Virginia State College, 1974.

Art Salon, New York, NY, 1979.
Isobel Neal Gallery, Chicago, IL, 1988.
Clemson University Gallery, Genoa, Italy, 1989.
Douglass College Women Artists Series, NJ, 1989.
Newark Museum, Newark, NJ, 1990.
Bronx Museum, NY, 1991.
McIntosh Gallery, Atlanta, GA, 1991.
College of Wooster Art Museum, Wooster, OH, 1993.
Changing the Subject, Art in General, New York, NY, 1994.
Sherry Washington Gallery, Detroit, MI, 1996.
Emma Amos: Thinking Paint, Kenyon College, OH, 2001.
Emma Amos: New to New York: A Midcareer Survey, New York, NY, 2002.
Emma Amos: Paintings and Prints, 1983-2003, Antioch College, 2004.

Group exhibitions

Dream Singers, Story Tellers: An African American Presence, New Jersey State Museum, Trenton, 1992.
Reading Prints, Museum of Modern Art, New York, NY, 1992.
Engaged Vision, Terry Dintenfass Gallery, New York, NY, 1994.
Romare Bearden and Friends: Emma Amos, Charles Alston, Herbert Gentry, Norman Lewis, Alitash Kebede Gallery, Los Angeles, CA, 1994.
Interamerican De Artistas Plastico, Museum de las Artes, Universidad de Guadalajara, Mexico, 1994.
A Women's Place, Monmouth Museum, Lincroft, NJ, 1996.
Six Artists: The 1990s, New Jersey State Museum, Trenton, 1996.
Bearing Witness: Contemporary Works by African American Women Artists, Atlanta, GA, 1996.
Thinking Print: Books to Billboards, 1980-95, Museum of Modern Art, New York, NY, 1996.

Sources

Books

Contemporary Women Artists, St. James Press (Detroit, MI), 1999.
Gouma-Peterson, Thalia, and bell hooks and Valerie Mercer, *Emma Amos: Paintings and Prints, 1982-92*, Studio Museum in Harlem, 1993.
Farrington, Lisa E., *Creating Their Own Image: The History of African-American Women Artists*, Oxford University Press, 2007.

Periodicals

Art in America, January 1, 1996, p. 103.
Essence, September 1994, p. 56.
New York Times, March 3, 1995, p. C21; November 1, 2002, p. E2.
Woman's Art Journal, spring-summer, 1996, pp. 43-45; spring-summer, 2007.

On-line

"Emma Amos: Paintings and Prints, 1983-2003," *Antioch College*, www.antioch-college.edu/herndon/html/amos.html (September 5, 2007).
"Emma Amos: Thinking Paint," *Kenyon College Art Gallery*, www2.kenyon.edu/ArtGallery/exhibitions/0001/amos/amos.htm (September 5, 2007).
"Interview with Emma Amos," *Smithsonian Archives of American Art,* www.aaa.si.edu/collections/oral-histories/transcripts/amos68.htm (September 5, 2007).

Other

Emma Amos: Action Lines, L&S Video.

—E. M. Shostak

Mike Anderson

1959—

Basketball coach

Mike Anderson's basketball teams are known for playing in high gear for the full 40 minutes of a game. That approach also characterizes Anderson's own career. From humble beginnings in a house too small for his family, Anderson has risen to become one of the most successful head coaches in college basketball. He currently coaches at the University of Missouri, where he is the only African American ever to hold the school's top basketball job.

Anderson was born on December 12, 1959, in Birmingham, Alabama. He grew up at the epicenter of the civil rights movement's most critical sites during some of its most critical moments. His family's house on Avenue J in Birmingham's Ensley neighborhood was a mere 10 minutes away from the scene of the 16th Street Baptist Church bombing and where police commissioner Bull Connor set police attack dogs and fire hoses on peaceful protesters. Nevertheless, the Anderson home was a peaceful, if overcrowded, refuge from the nearby tumult. Eight children had to share one room, and three or four of the six boys often had to sleep in a single bed, in head-to-toe fashion. The dinner table was not big enough to accommodate the whole family, so they ate in shifts. In spite of the cramped living conditions, Anderson remembers the family home mainly as one filled with love and support. "I remember a lot of love, a lot of caring and a lot of sharing," he was quoted as saying in a November 2006 *St. Louis Post-Dispatch* article. "You are who you are, and you never forget where you come from."

Junior College Served as Stepping Stone

Anderson starred in basketball at Jackson Olin High School in Birmingham, winning all-city and all-state honors as a guard. In his junior year, he led his team to the state semifinals. After graduating from Jackson Olin in 1978, Anderson enrolled at Jefferson State Junior College in Birmingham. While playing on the Jefferson basketball team, he caught the eye of Nolan Richardson, the coach of one of Jefferson's opponents, Western Texas Junior College. When Richardson landed the head coaching job at the University of Tulsa the following season, one of his first moves was to recruit Anderson to play for his new team.

With a basketball scholarship in hand, Anderson enrolled at Tulsa in 1981. He was a starter on the Tulsa team for two seasons. In his first year there, Tulsa won the National Invitation Tournament (NIT), and Anderson was named to the all-tournament team. The following year, Tulsa earned a spot in the NCAA Tournament.

By the time he graduated from Tulsa in 1982, Anderson had set his sites on a coaching career. While working as a substitute teacher, he started looking for coaching jobs. Richardson brought him on board as an assistant coach at his alma mater, Tulsa. During Anderson's two years as an assistant there, the team had a combined record of 50 wins and 12 losses, and appeared in the NCAA Tournament both seasons.

At a Glance . . .

Born Michael Anderson on December 12, 1959, in Birmingham, AL; married Marcheita Anderson; children: Darcheita, Michael, Jr., Yvonne. *Education:* Attended Jefferson State Junior College, Birmingham, AL, 1978-80; University of Tulsa, BA, 1982.

Career: University of Tulsa, assistant men's basketball coach, 1982-85; University of Arkansas, assistant men's basketball coach, 1985-2002; University of Alabama at Birmingham, head men's basketball coach, 2002-06; University of Missouri, head men's basketball coach, 2006–.

Awards: Conference USA Coach of the Year, 2004.

Addresses: *Office*—University of Missouri, 230 Mizzou Arena, Columbia, MO 65211.

When his mentor Richardson was hired as head coach at the University of Arkansas, he brought Anderson along with him. Anderson quickly moved up the ranks on Richardson's staff. In 1985 and 1986, he served as a volunteer assistant. The following year, he was a paid part-time assistant. He became a full-time assistant coach in 1988.

Groomed by Mentor Richardson

Anderson ended up serving as an assistant coach at Arkansas for 14 years. During his time there, Arkansas was a basketball powerhouse, recording the fifth highest number of victories (270) among all college basketball teams during the 1990s. The Razorbacks won two Southeastern Conference titles during Anderson's tenure there, appeared in the Final Four of the NCAA tournament three times, won the national championship in 1994, and were runners-up in 1995. A large part of Anderson's value to the time was his skill as a recruiter. Repeatedly, he was able to lure players to the school who fit well into Richardson's style of play, which emphasized an active, up-tempo approach to the game.

Anderson was apparently being groomed to succeed Richardson as head coach at Arkansas. However, when Richardson's relationship with the university suddenly went sour in 2002, Anderson's career path took an unexpected turn. In April of 2002, an offer to become the head basketball coach at the University of Alabama at Birmingham (UAB) brought Anderson back to his

hometown. In his first season at UAB, Anderson led the Blazers to a 21-13 record, marking the school's best ever improvement from one season to the next. That was good enough to earn the team a spot in the NIT tournament, the UAB's first postseason tournament invitation since 1998-99. The following year, UAB improved to 22-10, and tied for the Conference USA regular season championship. That was good enough to earn an invitation to the NCAA tournament, where the Blazers won two games, including a stunning upset of perennial powerhouse the University of Kentucky, the top-ranked team in the tournament. For his efforts, Anderson was named the 2004 Conference USA Coach of the Year.

The 2004-05 season was almost a carbon copy of the previous year. The Blazers made their second straight NCAA tournament appearance in spite of losing several key seniors to graduation after their breakthrough campaign a year before. Another 20-plus win season and another NCAA tournament berth followed in 2005-06, as Anderson continued to mold UAB into the type of team he had learned to lead under Richardson's tutelage. Anderson's swarming defenses and fast-paced style were eventually dubbed "The Fastest 40 Minutes in Basketball." Others called it "Forty Minutes of Hell."

First Black Head Coach at Missouri

Anderson's impressive results at UAB led to an offer from a bigger school with a better-funded athletic program. In March of 2006 he was named head basketball coach at the University of Missouri. In signing a five-year contract worth a reported $850,000 per year, Anderson became the first African-American head basketball coach in the school's history. As he was introduced to the media in his new hometown, Anderson made it clear that he intended to bring with him the scrappy style of play that had marked his teams at UAB. "If you ever see me in a fight with a tiger or a bear, you better help that tiger or that bear out," he was quoted as saying on the ESPN online report about his hiring. "If you watch my basketball team, that's the same mind-set...."

Anderson's first season at Missouri was unremarkable, though the team's 18-12 record exceeded the expectations of many college sports commentators, who picked them to finish last in the Big 12 conference. It also tied the team record for the most victories in a season by a rookie coach. Unfortunately, that record was not good enough to qualify Missouri for postseason play. Nevertheless, it further established Anderson as one of the top coaches of any race in college basketball, and one of the small handful of black head coaches thriving in a major university setting.

Sources

Periodicals

Columbia Daily Tribune (Columbia, MO), March 12, 2007; April 9, 2006.

Jet, April 17, 2006, p. 50.

St. Louis Post Dispatch, November 5, 2006, p. D1.

On-line

"Mike Anderson: Former UAB Coach Happy to Give Back," *Special, The Birmingham News,* blog.al.com/bn/2007/05/mike_anderson_former_uab_coach.html (July 3, 2007).

"Mike Anderson Profile," *CSTV.com,* www.cstv.com/printable/schools/miss/sports/m-baskbl/mtt/anderson_mike00.html (August 8, 2007).

"Mizzou Hires Former UAB Coach Anderson," *ESPN.com News Service,* http://sports.espn.go.com/espn/print?id=2385253&type=story (August 8, 2007).

"Mizzou Tabs Mike Anderson New Head Men's Basketball Coach: Anderson Becomes First African-American Head Coach in University of Missouri History," *Mizzou: The Official Athletic Site of the University of Missouri,* http://mutigers.cstv.com/sports/m-baskbl/spec-rel/032606aae.html (August 8, 2007).

—Bob Jacobson

Trey Anthony

1974—

Playwright, actor, comedienne, director, producer

"If you want to know a woman, a black woman, that is, touch her hair. Cause our hair carries our journey." With these words, Novelette, the irrepressible West Indian hairdresser created and brought to life onstage by Trey Anthony in *da Kink in my Hair*, describes how the roots of black women's hair go deeper than flesh and fashion. Indeed, the funny, brave, and moving stories of the women in Anthony's dynamic play demonstrate that, for women of African descent, hair can represent culture, identity, and self-acceptance.

A queer woman of Jamaican heritage, born in England and raised in Canada, Anthony learned to accept and appreciate her African hair just as she learned to accept and value her plus-size body and her lesbian sexual orientation. A creative thinker and entertainer since childhood, it seemed natural to her to turn her own search for identity into a theatrical performance that celebrates both the diversity and the commonality of black women's experience. Following the success of *da Kink in my Hair*, Anthony has continued to write and produce plays that tell the stories of the people of color, the poor workers, and the sexual minorities who are often silent and invisible in mainstream media.

Anthony was born on February 18, 1974, in London, England, one of three children of immigrant parents who had come to the United Kingdom from Jamaica as children. Her father, Hortnele Dennie, worked as an electrician, and her mother, Angela, was a resourceful woman who worked a wide variety of jobs to support her family. When Anthony was 12 years old, her parents divorced, and her mother took the children to Toronto, Canada. There, they lived in an apartment building in a working-class neighborhood with many other West Indian families.

Put on Shows as a Child

Growing up in Toronto, Anthony spent much of her time in the care of her grandmother, who not only supervised her grandchildren, but encouraged their creativity. A funny and imaginative woman herself, Anthony's grandmother was an appreciative and supportive audience for the many neighborhood shows Anthony organized, frequently spending her limited funds on records to help her granddaughter practice singing. From an early age, Anthony had an active imagination, which she nurtured by constant reading. Soon, she began writing her own stories.

In school, Anthony was an enthusiastic student in her English and drama classes, though she had no love for math or sports. During the late 1980s, the family moved from Toronto to Brampton, a suburban town on the outskirts of the city. Anthony graduated from Brampton's Notre Dame High School and entered college at York University in Toronto. During the summer after her third year at university, she entered a six-week summer program at the Academy of Arts in New York City.

While in New York, Anthony heard that auditions were being held for the *Chris Rock Show*, a cable program featuring the successful African-American comedian comic whose intelligent and often outrageous act includes social commentary about issues of importance

At a Glance . . .

Born on February 18, 1974, in London, England; partner, Sherrisse Solomon.

Career: HBO, *The Chris Rock Show,* intern, 1998-99; Plaitform Comedy Troupe, founder, 1999–; CTV, *After Hours,* writer and performer, 1999-2000; Trey Anthony Productions, founder, 2001–; Kinky Dinner Productions, co-founder, 2005–.

Awards: National Association for the Advancement of Colored People, Beverly Hills, Theater Award, Best Playwright—Equity, 2007.

Addresses: *Office*—Trey Anthony Productions, 23 Buckingham Street, Main Floor, Toronto, Ontario M8Y 2W2. *Web*—www.treyanthony.com.

to African Americans. Though students in Anthony's summer program were not supposed to audition for shows, she could not resist giving it a try. When she arrived at the audition and saw the long line of hopeful actors, Anthony realized it was unlikely that she would be cast in the show. However, her resourceful and creative nature helped her to turn her disappointment into opportunity. She struck up a conversation with one of the interns at the audition and learned that there was an opening for a new intern. Though interns are more likely to do office work and errands than participate in the creative process, an internship would allow her to work on a real show. Anthony applied, got the job, and remained in New York for a year, learning about both comedy and production on the set of a successful television show.

Started Comedy Troupe in Toronto

After her year in New York, Anthony returned to Toronto, full of creative energy and ideas. Anthony liked the sketch comedy format of the *Chris Rock Show,* and she too wanted to create comedy that addressed serious issues in the lives of people of color. With other like-minded performers, she formed a sketch comedy troupe called Plaitform, dedicated to creating black urban comedy. Plaitform performed throughout Toronto in whatever venues they could find, from libraries to theaters to comedy clubs. Yuk Yuk's, a well-known Toronto comedy club, sponsored an African Nubian comedy night, and Anthony became a regular performer there. One of her best-loved characters was Carlene, the dance hall queen, an irrepressible, fast-talking West Indian woman. In other sketches with titles like, "Rice and Peas on Sunday"

and "You Know You Have a Black Mother When...," she did humorous and touching imitations of her mother and grandmother, complete with Jamaican accents.

Anthony was working with Plaitform when she attracted the notice of a producer from the Canadian television network CTV. He hired her to work on the late-night comedy series *After Hours* with black Canadian comic Kenny Robinson. She spent the next year writing and performing on the show while continuing to perform at Yuk Yuk's as part of Robinson's Nubian Disciples of Pryor.

As Anthony's professional career progressed, she experienced dramatic changes in her personal life. She had been in a romantic relationship with a man for almost a year and was engaged to be married when her feelings began to take her in another direction. During her off-hours, she volunteered at a Toronto shelter for homeless women where she met some lesbians and other queer women. The word queer was once used as an insulting term for homosexuals. However, after the gay liberation movement of the 1970s, some radical gays and lesbians began reclaiming the word, using it proudly to describe themselves. During the 1990s, other sexual minorities expanded the use of queer, using it to describe not only gays and lesbians, but also bisexuals and transgender people. Even straight people who have an open-minded attitude toward monogamy and sexual orientation sometimes call themselves queer.

Wrote, Directed, Produced, and Acted

As Anthony grew to understand her attraction to other women and define herself as queer, she broke off her engagement. She also began writing a series of monologues about many different issues of importance to working-class women of color. She wanted to write her own show in part because she had begun to feel that there was no place on stage for women like her, that is, black, fat, articulate, and queer. Theatrical agents had even told her that she was not a marketable talent because she did not fit into the stereotypical roles of mammy or prostitute usually available to black women, and she did not sound "black enough."

Anthony determined to create a theatrical piece that would respectfully showcase the many different sides of black women. The result was *da Kink in my Hair,* a series of conversations between women and their hairdresser, set in Novelette's, a beauty salon in a West Indian neighborhood of Toronto. Novelette (played by Anthony herself) and her customers laugh, cry, sing, and dance about the issues of their lives, including child abuse, homophobia, abandonment, betrayal, and loss. The show premiered in 2001 at the Toronto Fringe Festival. The festival's producers warned Anthony that her play might not get a warm reception, because the Fringe audience was largely white and middle class.

However, Anthony was undaunted. Used to taking risks, she tried an innovative approach to publicizing her play—giving the responsibility to the audience. On opening night, she offered free tickets to all hairdressers and barbers, asking in return that they tell their friends and customers about the show.

Anthony's gamble paid off. In exchange for a few free seats, she got a full house on opening night and priceless publicity. *Da Kink in my Hair* was not only one of the most successful plays in the Toronto Fringe Festival, but it was chosen as one of the five outstanding works of the New York Fringe Festival in 2002. When Toronto's Theatre Passe Muraille produced *da Kink* in 2003, the play sold more tickets than any other in the theater's history. In 2005, an expanded version of *da Kink* became the first Canadian play produced by the elite Princess of Wales Theatre in Toronto. However, as her success began to grow, Anthony did not forget her working-class roots, and, even in the lavish Princess of Wales production, she insisted that 20 prime seats be offered to low income patrons at an affordable price.

Formed Production Companies

In addition to wowing audiences from the fringe to the elite, *da Kink* received critical acclaim and international notice. The Toronto production received four Dora theatrical award nominations, and, in the United States, a San Diego production won awards from the NAACP Beverly Hills chapter for best ensemble, best director, best sound, and best playwright. In 2004, a Canadian television company produced a pilot film for a proposed television series based on *da Kink in my Hair*.

Anthony has continued to create plays that tell the unheard stories of forgotten women. In 2005, with Rachael Lea Rickards, a writing partner and friend since high school, Anthony produced her second major play, *I am NOT a Dinner Mint: The Crap That Women Swallow to Stay in a Relationship*. The title of the play expresses the writers' idea that women are often defined in their relationships the way a dinner mint is defined in relationship to dinner, a pleasant afterthought. *Dinner Mint* brings together onstage five women of different ethnic backgrounds to share the stories of the many different kinds of relationships in their lives.

In addition to writing her own plays, Anthony's production companies, Trey Anthony Productions and Kinky Dinner Productions also showcase other works by performers of color, such as Indian American comic Vijai Nathan's one woman show *Good Girls Do, Indian Girls Don't* and Darren Anthony's *Secrets of a Black Boy*. She has also continued to share her success with her community, giving dozens of free tickets to youth groups and shelters and doing volunteer work with Toronto youth groups such as Support Our Youth and Black Queer Youth.

Sources

Periodicals

Back Stage East, April 12, 2007, pp. 11-13.
Canadian Ethnic Studies, (Calgary), 2006, pp. 212-14.
Flare (Toronto) November 1999, p. 84.
Toronto Life, January 2005, p. 23.
Variety, February 7, 2005, p. 86.

On-line

Trey Anthony Productions, www.treyanthony.com (July 16, 2007).
"Kink in My Hair," *VisionTV,* http://visiontv.com/Programs/drama_kinkinhair.html (July 16, 2007).
"VisionTV Drama *Kink In My Hair,*" *Black Canada,* www.blackcanada.com/news_103.htm (July 16, 2007).
"Five Women, Five Hearts, One Story," *Afrotoronto. com,* www.afrotoronto.com/Articles/July06/Dinnermint.html (July 16, 2007).
"Playwright Trey Anthony Celebrates Black Women And Her Free-At-Last Hair," *Eye Weekly,* www. eyeweekly.com/eye/issue/issue_06.12.03/arts/dakinkinmyhair.php (July 16, 2007).
"New Twist in Kink's Story," *George Brown College,* www.georgebrown.ca/theatre/alumni/alumni_press_Trey_Anthony.aspx (July 16, 2007).
"What Comes Around Comes Around Again," *TorontoStage.com,* www.torontostage.com/reviews/dinnerMint.html (July 16, 2007).

Other

Information for this profile was obtained through an interview with Trey Anthony on July 16, 2007.

—Tina Gianoulis

Tichina Arnold

1971—

Actor

Tichina Arnold stars in the top-rated, critically acclaimed television sitcom *Everybody Hates Chris,* portraying a 1980s version of comedian Chris Rock's real-life mother. The no-nonsense, working-class New York City household depicted on the show is not very different from Arnold's own background as a kid in South Ozone Park, Queens. "The TV family just clicked," Arnold said of her first days on the job in an interview with *New York Times* journalist Felicia R. Lee. "It was like we had the same memories."

Arnold, Tichina, photograph. Charley Gallay/Getty Images.

Arnold's mother enrolled her in dance school before she started kindergarten, at the age of four. "I was a child with a lot of energy and my mom said, 'We've got to channel this energy. You're getting on my nerves,'" she recalled in an interview with *Jet* contributor Aldore D. Collier. Singing and acting came naturally to Arnold, and she flourished at her school's music and drama departments. She began auditioning for professional jobs, and won her first acting role in a 1983 made-for-television movie about clinical depression, *The Brass Ring.*

Arnold was born in 1971 as the first of two daughters in that Queens household. Her father was a New York City police officer, and her mother worked for the municipal department of sanitation. The Arnolds shared more than a few similarities with the fictional one the actress would later head on television, especially their income level. "My parents made just enough for me not to get free lunch," she told Sherri McGee McCovey in *Essence.* Her mother also chose to have her bused to a predominantly white school in Flushing, another part of Queens, where most of her classmates came from the predominantly Jewish surrounding neighborhood.

Arnold's breakout role came in 1986 when she was cast in the film version of a popular off-Broadway musical, *Little Shop of Horrors,* which was an updated version of a campy 1950s horror movie about a menacing talking plant that grows enormous thanks to a steady diet of human blood. The stage remake added a trio of young female singers who provided narration and commentary, with *New York Times* critic Janet Maslin noting that the trio of pre-teens "sashay through the film as...one of the only known Greek choruses to perform doo-wop material."

Despite that auspicious start, Arnold struggled to move forward with her career as she progressed from her

At a Glance . . .

Born June 28, 1971, in Queens, NY; daughter of a police officer and a municipal employee; married once; children: daughter Alijah Kai Haggins (with Carvin Haggins, a songwriter and music producer).

Career: Actor, 1983–; China Moon Rags, a hair-accessories company, founder.

Addresses: *Office*—c/o Chris Rock Entertainment, 5555 Melrose Ave., Bldg. 213, Rm. 320, Hollywood, CA 90038. *Web*—www.chinamoonrag.com.

teens into young adulthood. She appeared on two ABC daytime dramas, *Ryan's Hope* and *All My Children,* and appeared in a few little-seen films or briefly in more successful projects, such as a ticket seller in the 1991 Bette Midler-Woody Allen comedy *Scenes from a Mall.* She finally landed a much more visible part in 1992 when she began appearing as Pam James on the hit Fox television sitcom *Martin* alongside comic Martin Lawrence. When the show ended in 1997, she once again found herself searching for meaningful roles. Her credits for the year 2000 provide a glimpse into her working life: she appeared in the box-office hit *Big Momma's House* as well as a critically acclaimed and Emmy-nominated HBO film, *Dancing in September,* which starred Nicole Ari Parker as a beleaguered Hollywood studio executive. A year later, Arnold won a recurring role on the UPN sitcom *One on One* as Nicole Barnes.

Arnold was invited to audition for the role of Rochelle Rock, the television version of comedian Chris Rock's real-life mother Rose, for a planned new series on UPN, *Everybody Hates Chris.* She was only half-interested in the job, and was hoping to land another role in a more blockbuster television project. When she arrived at the audition, she was surprised to find Rock there himself—somewhat of a rarity in television, where celebrity producers are often attached to projects but uninvolved in the gritty business of casting. "I found out later he had already made up his mind to use me for the part," Arnold told McCovey in the *Essence* article.

Everybody Hates Chris debuted on UPN for its fall 2005 line-up to excellent reviews. Its storylines take place in the early 1980s just as Rock's television family moves from public housing to an apartment in the Bedford-Stuyvesant neighborhood of Brooklyn—a dynamic, predominantly African-American community best known as the setting for some of Spike Lee's earlier films. Arnold played mother to the 13-year-old television version of Chris Rock (Tyler James Williams),

with former professional football player Terry Crews as her husband Julius. Like Arnold herself, the television Chris has a long daily bus trip to and from a middle school in mostly white—in this case, Italian-American—neighborhood elsewhere. And as with her own upbringing, the hardworking Julius and Rochelle's struggle to provide a stable home for their children is at the forefront of most household battles between parents and offspring. "I pull from my mom for the character—a woman doing her best to keep her family together," Arnold told Lee, the *New York Times* writer. "Our show takes place during a time when there were no time-outs, there were spankings."

Arnold's character was singled out by some reviewers, nearly all of whom heaped praise on the sitcom and heralded it as a newer, more realistic version of *The Cosby Show.* "The most touching aspect of 'Chris' is its depiction of the parents," noted the *New Yorker*'s television critic, Nancy Franklin. "Chris's mother is a piece of work: a fount of colorful expressions describing what she'll do to her kids if they don't behave, and openly proud of her family's relative prosperity." *Entertainment Weekly*'s Jeff Jensen called *Everybody Hates Chris* "poignant, pointed, and raucous," and "the best sitcom ever...to air on UPN."

That network home changed in 2006 with the show's second season, when UPN merged with the WB (Warner Brothers) network to become a new broadcast entity, CW. The show's Thursday-night slot was changed to Sunday then finally Monday nights, and ratings took a hit as a consequence. Arnold could be assured of at least a few more seasons on the show thanks to its early success, however, and her higher profile had already brought some new acting jobs, such as a role as Martin Lawrence's wife in the 2007 comedy *Wild Hogs.* In her leaner years, she had started her own Web-based business, China Moon Rags, which made hair accessories. The extra income helped provide for her daughter Alijah, born in 2004, whose father was songwriter and music producer Carvin Haggins. Arnold and Haggins had had an on-again, off-again relationship that began when Arnold recorded some demo tracks years before, and though they were no longer romantically involved they remained cordial and committed co-parents. Arnold is still close to Tisha Campbell, her fellow *Little Shop of Horrors* castmate, who is now Tisha Campbell-Martin and another Fox/UPN/CW sitcom veteran. "When we'd see each other at auditions, I would say, 'If I don't get it, I hope you do.' And she would say the same to me," Arnold told Collier in the *Jet* interview about their decades-long friendship. "That's where it started.... You see people come and go, but she is not one of them."

Selected works

Films

Little Shop of Horrors, 1986.

Starlight: A Musical Movie, 1988.
How I Got Into College, 1989.
Scenes from a Mall, 1991.
Fakin' Da Funk, 1997.
A Luv Tale, 1999.
Big Momma's House, 2000.
Dancing in September, 2000.
Yo Alien, 2002.
Getting Played, 2005.
Wild Hogs, 2007.

Television

The Brass Ring (movie), 1983.
House of Dies Drear (movie), 1984.
Martin, 1992-97.
One on One, 2001-05.
Everybody Hates Chris, 2005.

Sources

Periodicals

Daily Variety, June 8, 2006, p. A4.
Entertainment Weekly, September 9, 2005, p. 94.
Essence, March 2006, p. 70.
Jet, January 30, 2006, p. 52.
New Yorker, November 7, 2005, p. 146.
New York Times, December 19, 1986; October 30, 2006.
Star-Ledger (Newark, NJ), September 21, 2005, p. 35.
USA Today, September 22, 2005, p. 1D.

—Carol Brennan

Evelyn Ashford

1957—

Athlete

Sprinter Evelyn Ashford once told the *Washington Post*, "There's nothing wrong with second, but I only want to be first," and for most of her career, that is exactly what she was. In 17 years on the track, the five-foot-five sprinter broke world records, was ranked best in the world 14 times, and earned five Olympic medals. Known for her record-breaking speeds in the 100-meter run, the event in which she earned her first gold medal, Ashford was also a powerhouse in the 100-meter relay, helping the Team U.S. win three consecutive gold medals in the 1984, 1988, and 1992 Olympic Games. This final medal was earned when Ashford was 35 years old, a testament to her impressive longevity. Nearly 15 years after retiring from the track, Ashford's name is still carved on the record books, emblazoned in Halls of Fame, and revered by fans of track and field worldwide.

Outran the Boys to Break World Record

Evelyn Ashford was born on April 15, 1957, in Shreveport, Louisiana, the first of Samuel and Vietta Ashford's five children. Because Samuel's Air Force career kept the family on the move, it wasn't until they settled in Roseville, California that Ashford, whose long-time hero was the great African-American sprinter Wilma Rudolph, got serious about running. There was just one catch. Roseville High School did not have a girls' track team. However, when a school coach noticed Ashford's speed on the playground, he challenged her to race some of the football players. When she beat the school's star running back in a 50-yard dash, Ashford became a playground hero. Bucking gender lines, the school put her on the boys' track team and Ashford went on to place third in the Junior National Track Championships in 1975. In her senior year, she co-captained the team and upon graduation she became one of the first female athletes to win an athletic scholarship to UCLA.

As a collegiate runner, Ashford continued to draw attention for her speed on the track. UCLA track coach Pat Connolly, a three-time Olympian herself, saw Olympic potential in Ashford and took the young runner under her wing. Together, they worked on a training plan that primed Ashford for the 1976 Summer Olympics in Montreal. Just a freshman in college, Ashford came in fifth in the 100-meter race and 7th in the 4x100-meter relay, a team event that involves four runners completing a 100-meter leg of the race. Back at school, Ashford won national collegiate championships in both the 100- and 200-meter runs and the 800-meter relay. However, the Olympic bug had bitten and after her junior year, Ashford dropped out of college to train full-time for the 1980 Olympics. That same year, she married Ray Washington, a UCLA basketball player.

At the 1979 World Cup, Ashford beat world-record holders in both the 100-meter and the 200-meter races. These wins pegged her as a favorite for the gold medal at the upcoming Summer Olympics in Moscow. Unfortunately, in December of 1979 the Soviet Union invaded Afghanistan. In response, then-U.S. president Jimmy Carter initiated a boycott of the Moscow games.

Ashford was devastated. She and husband Ray took off for a cross-country road trip where the runner found both the solace and the strength to set her sights back on the track. The following year, Ashford once again scored world titles in both the 100-meter and 200-meter races at the World Cup in Rome. Then in 1983, she stunned even herself with a 100-meter race at the National Sports Festival in Colorado Springs. "I wasn't thinking about anything; I just ran," she told *Sports Illustrated*. "When I crossed the line, I thought, 'That was nothing special. Maybe 11.1.'" She soon found out that she had clocked in at 10.79 seconds, a world record that earned her the nickname, "world's faster woman."

Became Track Legend with Five Olympic Medals

Following her world record run, Ashford was the favorite to win the upcoming World Championships in Helsinki, Finland, however a pulled hamstring muscle kept her from finishing the finals. Later that year, running in the 1984 Olympic trials, she once again felt a tug in her hamstring. Though she still managed to qualify for the games, the injury made her rethink her running strategy. She decided to stick only with the 100-meter race as the 200-meter carried too much potential for damage. Her plan worked. When the gun went off marking the start of the 100-meter Olympic run, Ashford flew. "I didn't feel that much in control," she later told *Sports Illustrated*. "I felt that my legs were moving too fast for my body." When it was over, Ashford had not only won the gold, but she had set a new Olympic record for the event, 10.97 seconds. As the medal was placed around her neck in front of a stadium full of her screaming hometown fans, the normally reserved Ashford wept openly. "The response in the Olympic stadium today tells me that I'm very much appreciated," she told *Sports Illustrated*.

Before the Los Angeles games were over, Ashford scored a second gold medal with the American 4x100 relay team. However, she was not done yet. Later that year, she broke her own world record in Zurich when she clocked the 100-meter run in at 10.76 seconds. As of 2007, her time still stood as the fifth fastest in the history of the event. In 1985, Ashford slowed down just enough to have a baby. By the following year, she was back on track, her feet flying directly towards the 1988 Olympics. Despite another hamstring injury which kept her out of the 1987 World Championships, Ashford won all but two of the races she entered. She expected to do the same at the Seoul Olympics, however a new force was about to be unleashed on the track. During the 100-meter race, teammate Florence Griffith-Joyner stunned the world with an unprecedented finish of 10.54 seconds, good for the gold medal. Ashford took home the silver. "I'd never been beaten in a major competition before," she later told the *Washington Post*. "In 1976, I ran in the Olympics at 18 and finished fifth. After that, I won. I'm a winner." Ashford did win one gold in Seoul as part of the 4x100 relay.

With three Olympic gold medals, one silver, two world records, and several world championships under her cleats, Ashford could have retired a champion just then. By the time the next Olympics rolled around, she was 35, well beyond gold-winning age for track. Ashford, however, was not ready to quit. She made the Olympic trials and joined the U.S. track team as the oldest runner at the 1992 Barcelona Games. Though she was edged out of the 100-meter semi-finals by 1/1000th of a second, she finished first with the 4x100 relay team, winning her fourth Olympic gold medal. A year later, she finally retired, dedicating her life instead to raising her daughter and promoting literacy causes. Along with her old coach Connolly, she also became a vocal activist against the use of steroids in Olympic sports. Within a decade, Ashford had become a legend. She was inducted into the National Track and Field Hall of Fame in 1997 and into the U.S. Olympic Hall of Fame in 2006. Her picture has now joined that of her old idol

Rudolph on the bedroom walls of girls across the country who hope to one day fly in Ashford's footsteps.

Sources

Books

Connolly, Pat, *Coaching Evelyn: Fast, Faster, Fastest Woman in the World*, HarperCollins, 1991.

Periodicals

Sports Illustrated, July 11, 1983, p. 28; August 13, 1984, p. 60.

Washington Post, September 17, 1988, p. D8; January 12, 1989, p. B1.

On-line

"Ashford, Evelyn," *Hickok Sports,* www.hickoksports.com/biograph/ashforde.shtml (September 7, 2007).
"Class of 2006: Evelyn Ashford," *United States Olympic Committee,* www.usolympicteam.com/36370_37535.htm (September 7, 2007).

—Candace LaBalle

Jim and Gloria Austin

1951—

1956—

Co-founders of the National Cowboys of Color Museum and Hall of Fame

When Jim Austin and Gloria Reed met in Fort Worth, Texas, during the early 1990s, they discovered that they had a lot in common. Not only were they both interested in assisting the development of their city by working in the real estate business, but they were also deeply committed to promoting a strong, diverse, and compassionate community. Together, they participated in the formation of the Renaissance Cultural Center, which offered educational and cultural programs, scholarships, and other services to support the young, the old, and the poor within Fort Worth's inner city.

The Austins continued to work together on community projects after their marriage in 1997, and in 2001 they founded the National Cowboys of Color Museum in Fort Worth. As African Americans, they had a special interest in preserving and publicizing the largely unrecognized role that people of color played in the settlement and development of the Old West. In an October 2003 edition of *Realtor Magazine*, Jim Austin explained the importance of preserving such hidden history, "At least a third of all working cowboys were African American, Hispanic, or Native American. Minority cowboys weren't shown in movies or on TV. Youngsters need to know about them and what they did in order to fully appreciate their own history and know how much they have to be proud of."

Jim Grew Up Back East

Austin himself grew up over a thousand miles from the western frontiers that gave birth to the famous historic image of the cowboy. The son of James Nelson Austin, a brick mason, and Beatrice Austin, a social worker, James Nelson Austin, Jr. was born on May 16, 1951, in the city of Wilmington, near the Atlantic coast of North Carolina. When he was twelve years old his family moved to New Jersey, where his mother took a job with the New York City Department of Welfare and his father worked on the grounds crew at William Paterson University. Jim Junior returned to North Carolina each summer to visit his mother's brother, John Bernard Carter. His uncle Bernard was a farmer, storekeeper, and bail bondsman who was well known in Wilmington for his service to the African-American community. He became one of Jim Austin's childhood heroes, and his uncle's sense of civic duty would inspire Austin to make community service part of his own career.

Austin graduated from Bloomfield High School in New Jersey, then entered Howard University, the distinguished historically black Washington D.C. college. During his high school years he had worked part time in a neighborhood pharmacy, and he planned to study to become a pharmacist. Once at Howard, however, he

tions. He accepted a job with the financial corporation American Express, commuting to New York City for the company's nine-month training program.

After completing the training program, Austin went to work in American Express's travel division, becoming assistant manager in the company's New Orleans office. He performed so well there that he was soon made manager of his own office in Fort Worth, Texas. Austin was an able manager and enjoyed working in the travel business. Before long, he was promoted to district manager and, under his management, business in the Fort Worth office increased from $700,000 per year to $1.7 million.

Made Fort Worth His Home

Fort Worth is a dynamic city in north central Texas with a colorful past and a lively mix of modern cultures. Austin loved living in Fort Worth and felt that he had found his permanent home. Unfortunately, to remain in the American Express corporation, he would have had to move every few years as the company transferred him to different branches. He felt that he would rather devote himself to his community than to a corporation, so in 1981 he left American Express and opened his own company, Austin Company Commercial Real Estate.

While achieving success in business, Austin did not forget his uncle's example of service to the community. In 1991, he and another Fort Worth businessman named Timothy Grace converted a former grocery store into an organization to help those members of society who had few resources. The Renaissance Cultural Center they created offered services for youth, elders, and the poor, as well as educational scholarships and cultural events.

While working to launch the Renaissance Cultural Center, Austin met another community-minded realtor named Gloria Reed. Unlike Austin, Reed was a Texan by birth, born on January 7, 1956, in Brownwood, in the west central part of the state. Her mother, ParaLee Washington Reed, was a domestic worker, and her father, Kelly Miller Reed, Sr. worked as a porter on the Santa Fe Railroad for many years before becoming maitre d'hotel at a Houston restaurant. The Reeds had five children, although two died in childhood.

Gloria Did Volunteer Community Work

Gloria Reed grew up in a predominantly African-American neighborhood in Brownwood. Her family placed great importance on education, and she loved school, becoming an avid reader as well as joining the band, the drill team, and the civic club. During the summers she took part in the local library's summer

realized that a career in business interested him more than pharmacy, and he changed his major. Austin had a distinguished academic career, proving his leadership skills by serving as president of the student body, and when he graduated in 1976 with a bachelor's degree in business, he was recruited by a number of corpora-

reading club and attended vacation Bible school at every local church. As she grew older, she held several part time jobs, including secretarial and clerical work in the community center and the courthouse.

After graduating from Brownwood High School, Gloria Reed attended classes at both Howard Payne College in Brownwood and El Centro College in Dallas before earning her real estate license at the George Leonard Real Estate Institute. ParaLee Reed had taught her children the importance of community service, and, as Reed began building her real estate career, she began to look for ways to share her success. One of the programs she worked with during the early 1990s was the newly forming Renaissance Cultural Center. Reed used her business skills to do the complex paperwork that enabled the organization to gain tax-free status as a non-profit corporation.

Austin and Reed enjoyed working together, fell in love, and married on August 19, 1997. They continued to take leadership roles in the Renaissance Cultural Center, which was quickly growing and becoming an important community resource. Impressed with the center's work, Cleo Hearns, organizer of black rodeos since the 1970s, suggested a Cowboys of Color Rodeo as a fundraising event for the Renaissance Cultural Center.

Together the Austins Founded a Museum

Hearns had begun organizing the Cowboys of Color Rodeo in 1996 to honor the often-invisible black, Latino, Native American, and Asian people who had helped to settle the old West. The rodeo featured traditional competitions in calf roping, and steer and bronco riding, and also showcased cultural contests such as Native dancing and Spanish-style sidesaddle riding for women. The rodeo and the Renaissance Cultural Center shared many of the same goals of education and cultural pride, and soon the rodeo became one of the center's regular events.

Working with the rodeo, Jim and Gloria Austin became very interested in the forgotten history of people of color in the west. The history of the American West, of which Texas was a major part, has fascinated readers and moviegoers all over the world, and the image of the cowboy riding the range on his horse, is a major part of that image. The romantic fictional image of the cowboy is rugged, independent, plainspoken...and white. In reality, men and women of all races lived and worked throughout the western states. Native Americans and Latinos had long lived in those areas when white and black settlers, black slaves, and Asian workers arrived during the second half of the nineteenth century. People of all races worked at a wide variety of jobs, including tending the huge herds of cattle that formed a large part of the Western economy. The roping and

riding skills that helped those workers do their job became the basis for the rodeo.

The Austins grew to believe that it was important that youth of color learn that the history of the West included people who looked like them. In 2001 they opened the National Cowboys of Color Museum to showcase the true history of the diverse American West. The museum houses art, historical records, and artifacts such as tools, musical instruments, and furniture. In 2002 the Austins added a Hall of Fame to salute individuals such as "Stagecoach Mary" Fields, an African-American woman who ran a laundry and a café and delivered mail in nineteenth-century Montana, and could hitch up a team of six horses faster than anyone else in her community.

For both Jim and Gloria Austin, reclaiming the history of people of color in the West was closely tied to the work they had always done to support and mentor young people. They felt it was important that youth of color realize that they were part of the legendary Old West. The Austins were especially concerned about African-American youth, whose history too often skipped straight from slavery to the civil rights movement, with little mention of the powerful stories of the men and women who lived between those times. As Gloria Austin explained, "It is important to dig into history to find the people of color who forged their way West and made a big impact on the growth of this country.... They faced adversity and overcame it, and that's a good lesson for kids today. Learning about that pioneer spirit can encourage young people to take their own challenges and see their own resources."

Still headed by the Austins, the Renaissance Cultural Center and the National Cowboys of Color Museum have continued to grow and contribute to the community. By the early 2000s, the Renaissance Cultural Center had awarded more than $200,000 in educational scholarships and offered full yearly schedules of artistic events, poetry readings, and film festivals. The National Cowboys of Color Museum welcomes thousands of visitors a year and plans to move to a larger and more accessible location in Fort Worth. The museum still sponsors the Cowboys of Color Rodeo, which has expanded from a yearly event to a six-city touring fundraiser. By 2007 the rodeo featured over three hundred professional cowboys and cowgirls of color competing for $25,000 in prizes. Each year, the museum's Hall of Fame inducts new members, making sure that Western heroes of color from both the past and the present are not forgotten.

Sources

Books

Porter, Kenneth Wiggins, *The Negro on the American Frontier,* Arno Press, 1971.

Periodicals

Business Wire, September 10, 2004, p. 32-3.
Dallas Business Journal, January 21, 2000, p. 13.
Realtor Magazine, November 2003, p. 50-2.

On-line

"African-Americans and the Old West," *Long Island University, C.W. Post Campus,* www.liu.edu/cwis/CWP/library/african/west/west.htm (July 6, 2007).
Frazier, Matt, "Renaissance Cultural Center to Honor 5," *Star Telegram.com* www.realcities.com/mld/dfw/news/local/17404288.htm?source=rss&channel=dfw_local (July 6, 2007).
National Cowboys of Color Museum and Hall of Fame, www.cowboysofcolor.org (August 12, 2007).
"Realtor Magazine Announces Winners of Fourth Annual Good Neighbor Awards," *RISMedia,* www.rismedia.com/wp/2003-10-24/realtor-magazine-announces-winners-of-fourth-annual-good-neighbor-awards (July 6, 2007).
Renaissance Cultural Center, www.renaissanceculturalcenter.org (July 6, 2007).
Rockwell, Lilly, "Cowboys of All Colors Rodeo through Town," *The Daily Texan,* http://media.www.dailytexanonline.com/media/storage/paper410/news/2003/07/14/StateLocal/Cowboys.Of.All.Colors.Rodeo.Through.Town-493301.shtml (July 6, 2007).

Other

Additional information for this profile was obtained through interviews with Jim Austin on June 19, 2007, and Gloria Austin on June 25, 2007.

—Tina Gianoulis

Philip Bailey

1951—

Musician

Bailey, Philip, photograph. Robert Pitts/Landov.

Lead falsetto singer in the 1970s funk supergroup Earth, Wind & Fire, Philip Bailey is a multiple Grammy Award winner who sang on over 70 Earth, Wind & Fire singles and album tracks. Between 1972 and 1983, when the band went on "hiatus," their tally of 50 gold and platinum disks made them one of the biggest selling groups of all time. Bailey began his solo career in 1982, signing that year with Columbia Records. But he continued to work with Maurice and Verdine White, founding members of Earth, Wind & Fire, and has made records and toured with them since then. In 1984 Bailey became famous as a solo artist when he performed a duet with Phil Collins on the global hit "Easy Lover," a song from Bailey's album *Chinese Wall*. Since the 1980s Bailey has experimented with many different styles and genres, from gospel and R&B to smooth jazz and upbeat pop. He is one of the most successful recording artists of his generation with a voice that is familiar even to people outside of his regular fan base.

Philip Bailey was born on May 8, 1951, in Denver, Colorado and claims his first memories of music come from exploring the jazz record collection of the mother of a friend. He lists Thelonious Monk, Art Blakey, and especially Miles Davis as his main influences. He told *Billboard* magazine in 1999 "Because of my register, Miles Davis' trumpet playing has always been a big influence on my singing. I've always been intrigued by the way he can start anywhere and make it right." Bailey's first performances were with Phoenix Horns, playing gigs around his home town. Bailey recalled on his Web site that playing those countless gigs "was really such a valuable workshop. When I think back on it now, and I look at the musicians of today, I realize that we had a place to hone our skills, playing all those gigs in all those clubs." After several years of singing and playing drums in clubs while attending college, in 1971 Bailey's four octave range, distinctive falsetto, and natural adaptability found him a place as a core member of the group Earth, Wind & Fire.

Under the leadership of Maurice White, Earth, Wind & Fire became a group that crossed cultural and musical boundaries and became known for their fusion of different musical styles. The band's members changed frequently over the next decade, but Bailey and the White brothers remained at its core. Bailey's voice was

At a Glance . . .

Born Philip Bailey on May 8, 1951 in Denver, Colorado; married to Krystal Bailey. *Religion:* Christian.

Career: Phoenix Horns, vocalist; Earth Wind & Fire, vocalist, 1971–; solo recording artist, 1983–, including R&B, gospel, and jazz albums.

Awards: Grammy for Best R&B Vocal Performance By a Duo, Group or Chorus (with Earth, Wind & Fire), 1975, 1978, 1979, 1982; Grammy for Best R&B Instrumental Performance (with Earth, Wind & Fire), 1978, 1979; Grammy Award for Gospel Male, 1986; inducted into the Rock and Roll Hall of Fame with Earth, Wind & Fire, March 2000; Hollywood Walk of Fame, 2003.

Addresses: *Agent*—Damien Smith, Azoff Music Management, 1100 Glendon Ave., Ste. 2000, Los Angeles, CA 90024. *Web*—www.philipbailey.com.

the key to the band's distinctive sound, which has been described as "harmony and horns." In 1974 their album *Open Your Eyes* hit number 15 in the American album charts and in 1975 they starred in the film *That's the Way of the World*. "Shining Star," the single from the soundtrack album, was their first number one hit. That song also won a Grammy for Best R&B Vocal Performance by a Group. Although known primarily as an R&B outfit, most of their singles also topped the pop charts.

By the late 1970s Earth, Wind & Fire had become famous not only for their music but for their stage shows, which included fireworks and dramatic illusions and disappearing acts created by Doug Henning. They performed in large stadium venues, bringing disco to audiences of the size usually enjoyed by rock performers such as Bruce Springsteen. The influence of Earth, Wind & Fire on pop music in the 1970s and 1980s can hardly be overestimated. Drawing on Latin, African, and jazz rhythms and sounds, the group's versatility and creativity brought them to a wide and loyal audience. By 2005, when their 23rd album *Illumination* was released, Earth, Wind & Fire had won eight Grammy Awards and four American Music Awards to go with their 38 gold and platinum disks, and a star on the Hollywood Walk of Fame. *Illumination* itself was nominated for a Grammy Award in 2006. The band has sold over 19 million albums in a career spanning more than 35 years.

In 1983 Maurice White decided to suspend his work with Earth, Wind & Fire while he concentrated on producing and composing for others. Bailey, who had already released his first solo album, *Continuation*, in 1982, began a solo career that has included R&B, gospel, and jazz. *Chinese Wall* (1984) was co-produced by Bailey with fellow-drummer Phil Collins. It included the single "Easy Lover," a duet with Collins which became one of the year's biggest hits, Bailey's first gold solo release, and one of Collins's best known recordings. The Grammy-winning *Triumph* (1986) and *Philip Bailey* (1994) established Bailey as an important Gospel artist. After 1998's *Life and Love*, Bailey changed direction again, working with jazz greats Pat Metheny, Grover Washington Jr., and others on the album *Dreams*. In 2002 he released another jazz album, *Soul on Jazz*.

Although Bailey has pursued a successful solo career since the early 1980s, he has also toured and recorded albums with Earth, Wind & Fire. In the case of the album *Philip Bailey*, Earth, Wind & Fire concerts in Japan coincided with promoting his solo work. Since the early 1970s Bailey has been one of the most influential black pop musicians, his voice giving Earth, Wind & Fire the distinctive sound that is credited with changing black music in that decade. The band's upbeat brand of pop has survived perhaps because of its emphasis on positive thinking, but also because of willingness of its members to develop. Bailey told *Jet* in 2006, "You just hope to do music that people will embrace…music that will be cutting edge and will be recognized." In 2003 Bailey was one of four members of Earth, Wind & Fire to leave his hand-print on Hollywood's Walk of Fame.

Selected discography

Albums (with Earth, Wind & Fire)

Last Days and Time, 1972.
Head to the Sky, 1973.
Open Our Eyes, 1974.
That's the Way of the World, 1975.
Spirit, 1976.
All 'N All, 1977.
I Am, 1979.
Faces, 1980.
Raise!, 1981.
Powerlight, 1981.
Electric Universe, 1983.
Touch the World, 1987.
Heritage, 1990.
Millennium, 1994.
In the Name of Love, 1997.
The Promise, 2003.
Illumination, 2005.

Albums (solo)

Continuation, 1983.
Chinese Wall, 1984.
The Wonders of His Love, 1985.
Triumph, 1986.
Inside Out, 1986.

Family Affair, 1989.
Philip Bailey, 1994.
Dreams, 1999.
Life and Love, 2002.
Soul on Jazz, 2002.

Sources

Periodicals

Billboard, March 12, 1994, p21; June 26, 1999, p40.
Jet, July 28, 2003, p. 55; March 13, 2006, p. 54.

On-line

Earth, Wind & Fire, www.earthwindandfire.com (August 11, 2007).
"Philip Bailey," *allmusic*, www.allmusic.com/cg/amg. dll?p=amg&sql=11:wifoxqq5ldhe~T1 (July 19, 2007).
"Philip Bailey," *Biography Resource Center*, www. galenet.com/servlet/BioRC (July 18, 2007).
Philip Bailey, www.philipbailey.com (July 18, 2007).

—Chris Routledge

Dean Baquet

1956—

Journalist

Dean Baquet lost his job as editor of the *Los Angeles Times* in a drawn-out, headline-making showdown with the newspaper's owners in the late summer and autumn of 2006. Baquet was a veteran journalist who became the first African-American ever to head the *L.A. Times*, considered one of the top five dailies in the United States. His refusal to reduce the ranks of his editorial staff eventually cost him his job, but Baquet became a hero to newsroom journalists across the United States for his bold move. "I got defiant when I thought it was mindless," he told Katharine Q. Seelye in the *New York Times* about the reasons behind his firing. "I understand the reality of newspapers, but they shouldn't eat themselves alive."

Toiled in Family Business

Baquet hails from a family renowned in his hometown of New Orleans, Louisiana, for producing both jazz musicians and restaurants. The Baquets trace their lineage in the Southern city back 200 years, making them one of the older Creole clans of mixed African and French or Spanish heritage who settled in Louisiana when it was still a colonial possession of France and, later, Spain. Two of Baquet's great-uncles, Achille Baquet and George Baquet, were jazz clarinetists, while Baquet's father and brother own and operate several successful Creole eateries in town.

The first of these was Eddie's Place, which became a well-known Creole-food joint not long after Baquet's parents, Eddie and Myrtle, opened it in the Lakeview area of New Orleans. The senior Baquet had quit his job as a mail carrier and sold the family home to switch careers. Baquet—born in 1956—was quite young when this happened, and he and his four brothers lived behind the restaurant and spent their non-school hours cooking, cleaning, and serving customers. At one point, all five Baquet boys shared a single bed in the apartment attached to the living quarters. All of them attended a local Roman Catholic boys' high school, St. Augustine.

Baquet studied English literature at Columbia University in New York City, and returned home to New Orleans during his summer breaks. Likely as a way of avoiding long hours of work at the family business, he landed a summer internship with a daily newspaper, the New Orleans *States-Item,* which eventually led to an offer of a full-time reporter's job. He quit Columbia and New York City, and began at the paper in 1978 as a police-beat reporter. Two years later, the paper merged with another daily to become the New Orleans *Times-Picayune,* and Baquet soon gained a reputation as a top investigative reporter. In 1984, he was hired by the *Chicago Tribune* as an investigative reporter, and three years later became the paper's chief investigative reporter and associate metropolitan editor for investigations. In this capacity he shared a prestigious Pulitzer Prize for investigative reporting with two colleagues for their series of articles that exposed the financial wrongdoings of some Chicago City Council members.

At a Glance . . .

Born Dean Paul Baquet on September 21, 1956, in New Orleans, LA; son of Eddie Sr. (a restaurateur) and Myrtle (Romano) Baquet; married Dylan F. Landis (a writer), September 6, 1986; children: one son, Ari Theogene Landis. *Education:* Attended Columbia University, NY, c. 1974-78.

Career: *The States-Item,* New Orleans, LA, summer intern, mid-1970s; *Times-Picayune,* New Orleans, began as police-beat reporter, became investigative reporter, 1978-84; *Chicago Tribune,* investigative reporter, 1984-87, associate metropolitan editor for investigations and chief investigative reporter, 1987-90; *New York Times,* metropolitan reporter, 1990-92, special projects editor for the business desk, 1992-1994, special project editor for the office of executive editor, 1994-1995, deputy metropolitan editor, 1995, national editor, 1995-2000, assistant managing editor and Washington bureau chief, 2007–; *Los Angeles Times,* managing editor, 2000-05, editor and executive vice president, 2005-06.

Memberships: Fellow, Academy of Arts and Sciences.

Awards: Pulitzer Prize for investigative reporting (with William Gaines and Ann Marie Lipinski), 1988.

Addresses: *Office—New York Times,* Washington Bureau, 1627 I St., 7th Fl., Washington, DC 20006.

Rose to the Top

In 1990, Baquet joined the nation's top newspaper, the *New York Times,* as a metropolitan reporter. Two years later he became special projects editor for the business desk, and then spent a year in a similar post in the office of the paper's executive editor. In 1995 he was named the new national editor, overseeing a staff of 45 other editors and journalists. He was recruited by the *Los Angeles Times* in 2000 to become the paper's managing editor, and rose to the top job at the paper as its editor and executive vice president in July of 2005 after the resignation of his boss, Joseph S. Carroll. The *Los Angeles Times* was one of the top dailies in the country, and Baquet's elevation to the top editorial job made it the largest U.S. newspaper with an African-American editor—as well as making him the only African-American journalist to lead a major newspaper.

The *Los Angeles Times* had recently suffered a few well-publicized scandals, and was plagued with an increasingly contentious relationship with its corporate parent, the Tribune Company, which also owned the *Chicago Tribune* as well as Long Island's *Newsday* and the *Baltimore Sun,* among other media properties. As managing editor, Baquet had worked with Carroll to make the drastic staff reductions ordered by the Tribune Company board and top executives, cutting some 200 jobs in all. Like most print dailies, the *Times* had been suffering from declining readership numbers over the past decade, but unlike some competitors was actually operating with a healthy profit margin. Baquet's boss, Carroll, reportedly resigned when the Tribune Company pushed for more cuts, and Baquet succeeded him in the summer of 2005.

Faced with Biggest Story of 2005

The first challenge that Baquet faced as the *Times*'s new steward came just weeks into the new job when Hurricane Katrina devastated New Orleans and the surrounding Gulf Coast. The story made national headlines for days, but Baquet had a more personal stake in the story, with the entirety of his family having to flee to Atlanta, and his brother Wayne's restaurant in the Treme neighborhood, Lil' Dizzy's, seemingly ruined by the flood. Covering the environmental disaster and its catastrophic aftermath became "the most emotionally difficult story I've ever been involved with," he told a former colleague of his from the *New York Times,* Shaila Dewan.

Another crisis loomed barely a year after Baquet took over in Los Angeles, when management in Chicago told Baquet and the other top executive of the *Los Angeles Times,* publisher Jeffrey M. Johnson, to find a way to trim the paper's budget further. They refused, and then explained their decision in a *Times* story that ran on September 14, 2006; this move turned the conflict into a rare public glimpse of the routine "long-simmering conflict between many newsrooms and boardrooms around the country as newspapers face an industrywide economic slump and continued demands by Wall Street for improved financial results," noted Seelye, the *New York Times* journalist.

Baquet and Johnson became overnight heroes to an entire generation of working American journalists, and their stance against an unfriendly, out-of-town corporate owner was perceived as a long-overdue David vs. Goliath-type of battle. In Los Angeles, reporters and editors of the legendary *Times* felt that executives in Chicago had done little to dispel fears that there was a secret plan to diminish the *Los Angeles Times*'s esteemed reputation. The situation was further complicated by the Tribune Company's decision to place the paper up for sale, and many hoped that the new owners would be one of a few Southern California-based investors rumored to be interested in the *Times.*

Ordered to Resign

A stand-off ensued between the Chicago-based management and Baquet's newsroom in Los Angeles, and this took an ominous turn when Johnson was ousted on October 5 and replaced by David Hiller. In late October, Baquet spoke at the annual convention of the Associated Press Managing Editors organization, and told his fellow journalists, "It is the job of an editor of a newspaper to put up a little bit more of a fight than we have put up in the past," he said that day, according to *Editor & Publisher*. "Your newsroom wants you to lead them." On October 31, Baquet was ordered to hand in his resignation in ten days' time. Word leaked out, however, and the speculation over his future at the paper emerged as an Internet news item alleging he was about to leave the paper; the rumor appeared on Election Day, and Baquet handed in his resignation a few days earlier than planned, on November 7, 2006.

Baquet's leave-taking prompted an outpouring of support for him among newsroom and other staffers at the *Times*, who had political campaign-style buttons and posters made of his image to show their solidarity with his stance against further budget cuts. The paper was still on the auction block, and hopeful employees and Angelenos alike theorized that a more friendly owner would most likely rehire him. Late in January, 2007, Baquet instead announced his return to New York City and the *New York Times* as its new Washington bureau chief and assistant managing editor, telling the paper's Seelye that the past few months were "a long time for me to be outside a newsroom, and it's starting to make me nuts."

Sources

Periodicals

Daily Variety, January 31, 2007, p. 4.
Editor & Publisher, December 1, 2006.
Los Angeles Magazine, November 2005, p. 70.
New York Times, February 20, 2006; September 15, 2006; September 28, 2006; January 31, 2007.
Washington Post, July 21, 2005.

On-line

"Interviews: Dean Baquet," *Newswar Frontline*, www.pbs.org/wgbh/pages/frontline/newswar/interviews/baquet.html (August 6, 2007).
Smolkin, Rachel, "Nothing but Fans," *American Journalism Review*, August/September 2005, www.ajr.org/Article.asp?id=3912 (August 6, 2007).

—Carol Brennan

Black Thought

1972—

Rapper

Black Thought, photograph. Vince Bucci/Getty Images.

As the MC for the hip-hop act the Roots, Black Thought has been unconventional even by the standards of that iconoclastic group. Where most rappers seek out publicity, Black Thought has avoided it and has rarely even been interviewed over the group's 20-year existence. "Some people—they like to talk, they like to interview…," Black Thought pointed out to Paul Farber of *Philadelphia Weekly*. "I come from a household where it's like, 'Close that door.' As soon as the sun goes down and the street lights come on, you close the curtains so people can't be lookin' up into your s–t. I'm that way in life." Despite his reticence, however, Black Thought's creative contributions were central to the success of the Roots and became even more important as the group set hip-hop longevity records in the 2000s and approached their third decade of existence.

Black Thought was born Tariq Luqmaan Trotter on October 3, 1972. He grew up in the Point Breeze neighborhood in south Philadelphia, Pennsylvania. Although he concealed them from public view for many years, the facts of his childhood were grim. His father, a member of the Nation of Islam's Fruit of Islam policing arm, was killed while he was a baby, and his mother was also killed when he was in the 11th grade. Black Thought's brother Keith amassed a long criminal record.

Black Thought himself, however, seems to have channeled his reactions into creativity. He started rapping at age nine and won admission to Philadelphia's prestigious High School for the Creative and Performing Arts (CAPA). At first he studied visual arts and thought about becoming an architect. He had an instinct for commercial success from the start—he made African medallions and sold them for ten dollars each to his fellow students. Black Thought had disciplinary run-ins at CAPA, starting on his first day with an incident in which he was said to have been caught in a bathroom with a senior girl dance student, and he was eventually expelled. He graduated from Germantown High School and went on to study at Millersville University and to take journalism courses at Temple University in Philadelphia.

By that time he was already a star with a local reputation. "What set Tariq apart was that he had an amazing talent to play the dozens [competitive impro-

At a Glance . . .

Born Tariq Luqmaan Trotter on October 3, 1972; grew up in Philadelphia, PA; children: several. *Education:* Attended High School for the Creative and Performing Arts, Philadelphia, PA; graduated from Germantown High School, Philadelphia; attended Millersville University, Lancaster County, PA, and Temple University, Philadelphia.

Career: Square Roots (musical duo), Philadelphia, PA, cofounder (with Ahmir-Kalib "Questlove" Thompson), rapper, 1987; group expanded and changed name to the Roots, early 1990s–; recorded unreleased solo album, 2000; numerous guest appearances on albums.

Awards: (with the Roots) Best Rap Performance by a Duo or Group, for track "You Got Me," 1999.

Addresses: *Label*—Def Jam/Universal, 2220 Colorado Ave., Santa Monica, CA 90404. *Web*—www.black-thought.com.

vised insult rhyming]," fellow Roots member Ahmir-Kalib "Questlove" Thompson told Farber. In 1987 the pair formed a duo called the Square Roots and took their drum-and-rap act to clubs and talent shows. Not needing electronics, they were also free to take their act to the corner of Fifth Street at Passyunk Avenue in downtown Philadelphia, and in the summer of 1992 they earned some $4,000 in tips.

The Square Roots became the Roots, took on additional members (bassist Hub [Leonard Nelson Hubbard], rapper Malik B. [Malik-Abdul Basit], and "beat boxer" human percussionist Rahzel), and gained a regional reputation for its live, non-electronic take on hip-hop music. Around 1993 things started to happen quickly for the Roots. They were invited to play at a German festival, recorded an album, *Organix,* and parlayed the original appearance into a European tour. Word filtered back to the United States, and the Roots were signed to the DGC/Geffen label and released the album *Do You Want More?!!!??!* in 1995.

The group gained attention for its use of live instruments and limited recourse to such staples of hip-hop language as digital sampling (sometimes they sampled and looped their own rhythmic patterns, but the collage-like aspect of many hip-hop recordings was absent from their music). The Roots won fans among both urban and modern rock audiences. Although the loquacious Questlove was often seen as the group's public face, it was Black Thought (after the departure of

Malik B.) who provided most of the text content. His boasting raps reflected his early background in street and club "battle" performance, but there was also an element of social critique in his music. Some of his raps attacked the materialistic and misogynistic qualities of other hip-hop acts.

After the Roots continued to gain popularity with the albums *Illadelph Halflife* (1996), *The Roots Come Alive* (1999), and *Things Fall Apart* (1999), Black Thought planned to release a solo album of his own, tentatively entitled *Masterpiece Theater.* The album was eventually shelved because of disagreements between the Roots and their label (at the time) MCA; a solo Black Thought album would not have counted toward the group's contractual obligation toward the label. Much of the material Black Thought had written, however, showed up on the next Roots album, *Phrenology* (2002). Black Thought also contributed raps and background vocals to recordings by other artists including the Pharcyde (*Plain Rap*), Common (*Like Water for Chocolate,* which also featured several other members of the Roots), and Jill Scott (*Who Is Jill Scott?*).

Indeed, Black Thought's continuing development as a wordsmith was partly responsible for the ongoing success of the Roots, long after most of their hip-hop contemporaries had disappeared from the scene. The Roots returned with *The Tipping Point* (2004) and *Game Theory* (2006), ranging ever more widely in their subject matter. Black Thought's more serious attitude, Questlove told Peter Rubin of *XXL* magazine, was the key to *Game Theory:* "Mostly, this is Tariq's ongoing evolution," he said. "Once you've mastered battling about your MC prowess, what do you do? I think Tariq has come to grips with his life. I slowly see him starting to open himself more and more and more."

Partly Questlove was referring to the unreleased but widely circulated track "Pity the Child," on which Black Thought, for the first time, addressed the tragedies of his childhood. "Certain joints are a lot more personal, self-reflective, than I may have pulled out before," he pointed out to Rubin. A family also brought Black Thought to a new level of commitment; his son, and the boy's mother, were trapped in New Orleans during Hurricane Katrina, and for several days Black Thought did not know where they were. Asked by the website thaFormula in 2007 about what motivated him, he answered, "I got a family to take care of and kids to feed. That's my motivation, this is my job."

But continuing curiosity also played a role. "I strive for improvement," he told Farber. "I want to be a master of my craft. And I don't know if that's a work ethic that transferred over from the musicians I was around in high school, but that's how I get down. I want to be at the top of my game. That's what pushes me to go back to the drawing board and try to come up with some s–t that's going to be fresher." With a new Roots album on the way and a collaboration with producer Danger Mouse on the way in 2007, Black Thought seemed far from exhausted creatively.

Selected works

Albums (with the Roots)

Organix, Cargo, 1993.
Do You Want More?!!!??!, DGC, 1995.
Illadelph Halflife, DGC, 1996.
The Roots Come Alive, MCA, 1999.
Things Fall Apart, MCA 1999.
Phrenology, MCA, 2002.
The Tipping Point, Geffen, 2004.
Game Theory, Def Jam, 2006.

Albums (guest appearances)

Common, *One Day It'll All Make Sense,* 1997.
Pharoahe Monche, *Internal Affairs,* 1999.
Common, *Like Water for Chocolate,* 2000.
DJ Krush, *Zen,* 2001.
Soulive, *Next,* 2002.

Sources

Books

"The Roots," *Contemporary Musicians,* volume 55, Gale, 2006.

Periodicals

Gadfly, February 1999.
Philadelphia Weekly, August 30, 2006.
Seattle Times, February 2, 2007, p. H4.
XXL, October 2006, p. 88.

On-line

"Black Thought," *All Music Guide,* www.allmusic.com (July 15, 2007).
"History," *Black Thought,* www.black-thought.com/history.php (July 15, 2007).
"Q & A w/Black Thought of the Roots: Perception," *ThaFormula.com,* www.thaformula.com/black_thought_of_the_roots_perception_thaformula_music.html (July 15, 2007).

—James M. Manheim

Barry Bonds

1964—

Professional baseball player

Bonds, Barry, photograph. G Flume/Getty Images.

On August 7, 2007, outfielder Barry Bonds became professional baseball's greatest home run hitter of all time, yet he is often slighted as one of the game's great heroes. Bonds holds the game's two great power records: he topped Hank Aaron's lifetime home run record midway through the 2007 season with his 756th blast, and he set the single-season home run record with 73 in 2001. Bonds is more than a slugger, of course; he's a seven-time Most Valuable Player and the only baseball player to have won the MVP award for his league more than three times. Bonds won all his MVP honors in the National League, for the Pittsburgh Pirates and San Francisco Giants. Despite these accolades, controversy dogged Bonds as he approached Aaron's record, thanks to an ongoing scandal in which a federal grand jury indicted his longtime trainer for providing steroids to pro athletes. Many baseball purists allege that Bond's slugging prowess is the result of steroid use and that any of his records should be marked with the dreaded asterisk to call into question the legitimacy of his feats.

Bonds, the son of former major leaguer Bobby Bonds, has been around the big leagues most of his life. He approaches baseball as a job—with its own pitfalls and pleasures—and does little to enhance his personal image. He has been called uncooperative, arrogant, and selfish. He has quarreled openly with teammates, managers, and especially reporters who try to corner him for interviews. His image, particularly after steroid use made big headlines in 2005, has suffered to such an extent that he has become a favorite target for fan abuse on the road—and an occasional target of scolding from fellow players. Nothing has swayed Bonds to become more tolerant or easygoing. He points to his offensive numbers, eight Gold Glove awards for fielding, and MVP honors, saying they speak for themselves. "I'm not a media person," he told the *San Francisco Examiner*. "I don't like to answer the same questions. I just like to play baseball. I'm not into the other stuff. I turn down a lot of interviews. It's the United States of America. I have freedom of choice. It's two different jobs—keeping the media happy, and keeping yourself and your family happy. It's too much for one man."

If Bonds is unpopular elsewhere, he is popular in San Francisco. Since joining the Giants in 1993, he has helped turn the ballclub around. In 2002, the Giants made their first World Series appearance since 1990, losing to the Anaheim Angels in seven games. *Philadelphia Inquirer* correspondent Sam Carchidi wrote that Bonds has helped to energize a franchise that nearly moved out of town.

Destined for the Big Leagues

You might say that Barry Lamar Bonds inherited a family business. Born on July 24, 1964, in Riverside, California, he is the oldest son of baseball star Bobby Bonds and the godson of Hall of Famer Willie Mays. While other boys his age watched longingly from the bleachers, he used to shag fly balls in the Candlestick Park outfield with his dad and Mays. "I was too young to bat with them," Bonds told *Sports Illustrated*, "but I could compete with them in the field."

Bonds's father joined the Giants in 1968 and played there until 1974. Early in his career, Bobby Bonds was heralded as the successor to Willie Mays, especially since the two men were such good friends. Unfortunately, Bobby could never live up to expectations from fans and media. Even though he hit 30 home runs and stole 30 bases the same season five times, his performance never satisfied the critics. His other teams included the New York Yankees, California Angels, Chicago White Sox, Texas Rangers, and Cleveland Indians.

In the *San Francisco Examiner*, Larry Stone wrote: "The Bonds' ... know what it's like to never do quite enough to satisfy the fans and the media. Bobby was supposed to be the next Willie Mays. Barry was supposed to be the next Bobby Bonds. With both, the story line was always potential, and how it wasn't being fulfilled." Barry Bonds seemed to echo these sentiments when asked about his father by *Sports Illustrated*. "No one gives my dad credit for what he did, and they want to put me in the same category," he said. "He did 30-30 five times, and they say he never became the ballplayer he should have become. Ain't nobody else done 30-30 five times. Nobody. Zero. So I don't care whether they like me or they don't like me. I don't care."

The elder Bonds was an all-out competitor who liked to push his children to excel. Before he even attended school, young Barry could hit a Wiffle ball so hard it could break glass. He took to baseball naturally and learned from his father as well as his high school and college coaches. As a student at Serra High School in San Mateo, California, he played baseball, basketball, and football. When he graduated in 1982, he was offered a contract with his father's former team, the San Francisco Giants. The money was significant— $75,000—but Bonds asked for more. The offer was withdrawn, and Bonds went to college instead.

At Arizona State University, Bonds played baseball for coach Jim Brock. The young outfielder's talent was evident from the outset, and by his junior year he had been named to the All-Pac 10 team three consecutive years. He hit 23 home runs as a junior and compiled a career .347 average, and he was chosen for the *Sporting News* All-American Team in 1985. Brock recalled his years coaching Bonds in *Sports Illustrated*: "I liked the hell out of Barry Bonds. Unfortunately, I never saw a teammate care about him. Part of it would be his being rude, inconsiderate and self-centered. He bragged about the money he turned down, and he popped off about his dad. I don't think he ever figured out what to do to get people to like him."

Drafted by the Pirates

Bonds was drafted again in 1985 when the Pittsburgh Pirates made him the sixth pick in the first round. Bonds was sent to the minor leagues, where he played for the Prince William (Virginia) Pirates of the Carolina League. There he batted .299, hit 13 home runs, and was named league player of the month for July. The following season found him in Hawaii, where he batted .311 in just 44 games before being called up to Pittsburgh. All told, Bonds spent less than two years in the minor leagues. He was just 21 when he became a Pittsburgh Pirate.

Bonds quickly became the starting center fielder and leadoff hitter for the Pirates. On his second day with the team he smacked a double, and less than a week later he had his first home run. By year's end he led the National League rookies in home runs, runs batted in, stolen bases, and walks. The Pittsburgh front office rejoiced—it was hoped that Bonds could help the team back into playoff contention.

In 1987 Bonds was switched to left field and moved to fifth in the batting order because he could hit to all fields. His batting average shot to .261, he hit 25 home runs, and he stole 32 bases. The following year a knee injury kept his stolen base total down but did nothing to his average (.283) or home run total (24).

Bonds came into his own in 1990, the year he won his first National League Most Valuable Player award. He hit 32 home runs and stole 52 bases—prompting further comparisons with his father—and he led the National League in slugging percentage with .565. Largely due to Bonds, the Pirates finished first in the National League East, though the Cincinnati Reds defeated them in the National League Championship Series.

Personality Alienated Allies

In 1990 Pirate manager Jim Leyland told *Sports Illustrated*: "Barry's at the point in his career where he should be. If he handles himself the way he is capable of, he's going to be a consistent star for years." The "if" in Leyland's comment was important. Leyland recognized Bonds's talent but also found the young star temperamental and insensitive toward teammates. After he won the MVP award, Bonds asked for salary arbitration. He wanted a bigger raise than the Pirates were willing to give him. He lost.

Matters took a turn for the worse after the Pirates lost the 1990 NLCS. Bonds joined a group of other star players for a goodwill tour of Japan. Associated Press reporter Alan Robinson claimed that Bonds quit early in an exhibition game and then insulted his Japanese hosts by tossing aside a token gift during a post-game ceremony. Trouble followed Bonds back to the United States. During 1991 spring training in Florida, he engaged in a heated swearing match with Leyland and Pirates coach Bill Virdon after he refused to pose for photographs.

Bonds and Leyland reconciled, and once again the team advanced to the league championship series—this time losing to the Atlanta Braves—and Bonds hit .292 for the 1991 season. Bonds narrowly missed being voted League MVP again, finishing second to Atlanta's Terry Pendleton. In 1992 Bonds captured his second MVP award and a .311, 34-home run year,

though the Pirates missed the World Series yet again in an NLCS rematch with the Braves, when Atlanta rallied for three runs in the ninth inning.

Joined Father with the Giants

It is especially rare for a team to trade a Most Valuable Player. Almost any club will try every avenue to keep such a star happy. The Pirates made little effort to court Bonds when he became a free agent at the end of the 1992 season. It was essentially a foregone conclusion that Bonds would leave the team, and everyone acted accordingly. For some time in the fall of 1992 it looked as though Bonds would sign with the New York Yankees. Then, in December, he received a more tempting offer.

The San Francisco Giants had narrowly escaped being sold and sent to St. Petersburg, Florida. New ownership surfaced in San Francisco, one that wanted to make a fifth-place team a serious contender. The new owner/president, Peter Magowan, eyed Bonds as the most desirable free agent on the marketplace. Magowan offered Bonds a deal that would make him the highest-paid player in baseball. Then the president sweetened the deal by adding Bonds's father, Bobby, as a Giants hitting coach. Recognizing Barry's solitary personality, Magowan even offered the star private hotel suite accommodations on the road. Bonds's average salary for one year of the six-year deal came to more money than his father and godfather earned in their entire careers.

Together, Bobby and Barry Bonds hold the major league record for home runs from fathers and sons. Until the elder Bonds died in August of 2003, they worked side-by-side on the Giants, and were closer than ever. If anyone understood Barry's unwillingness to talk to reporters and sign autographs, it was Bobby. "For them to say my son is moody is not right," the elder Bonds once told the *San Francisco Examiner*. "How many days have they spent with my son? How many nights? They've met him for a couple of minutes, and because he might be busy that day, or they don't know his business-like attitude at the ballpark, they say, 'My god, he's got an attitude.' And that's wrong."

Fans and critics were not the only people that Bonds was having difficulties with in the early 1990s. In the summer of 1994, Bonds filed for divorce from his wife, Sun, and requested joint physical and legal custody of his children. After the divorce was final in 1995, Bonds vowed to the media as well as to his teammates that he had resolved to improve both his personal and professional lives. He began a rigorous off-season workout program and began to try to curb his famous "bad" attitude toward teammates and fans. He wanted to change the impressions of people who thought he was a bad person, for according to Bonds, "I feel the press puts a stamp on certain players and once they stamp you as a 'bad person' then that's what they feed on and there's nothing you can do about it. I know in my heart the type of ballplayer I am and the type of person I am." This transformation by Bonds would not be easily accepted, especially by the fans, who wanted not only a nicer Barry Bonds, but a better baseball playing Barry Bonds. Defending his demeanor on and off the field, Bonds asked *Sports Illustrated* interviewer Richard Hoffer: "Why can't people just enjoy the show? And then let the entertainer go home and get his rest, so he can put on another show?"

Soared to Greatness

Over the next few years, Bonds made sure to live up to his title as an entertainer, continuing to improve his game and his statistics to become one of the best players of the 1990s. In 1996 he become one of only four players to ever hit 300 home runs and steal 300 bases, sharing the honor with such greats as Willie Mays and Andre Dawson. The following year, he led the Giants to a National League West Division title, but San Francisco lost to the eventual World Series champion Florida Marlins in the National League playoffs. Bonds, though, continued to rise in prominence. By the end of the 1990s, *Sport* magazine named him Player of the Decade and he was starting to turn his image around.

Bonds, meanwhile, was restructuring his personal life. In 1998 he married girlfriend Liz Watson and in 1999 he became a father for the third time with the birth of his daughter, Aisha Lynn. The following year, he began to step up his on-field play, becoming the first player to ever hit 400 home runs and steal 400 bases. By the end of the decade, Barry Bonds had won three MVPs and eight Golden Glove Awards.

By the middle of the 2001 season, Bonds had already hit forty-five home runs and was on pace to make a run at Mark McGuire's record of 71 home runs set back in 1998. He was also chasing after Mickey Mantle's walk record as well as the all-time MVP record. The chase for the records would last all season, coming down to the last three games of the Giants' regular season.

On September 27, 2001, Bonds lost good friend and sometimes bodyguard Franklin Bradley and many were worried that this would hamper his play. Bonds proved to everyone, including himself, that nothing was going to stop him from slugging his way into the record books. On October 5, 2001, his first day back from leave, Bonds hit home run number 70, which he dedicated to Bradley. The next day, he would bat his way into history as he hit home runs 71 and 72. Bonds finished the 2001 season with an amazing 73 home runs, 177 walks, 137 runs batted in, and an outstanding average of .328.

Bonds broke every record he had been chasing all season, including the coveted MVP award. The Giants re-signed Bonds to a five-year, $90-million contract, ensuring them a powerful clean-up hitter for years to come. He signed with a team of agents to win endorsements, including having his face on the Wheaties box and being named a spokesman for Kentucky Fried Chicken. As the 2002 season began, many fans and players worried that Bonds could not match the feats of the previous season. Those fears seem to be unfounded however, for Bonds began the season with five home runs in six games and maintained a .375 average. He also surpassed Mark McGwire in career home runs when he batted his 576th home run in May of 2002. It was also his 400th home run with the Giants. In a *Sports Illustrated* interview Bonds said, "I'm shocked, as shocked as anybody." Barry Bonds had developed from a rough and tumble outfielder and outsider to one of the greatest players baseball has ever seen, on and off the field. Reggie Jackson said of Bonds during the awarding of the MVP award, "Bonds's burgeoning legacy is almost palpable in the air. Babe Ruth. Ted Williams. Henry Aaron. Sooner or later they'll have to end that list with Barry Bonds."

Bonds played in his lone World Series in 2002. The Anaheim Angels, intent on not letting Bonds beat them, walked the slugger 13 times in a seven-game series. Bonds did homer four times and had eight hits in 17 at-bats for a .471 average but the Giants, on the cusp of their first World Series title since 1954, blew a 5-0 lead late in the sixth game and dropped the seventh game as well. Anaheim came away with the championship.

Pursued the Ultimate Record

Bonds captured his sixth and seventh MVP awards in 2003 and 2004, respectively, but endured injuries and controversy the following year. After the 2004 season, he underwent arthroscopic surgery on his left knee. In December of that year, the *San Francisco Chronicle* reported that Bonds testified to a Bay Area grand jury that he used a clear substance and a cream given to him by his trainer, Greg Anderson, who was indicted in a steroid-distribution ring. Bonds insister, however, that he did not know they were steroids. The controversy did not die there, however, as a federal grand jury was convened to investigate amid widespread suspicion that professional baseball was permeated by steroid abuse. Anderson and Victor Conte, founder of the Bay Area Laboratory Co-operative (BALCO) that allegedly supplied the steroids, received prison sentences of less than six months for their roles in providing athletes with undetectable banned substances. Anderson was imprisoned again in 2006 and 2007 after refusing to testify before the grand jury.

Despite the near-continuous controversy that followed the 2003 BALCO case—controversy that included U.S. Congressional hearings that featured ballplayers past and present admitting to or denying their own steroid abuse—Bonds kept right on slugging. In 2004, he smacked another 45 home runs. In 2005, after having three operations on his right knee, Bonds played in 14 games for the Giants near the end of the season. He homered five times and batted .286. By the end of the season, he had 708 regular-season homers and trailed Aaron by 47 on the all-time list. On May 28, 2006, Bonds hit his 715th home run, off Byung-Hyun Kim of the Colorado Rockies. With this blast he passed pass Babe Ruth and reach second place behind Hank Aaron on the all-time home run list.

Pursued by Scandal

As the 2007 season opened, all of baseball awaited the day when Bonds would break Hank Aaron's record. Bonds's pursuit of the record was sporadic, with a flurry of towering home runs followed by several days of rest for his aching legs. News stations across the country kept the nation posted on every homer Bonds hit, and sports radio and TV programs buzzed with speculation as to when Bonds would hit the record, whether baseball commissioner Bud Selig would even recognize the achievement by attending games as the time drew near, and whether an asterisk should be placed next to Bonds's name in the record books.

Meanwhile, lawyers continued their pursuit of the slugger. In July of 2006 a federal grand jury had declined to indict Bonds on tax evasion and perjury charges related to his alleged steroid use, but prosecutors were not yet through. On July 21, 2007, the grand jury investigating Bonds's alleged steroid use was extended, and the U.S. Attorney's office claimed that it would soon have enough evidence to indict baseball's greatest slugger, perhaps as early as September. Bonds and his lawyers dismissed the extension, with lawyer Michael Rains calling it a "perjury trap."

On August 7, 2007, Bonds's chase came to a close. After tying Aaron's record two days before with a blast against the San Diego Padres, Bonds faced Washington Nationals pitcher Mike Bacsik with one out in the fifth inning. Bonds pounded Bacsik's 84-mile-per-hour pitch deep to right field as San Francisco fans erupted in applause. Bonds jogged around the bases, soaking in the adulation, and greeted his son and his teammates at the plate. Though commissioner Selig wasn't at the game, former home run champ Hank Aaron appeared in a taped message played on the massive center field video display, lauding Bonds for an accomplishment which required "skill, longevity, and determination."

While Bonds's chase of the mark was over, the media's pursuit of Bonds continued. *Sports Illustrated*'s Tom Verducci summed up the opinions of many sportswriters when he claimed that "756 settled nothing. It invited interpretation more than it provided certainty, making for an awkward kind of history. Bonds still faces the possibility of a federal perjury indictment as well as repercussions from the Mitchell report," an ongoing investigation by former Senator George Mitchell. Bonds, as ever, resisted the attempts to diminish his performance, telling reporters after the big game, "This record is not tainted. At all. At all. Period. You guys can say whatever you want."

As Bonds and the Giants continued their season— Bonds had hit number 761 at the time of this writing— speculation resumed as to what would come next in Bonds's tumultuous career. Would the aging slugger announce his retirement, or would he continue, perhaps reaching the 3,000-hit milestone to add yet another argument for his induction into the Hall of Fame? Would a grand jury finally provide compelling evidence that Bonds's pursuit of the ultimate baseball record was tainted by steroids—or driven by Bonds's undeniable drive and physical talent? Though Bonds holds the home run record, the jury is not yet in on how he will be regarded by fans of America's pastime.

Sources

Books

Bernstein, Ross, *Barry Bonds,* LernerSports, 2004.
Bloom, John, *Barry Bonds: A Biography,* Greenwood Press, 2004.
Fainaru-Wada, Mark, *Game of Shadows: Barry Bonds, BALCO, and the Steroids Scandal that Rocked Professional Sports,* Gotham Books, 2006.
Pearlman, Jeff, *Love Me, Hate Me: Barry Bonds and the Making of an Antihero,* HarperCollins, 2006.

Periodicals

Atlanta Constitution, May 28, 1993, p. H6.
Dallas Morning News, November 27, 2001.
Jet, December 10, 1990; August 17, 1992; December 28, January 4, 1993; June 20, 1994; February 4, 2002.
Los Angeles Times, November 19, 1992.
New York Daily News, March 5, 1991.
Newsday (Long Island, NY), April 4, 1993.
Newsweek, May 31, 1993, p. 64; September 20, 1993, p. 53.
Philadelphia Daily News, February 25, 1993.
Philadelphia Inquirer, April 28, 1993.
San Francisco Chronicle, May 5, 2002, p. B4.
San Francisco Examiner, October 8, 1990.
Sporting News, July 12, 1999, pp. 12-20; August 20, 2007, pp. 12-16.
Sports Illustrated, June 25, 1990; December 14, 1992, p. 9; April 26, 1993, pp. 19-21; May 24, 1993, pp. 13-21; October 11, 1993, p. 20; June 4, 2001, pp. 8-11; October 15, 2001, pp. 46-50; April 15, 2002, pp. 42-45; August 13, 2007, p. 44; August 20, 2007, p. 46.
Time, August 20, 2007, p. 20.

USA Today, June 19, 1991.

Washington Post, June 6, 1993, p. D1.

On-line

"Barry Bonds," *Baseball-reference.com,* www.baseball reference.com/b/bondsba01.shtml (July 23, 2007).

"Barry Bonds," *ESPN.com,* http://sports.espn.go.com/mlb/players/profile?statsId=3918 (July 23, 2007).

"BALCO Boss Conte to Serve Eight Months in Prison," *USA Today,* www.usatoday.com/sports/2005-10-18-balco-conte-sentencing_x.htm (August 31, 2007).

"Bonds Returns, Giants Win," *Washington Post*, www.washingtonpost.com/wp-dyn/content/article/2005/09/13/AR2005091300089.html (August 31, 2007).

"The Official Barry Bonds.com Site," www.barrybonds.com (August 31, 2007).

—Mark Kram, Ralph Zerbonia, and Tom Pendergast

Cupcake Brown

1964—

Lawyer, writer

An attorney at one of the leading law firms in San Francisco, California, Cupcake Brown spent 14 years as a drug addict and prostitute after leaving an abusive foster home. Involved with gangs and often homeless, she endured rape, alcoholism, serious injury in a drive-by shooting, and other assaults. As she struggled for many years to get clean and sober, Brown continually succumbed to the lure of street life. Finally, she found enough strength in her religious faith to succeed in beating the obstacles that had once seemed impossible to overcome. Putting herself through school, Brown established herself in an intensely competitive profession and began traveling throughout the country as a motivational speaker and advocate.

Though Brown was not born into a privileged family, her first years were stable and happy. She received her unusual name when her mother, not fully alert after giving birth in 1964, asked for a cupcake and the delivery room nurse wrote that down on the birth certificate. Brown grew up in San Diego, California, and enjoyed a fairly typical childhood until age 11, when she came home one day to discover her mother lying dead in bed from an epileptic seizure. As soon as she was taken away from her stepfather and placed in foster care, her troubles began.

Ran Away from Foster Homes

As she recounts in her memoir, *A Piece of Cake,* Brown was given alcohol and was physically and sexually assaulted within the first week in her foster home. She ran away, finding refuge with a young prostitute who gave her drugs as well as tips on how to sell her sexual favors on the street. "I actually never looked beyond tomorrow," Brown said in an interview with Margena A. Christian in *Jet.* "Being a child in the streets, it was always about today. I'm going to get high today. Where am I going to sleep tonight? I didn't have time to worry about tomorrow." Every time she was returned to foster care, she would run away again. By the time she was 13, Brown was selling drugs and had become pregnant. The pregnancy ended in a miscarriage after other foster girls in the home where Brown was staying attacked her.

Brown decided to hitchhike to Los Angeles, where she was soon introduced to members of the Crips, a notorious gang. The bond among gang members, she recalled to *Entertainment Weekly* contributor Karen Valby, was something she desperately craved. "To this day," she said, "I haven't felt that kind of love and camaraderie.... In a gang, they don't care if you're drunk, loaded, crippled, blind. But, yes...it's an unhealthy kind of camaraderie." The cycle of alcohol, drugs, and crime continued, intensifying over the years. Brown used crack, LSD, cocaine, alcohol, and anything else she could find. Shortly before she turned 16, she was shot in the back in a drive-by incident while celebrating her upcoming birthday. Two bullets lodged in her spine, and doctors warned her that she might never be able to walk again.

After a week in the hospital, Brown regained feeling in her legs and was discharged back to a foster home. "This time it was actually a blessing because it was my way out of a gang," she told Christian. "You don't just walk away from a gang. It's blood in and blood out." Though Brown did not graduate from high school she did receive some clerical training at school and managed to get and keep a job, supporting herself as a legal secretary starting in 1987. Her drug and alcohol addiction, however, continued to dominate her life. Obsessed with getting a fix one day in 1989, she stole from a dealer who beat her senseless, then raped her and left her body near a dumpster. He even took her shoes. When she woke up, she realized she would die on the street if she didn't get help—and get it fast. "You could see the imprint of my ribs—I was a size 1," Brown said in remarks quoted in the *San Francisco Chronicle.* " I had no shoes. My hair was sticking up like Buckwheat. My lips were cracked and burnt from the crack pipe." She walked 60 blocks to the law firm where she worked, and told her boss, Kenneth J. Rose, that she could not get straight on her own. He helped her check into a rehabilitation facility.

Put Herself Through College

Though she was happy to be clean and sober at last, Brown relapsed after about two months. "The new was unfamiliar," she told Christian, and she began seeing her old friends again, whose influence dragged her back into her old self-destructive habits. But she was able to emerge from this period with renewed determination to fight her addictions. Using her religious faith to guide her, and relying on the support of her stepfather, Tim Long, and other positive mentors, she made it. And as she pointed out to Valby, "I was not only able to change, but was able to make drastic changes." Without even a high school diploma or a GED certificate, she enrolled in San Diego City Community College. At times, she had so little money that she could afford tuition for only one class, but she persevered. She graduated in 1995 with honors, transferring to San Diego State University as a full-time student later that year. Brown earned a degree in criminal justice administration, magna cum laude, in 1998 and then enrolled at the University of San Francisco School of Law, working four part-time jobs while attending classes full-time. "I worked my ass off," she said, quoted by Valby. "Nothing was given to me, and I mean nothing." Brown earned a law degree in 2001 and was admitted to the California bar later that same year.

As a litigator with Bingham McCutchen in San Francisco, Brown focuses on antitrust and trade regulation, securities and corporate governance, and white-collar crime. In addition, she is a popular motivational speaker and advocate for children's rights. Encouraged by a former professor to write about her life, she began setting down her memories but worried that the near-constant haze of drugs and alcohol in which she had lived for so long had distorted her recollections. Determined not to misrepresent what really happened, she talked to people from her past to corroborate details. She even hired a private investigator, whom she paid out of her own pocket, to confirm that events as she depicted them were accurate.

The resulting book, *A Piece of Cake*, became a *New York Times* bestseller. Speaking to Christian in *Jet*, Brown said that her experiences taught her courage—because "it doesn't take courage for that which you are not afraid to do." God, she added, saved her "for a sense of motivation and encouragement to others because I am so normal. God makes the impossible possible. So there are no excuses but you."

Selected writings

Books

A Piece of Cake, Crown, 2006.

Sources

Books

Contemporary Authors, Thomson Gale, 2007.

Periodicals

Publishers Weekly, November 21, 2005, p. 36.
Jet, April 24, 2006, p. 52.

Entertainment Weekly, March 3, 2006, p. 72.
Ebony, March 1, 2006, p. 28.
New York Times Book Review, February 23, 2006, p. E8.
San Francisco Chronicle, July 14, 2000, p. A17; May 21, 2001, p. A17.

On-line

Cupcake Brown, www.cupcakebrown.com/index2.html (July 5, 2007).

—E. M. Shostak

Sheryll Cashin

1962(?)—

Law professor, author

Sheryll Cashin has become a prominent advocate for closing the racial and class divisions in America. Cashin's 2004 book, *The Failures of Integration: How Race and Class Are Undermining the American Dream*, received widespread attention for its revelations of the growing divisions within American society. A professor at Georgetown University Law Center and former White House advisor, Cashin wrote in her introduction: "I come to this as a scholar but also as a black woman who values black institutions and communities even as I advocate for race and class integration."

Raised in an Activist Family

Born and raised in Huntsville, Alabama, Sheryll D. Cashin was the daughter of Dr. John L. Cashin, Jr., and Joan Carpenter Cashin. Her father founded the National Democratic Party of Alabama and ran against the segregationist George Wallace in the 1970 Alabama gubernatorial election. Cashin's childhood experiences foreshadowed her future interest in racial integration. Cashin's family moved from their middle-class black neighborhood to an all-white neighborhood so that her brother could attend Huntsville's only elementary school with a program for the hearing impaired. However a few years later, for financial reasons, the Cashins returned to their home in the black neighborhood. There Cashin found "a happier, more supportive social environment" she recalled in *The Failures of Integration*.

Cashin told Jon Christensen of *Grist* in March of 2006: "My parents were activists, but also members of the Unitarian church, although both became Baptists later. I grew up in a household where the most fascinating people would come through. My parents lived a very diverse life, with friends from a lot of different realms. They modeled for me how they wanted to be in the world. These were two people with very strong black identities. They wanted me to value who I was as a black person and value black institutions, but also not cut myself off from exciting, interesting things." Cashin wrote in *Failures* that she "mastered the fundamentals of both black and mainstream culture in a way that enabled me to relate to many different social groups."

After graduating *summa cum laude* from Vanderbilt University in 1984, Cashin studied English law at St. Catherine's College, Oxford University, earning her master's degree with honors in 1986. She graduated with honors from Harvard Law School in 1989.

Joined the Clinton Administration

Cashin became a law clerk for U.S. Supreme Court Justice Thurgood Marshall, who had successfully argued for school desegregation before the 1954 Supreme Court in *Brown v. Board of Education*. She wrote of Marshall in *Failures*: "In his chambers he worried aloud about what he would say to a poor black kid about his life chances, given the schools and neighborhoods such kids were relegated to."

Cashin went on to clerk for Judge Abner Mikva of the U.S. Court of Appeals for the District of Columbia and was an associate at the law firm of Sirote & Permutt

At a Glance . . .

Born Sheryll D. Cashin in 1962(?) in Huntsville, AL; married Marque Chambliss, 2003(?); children: twin sons. *Education:* Vanderbilt University, BE, electrical engineering, 1984; Oxford University, MA, English law, 1986; Harvard University, JD, 1989. *Politics:* Progressive Democrat.

Career: U.S. Supreme Court, Washington, DC, clerk to Justice Thurgood Marshall, 1990-91; U.S. Court of Appeals, Washington, DC, clerk to Judge Abner Mikva; Sirote & Permutt, P.C., Washington, DC, associate; The White House, Washington, DC, Office of Transition Counsel, associate counsel, National Economic Council, Director for Community Development, 1993-95; U.S. Department of Housing and Urban Development, Washington, DC, Deputy Assistant Secretary for Empowerment Zones assigned to Vice President Al Gore, 1995-96; Georgetown University Law Center, Washington, DC, professor of law, 1997–; author, 2004–.

Memberships: Vanderbilt University, trustee, Public and Government Relations Committee, Academic Programs Committee chair.

Awards: Marshall Scholar at Oxford University; *Harvard Law Review.*

Addresses: *Office*—Georgetown University Law Center, 600 New Jersey Ave. NW, Washington, DC 20001.

before joining the administration of President Bill Clinton in 1993. As director of community development for the National Economic Council, she oversaw urban policy and community development initiatives and advised on community development in inner-city neighborhoods. As staff director for the Community Empowerment Board in the Office of Vice President Al Gore, Cashin worked on community-based revitalization strategies for urban and rural communities. A then-single woman, she bought a bungalow in Shepherd Park, an integrated but majority-black upper-middle-class neighborhood in Washington.

Frustrated by her inability to address issues of social injustice within the administration, Cashin left public service in 1997 and joined the faculty at Georgetown. She began researching the social and economic costs and consequences of racial segregation in urban and suburban America. Her analysis of census and school enrollment data revealed that the communities and schools of America remained segregated and unequal.

Published Failures of Integration

Aimed at a lay audience, *The Failures of Integration* was well-received. It was a *New York Times Book Review* editor's choice selection for three weeks. Cashin argued that "Integration is critical for the enduring strength of our democracy," as well as true equality of opportunity. Whites as well as blacks were hurt by segregation, as they struggled to pay for more expensive housing in all-white neighborhoods, enduring long commutes and diminished quality of life.

Cashin enumerated the numerous causes and consequences of continued racial and class segregation. At the Minnesota Meeting in September of 2006, Cashin explained: "Where you live determines whether you are going to be exposed to a host of models of success, what kind of schools you will go to, and whether you're going to have employment opportunities. And in America, in 2006, where a person lives is heavily influenced by race and class.... It was only after seven decades of very intentional public policies that we got to the point where separation by race and class seems like what is natural." But it was not only public policies that discouraged integration. Blacks, Cashin wrote, "have become integration weary."

Cashin called on civil rights activists to address discrimination in housing. She advocated breaking up inner-city ghettos with suburban housing vouchers, home-ownership incentives in high-poverty neighborhoods, requirements for low-income housing in new developments, and the promotion of school choice, including charter schools designed by blacks for blacks. In particular, she pointed to the need for regional solutions to the problems of metropolitan areas.

In addition to her teaching and writing, Cashin made frequent appearances as a radio and television commentator. She wrote in the *Washington Post* in 2004: "I am a champion of a transformative integration of the races and classes because I have become convinced that it is the only route to closing the egregious gaps of inequality that weaken our nation. I can acknowledge the benefits of a minority enclave and still hope to see the day when there will be less need for such a psychic haven. I dare to believe that America could be a society premised upon brotherly love and inclusion, rather than fear and exclusion."

Cashin told *Contemporary Authors* that *The Failures of Integration* "was written out of passion, or anger rather.... I was angry mostly about the raw deal many minority poor kids receive through no fault of their own. I decided to channel five years of academic research on the subject into a book for lay audiences. In the process, I found a voice as a writer and am now committed to the writing life." True to her word, in

October of 2007 Cashin published a memoir of her extraordinary family.

Selected writings

Books

The Failures of Integration: How Race and Class Are Undermining the American Dream, Public Affairs, 2004.
"Katrina: The American Dilemma Redux," in *After the Storm: Black Intellectuals Explore the Meaning of Hurricane Katrina*, David Dante Troutt, ed., New Press, 2006.
The Agitator's Daughter: Four Generations of One Extraordinary African-American Family, Public Affairs, 2007.

Periodicals

"Federalism, Welfare Reform, and the Minority Poor: Accounting for the Tyranny of State Majorities," *Columbia Law Review*, Vol. 99, No. 3, April 1, 1999, p. 552.
"Privatized Communities and the 'Secession of the Successful': Democracy and Fairness Beyond the Gate," *Fordham Urban Law Journal*, Vol. 28, No. 5, June 1, 2001, pp. 1675-1692.
"The American Dilemma Continues," *Education Week*, Vol. 23, No. 37, May 19, 2004, pp. 40-41.
"American Public Schools Fifty Years after Brown: A Separate and Unequal Reality," *Howard Law Journal*, Vol. 47, 2004, pp. 341-360.
"Race, Class and Real Estate: What We'll Get from Mixing It Up," *Washington Post*, August 1, 2004, p. B2.
"The Dilemma of the Black Middle Class," *Next American City*, November, 2005, pp. 31-35.
"Democracy, Race, and Multiculturalism in the Twenty-First Century: Will the Voting Rights Act Ever be Obsolete?" *Washington University Journal of Law and Policy*, Vol. 22, 2006, pp. 71-105.

On-line

"A Tale of Two Schools," May 13, 2004, *AlterNet*, www.alternet.org/story/18687 (June 29, 2007).

Sources

Periodicals

Washington Post, November 10, 2004, p. B1.

On-line

"Building an Integrated Society: A Community Conversation," *Minnesota Meeting*, www.minnesotameeting.com/disparities/mtg3.htm (August 12, 2007).
"Integrate Expectations: An Interview with Integration Advocate Sheryll Cashin," March 21, 2006, *Grist*, www.grist.org/news/maindish/2006/03/21/Christensen (August 12, 2007).
"Sheryll Cashin," *Contemporary Authors Online*, http://galenet.galegroup.com/servlet/BioRC (August 12, 2007).
"Sheryll D. Cashin," *Georgetown Law*, www.law.georgetown.edu/faculty/cashin (August 12, 2007).

Other

"Interview: Sheryll Cashin Discusses Her New Book *The Failures of Integration*" (Transcript), *National Public Radio: All Things Considered*, May 5, 2004.

—Margaret Alic

Presley Chweneyagae

1984—

Actor

South African actor Presley Chweneyagae became an internationally recognized star when his title role in the compelling drama *Tsotsi* helped the film win an Academy Award for Best Foreign Language Film of 2005. The story tracked the personal redemption of a tough Johannesburg gang leader in a violent, post-apartheid era. *New York Times* reviewer Manohla Dargis noted the "charismatic newcomer…delivers a fine, sympathetic performance, and you root for the actor even when his character inspires unforgiving thoughts."

Born Under Apartheid

Chweneyagae, whose name is pronounced "Shwen-NAY-ah-hi-eh," was born in October of 1984 in North West Province, the modern name of a newly created unit that merged parts of Transvaal and Cape Province with Bophuthatswana, one of the former Bantustans, or black areas, of South Africa's apartheid era. Chweneyagae was at a time when his nation was an international pariah for its draconian statutes that separated a ruling white minority from the majority black population, and denied the latter nearly all political rights. South Africa's blacks were confined to the homelands or townships adjacent to major cities, where they lived in abysmal, near-medieval conditions, and were required to carry a pass, or identity card, at all times and show it on demand. Under apartheid, South African law also provided for detention without trial for an indefinite period. All of this changed when Chweneyagae was 10 years old, as the apartheid system

was finally dismantled and South Africa's first free elections were held.

Chweneyagae was one of four children in his family, and his police-officer mother noticed that her son seemed to enjoy the roles he played in the religious dramas staged by their church. She decided to enroll him in acting classes. At the age of 14, he moved on to a drama school run by a well-known young playwright and stage director, Mpumelelo Paul Grootboom, and after several theater roles in his late teens he made his film debut in *Tsotsi*. The story was based on South African playwright Athol Fugard's only novel, and was updated for the screen by director Gavin Hood. Chweneyagae had auditioned for one of the supporting roles in the story of a violence-prone young South African, but Hood decided to cast the unknown actor as the lead instead.

Starred in Tsotsi

Chweneyagae's character calls himself "Tsotsi," a word that references a township patois called Tsotsi-Ttaal, which blends elements of Afrikaans, English, Zulu, Xhosa, Tswana and Sotho; the word "tsotsi" is also a term for a thug. Tsotsi's character and friends are denizens of Soweto, the black township attached to Johannesburg, South Africa's largest city, and in the post-apartheid, high-unemployment era they subsist by stealing and other criminal acts. After a particularly brutal subway robbery, one of Tsotsi's underlings makes a drunken comment that Tsotsi appears to have no remorse, which prompts another episode of brutal-

At a Glance . . .

Born Presley Oageng Chweneyagae on October 19, 1984, in North West Province, South Africa.

Career: Actor. Co-author of *Relativity*, a 2003 series of vignettes that had a run in Edinburgh, Scotland, as *Township Stories*.

Awards: American Black Film Festival, Black Movie Award for outstanding performance by an actor in a leading role, 2006, for *Tsotsi*.

Addresses: *Agent*–Moonyeenn Lee Associates, P.O. Box 41792, Craighall 2024, Johannesburg, South Africa.

ity. Fleeing the scene, Tsotsi finds himself in an affluent neighborhood, and comes upon a car with the engine running. Ignoring the pleas of the woman who had stepped out of it briefly, he takes off in it and shoots her as she clings to her vehicle as it speeds away.

Tsotsi realizes why the woman—a middle-class black South African—was so desperate when he finally spies the infant in its car seat. Ditching the luxury ride, he puts the baby in a shopping bag and furtively takes it back to his Soweto shanty. Realizing he cannot care for his new guest properly—an attempt to give the baby condensed milk results in an army of ants covering the infant—he seeks out a neighbor woman and single mother named Miriam (Terry Pheto) and demands that she nurse it. Soon, the newspapers have picked up on the story of the carjacking and the missing infant, and Chweneyagae's Tsotsi begins to realize that his long list of enemies have ample reason to turn him in to authorities. The plot and his decision to turn his life around are peppered with flashbacks that tell of his own harsh and tragic childhood.

Film Brought International Acclaim

Tsotsi caused a sensation when it premiered at the Edinburgh Film Festival in the summer of 2005, followed by another acclaimed showing at the Toronto Film Festival in September. It was released in South Africa that December and then internationally in early 2006. Some critics termed the gangster-plus-baby formula an overly simplistic, melodramatic one, but even the traditionally independent-minded trade journal *Variety* commended both the movie and its star. "Caring for the child gradually repairs Tsotsi's broken spirit, a trajectory that could have been mawkish or unbelievable in lesser hands, but which Hood and particularly Chweneyagae make utterly convincing," asserted the

paper's Leslie Felperin. The *Sunday Times* of London also weighed in favorably, with writer Cosmo Landesman conceding that the thug-turned-hero plot was "a little flimsy, as he gets in touch with feelings he has long suppressed. The idea is that what reforms him is his contact with humanity. But such is the performance of Chweneyagae—his ability to move from vicious killer to weeping child—that it all seems totally convincing."

Tsotsi made Chweneyagae a star in South Africa, and his standing was further boosted when Hood's movie won the 2006 Academy Award for Best Foreign Language Film of the past year. Later that year Chweneyagae traveled to Los Angeles for the Black Movie Awards, and was stunned to accept the honor for Outstanding Performance by an Actor in a Leading Role, besting contenders that included Denzel Washington and Cuba Gooding Jr. At the event, he was thrilled to meet so many African-American actors whose films he had watched all his life, including filmmaker Spike Lee, who sat next to him at the ceremony. Many of his idols greeted the newcomer with enthusiasm, saying they had seen *Tsotsi* and had been impressed.

Continued to Appear on Stage

Back in Johannesburg, Chweneyagae continued to work in theater and collaborated with Grootboom on a stage work that had a 2006 run at the Traverse Theatre in Edinburgh under the title *Township Stories*. *Tsotsi* and its Oscar win boosted the profile for South Africa's new, richly diverse cultural offerings on an international stage, Chweneyagae said in an interview with Alice Jones for the London *Independent* newspaper, which seemed to be propelling the post-apartheid cultural scene even further ahead. "People are starting to take work more seriously, be more creative. There's a different landscape now—the slums, kwaito music," referring to Johannesburg's hybrid of African beats with hip-hop and house music.

Chweneyagae even said that *Tsotsi* had altered his own perspective on life in South Africa, noting that he had been mugged just before filming started. "When you are a victim of crime, you do tend to think, 'if I ever come face to face with that person, I'll kill them or do something to get back at them,'" he told *Lexington Herald-Leader* writer Rich Copley. "But after watching the film, I can see that people do not choose where they come from. They do not choose their financial background or their social background. It's just circumstances that force them to be what they are."

Selected works

Films

Tsotsi, 2005.

Sources

Periodicals

Independent (London, England), August 22, 2006, p. 14.

Lexington Herald-Leader (Lexington, KY), April 21, 2006.

Mercury (South Africa), February 28, 2007, p. 4.

New York Times, February 24, 2006.

O, The Oprah Magazine, February 1, 2006, p. 42.

Observer (London, England), March 19, 2006, p. 14.

Star (South Africa), October 17, 2006, p. 5; January 25, 2007, p. 6.

Sunday Times (London, England), March 19, 2006, p. 12.

USA Today, February 24, 2006, p. 3E.

Variety, August 29, 2005, p. 71.

On-line

Balfour, Brad, "Tsotsi: An Interview with Pressley Chweneyagae," *Blackfilm,* www.blackfilm.com/20060217/features/chweneyagae.shtml (August 11, 2007).

—Carol Brennan

Albert B. Cleage, Jr.

1911-2000

Religious leader

Reverend Albert B. Cleage, Jr., who took the name Jaramogi Abebe Agyeman in the 1970s, spent five decades as a champion of black theology, during which time he built thriving congregations and played a significant role in strengthening African-American political activism. He emerged as a leader during the devastating riots of 1967 in Detroit, Michigan, and a 1968 *Detroit Free Press* poll confirmed him to be one of the most well-known and influential leaders in his community. Establishing member churches of his Pan African Orthodox Christian Church in cities across the United States helped win Agyeman respect on a national level in the decades to come. The congregations he founded were part of his Black Christian Nationalist Movement, which he launched in 1967. With its community service programs, the movement—as well as Cleage's Shrine of the Black Madonna—sought to provide a framework for the economic self-sufficiency of its members. Agyeman's energetic leadership style and development of a well-organized political action group called the Black Slate Inc furthered the careers of several African-American politicians, most notably the first African-American mayor of Detroit, Coleman Young. Esteemed for his spiritual leadership, he also "changed the face of political organizing," according to Kilpatrick writing in the *Michigan Chronicle* at the time of Cleage's death.

Inspired by Father

Agyeman was born Albert Buford Cleage, Jr., in Indianapolis, Indiana, on June 13, 1911, the first of seven children born to Albert, Sr., a physician, and Pearl Reed Cleage. The family relocated to Kalamazoo, Michigan, a few years later, and then to Detroit. Cleage's father became the first African-American doctor on the city payroll in 1930, a post he held for 16 years while at the same time operating his own practice. Dr. Cleage also helped found Detroit's first African-American hospital, and he worked tirelessly with a number of civic and church groups in his community. Inspired by his father's drive, Albert, Jr., studied sociology at Wayne State University in Detroit and was employed as a social caseworker for the Detroit Department of Public Health. He graduated in 1937 and earned a divinity degree from Oberlin College Graduate School of Theology in 1943.

By then Albert Cleage, Jr., had been ordained in the Congregational faith and was a minister at the Chandler Memorial Congregational Church in Lexington, Kentucky. He later moved to California, where he headed the Church for the Fellowship of All Peoples, a San Francisco interracial congregation, and attended film school at the University of Southern California. In 1946 Cleage was appointed pastor of St. John's Congregational Church in Springfield, Massachusetts. This was one of the oldest African-American congregations in New England and one that played an active role in the surrounding community.

Cleage became known as an outspoken activist during his tenure at St. John's for his involvement with the local branch of the National Association for the Advancement of Colored People (NAACP) and the overseeing of the church's extensive social service pro-

At a Glance . . .

Born Albert Buford Cleage, Jr., on June 13, 1911, in Indianapolis, IN; died on February 20, 2000, in Calhoun Falls, SC; renamed Jaramogi Abebe Agyeman, 1970s; son of Albert Buford (a physician) and Pearl (Reed) Cleage; married Doris Graham, 1943 (divorced, 1955); children: Pearl, Kristin. *Education*: Wayne State University, 1929-31; Fisk University, 1931-32; Wayne State University, BA, sociology, 1937; Oberlin College Graduate School of Theology, BDiv, 1943; University of Southern California Film School, mid-1940s.

Career: Detroit Department of Public Health, Detroit, MI, social caseworker, 1936-38; Union Congregational Church, Painesville, OH, minister, late 1930s; ordained Congregational minister, 1943; Chandler Memorial Congregational Church, Lexington, KY, minister, 1942-43; Church for the Fellowship of All Peoples, San Francisco, CA, pastor, 1943-44; St. John's Congregational Church, Springfield, MA, pastor, 1946-51; St. Mark's Community Church, Detroit, pastor, 1951-53; Central Congregational Church, Detroit, MI, pastor, 1953; Michigan Freedom Now Party (political party), co-founder, 1957; Black Christian Nationalist Movement, founder, 1967; Shrine of the Black Madonna, 1967, founder and first Holy Patriarch, 1967-2000; Pan African Orthodox Christian Church denomination, founder, 1970s; Black Slate Inc (political organization), founder, 1970s; Beulah Land (church farm), Calhoun Falls, SC, founder, 1999.

grams. In a published history of St. John's that was excerpted in Hiley S. Ward's biography of Cleage titled *Prophet of the Black Nation*, the minister was recalled as "a courageous fighter for equal opportunities for Negroes in the field of employment, and he did much during his ministry at St. John's to open up new avenues of work for qualified job applicants." The examples set by the community service programs at the esteemed church, such as its youth athletic leagues, provided valuable lessons for Cleage when he arrived back in Detroit to head another church.

Community Service Led to Political Activism

Cleage was named pastor of St. Mark's Community Church, a Presbyterian ministry on Detroit's west side,

in 1951. Two years later, he led a portion of its congregation in the formation of a new religious organization called the Central Congregational Church (renamed the Central United Church of Christ (CUCC) in 1965). Cleage's concept of a church as the focal point of the community—especially in the political and educational spheres—was increasingly put into practice. In 1957, politicians tried to rezone a primarily African-American congressional district in an attempt to diminish its influence. Cleage and his congregation were vocal opponents of the gerrymandering. They also opposed the reclassification of certain school zones, a move seen as a step toward a more segregated, and therefore unequal, educational system.

The civil rights movement found an increasing base of support among Cleage's churchgoers. In June of 1963 Cleage, along with civil rights leader Reverend Martin Luther King, co-directed a "Walk to Freedom" through Detroit. By the mid 1960s, both Cleage's church and the surrounding community had changed; in some ways, African Americans in Detroit had benefited from the prosperity provided by the automobile industry and become more affluent, educated, and politically aware. Such gains only exacerbated the always-present hostilities between the black and white communities of the city.

Cleage believed in the power Black spirituality could offer to realize Black liberation and sought ways to make Black churches politically active. He was one of the founders of the Freedom Now Party in Michigan, an all-black political party, in 1964 and ran as the first African-American candidate for Michigan governor that same year. Though he ran for several political offices over the years, he did not win an election himself. Instead, his political power developed through his ability to mobilize others. In 1967 he helped to found such groups as the City Wide Citizens Action Committee and the Federation for Self Determination.

As Cleage took note of the increasing politicization of black communities, he began studying earlier African-American religious movements. The tenets of Malcolm X, then an important leader in the Nation of Islam, held great relevance for Cleage. Malcolm X warned of the pitfalls of the integration that King espoused in the struggle to become fully equal members of American society. He pointed out that such integration was not possible without also giving up a part of one's own heritage.

Started Movement with Installation of Black Madonna

In March of 1967, Cleage took a step that was to have far-reaching implications for both his parish and the city: he installed an 18-foot religious painting that depicted a black Madonna and infant Jesus. The work was officially dedicated on Easter Sunday. During the service, Cleage spoke of the need for a separate Christian denomination for the African-American community, one that worshipped a savior who, according to biblical references, may have indeed been of African heritage. "For nearly five hundred years the illusion that Jesus was white dominated the world," the pastor said that day. "The resurrection which we celebrate today is the resurrection of the historic black Christ and the continuation of his mission. The church which we are building and which we call upon you to build wherever you are, is the church which gives our people, black people, faith in their power to free themselves from bondage, to control their own destiny, and to rebuild the Nation."

The Black Christian Nationalist Movement that Cleage established soon attracted legions of followers in Detroit. Cleage's new creed took the tenets of Black separatism—drawn from the teachings of Marcus Garvey, Nation of Islam leader Elijah Muhammad, and Malcolm X—and joined them with religious inspiration from the Bible to give birth to a new Christian denomination that spoke directly to the African-American community. A few months after the movement's inception, the city of Detroit was ravaged in vicious rioting that lasted four days in the summer of 1967. A mostly white police force, notorious for its racism and aided by a National Guard culled from the state's rural counties, seemed to take advantage of the lawlessness of the situation to brutalize—and fire on—members of the city's African-American community. The devastation left by the mayhem galvanized Detroiters to an even greater degree: whites began moving out en masse to the suburbs, and membership in African-American political and social organizations skyrocketed. Cleage and the Shrine of the Black Madonna, as his congregation was soon christened, became the focal point of a new era for the city.

One of the most important tenets proposed by Cleage, based on his own scholarship and writings, was that Jesus was a black revolutionary. He wrote that the religious leader was descended from a dark-skinned tribe of Israelites and that his teachings preached a radical new order. Such tenets eventually made Jesus a political prisoner and a martyr for his cause, and whites had appropriated his teachings to establish a creed for themselves alone. In Cleage's biography, Ward quoted the minister as saying: "Jesus was the nonwhite leader of a nonwhite people struggling for national liberation against the rule of a white nation.… That white Americans continue to insist upon a white Christ in the face of all historical evidence to the contrary and despite the hundreds of shrines to Black Madonnas all over the world, is the crowning demonstration of their white supremacist conviction that all things good and valuable must be white."

For a 1990 *Detroit Free Press* article on the history and influence of the Shrine, reporter Dori J. Maynard interviewed local educator Clifford Watson. "It got to your psyche," Watson said of the Black Madonna mural in Cleage's church. "If you thought you were…nothing and you walked into the church and you saw a black woman holding a black baby, the Mother Mary, it got to your psyche. And [when] you saw a picture of a black man being crucified on the cross, that had to hit your psyche. Those kind of impressions stayed with you for a lifetime."

Such declarations, combined with Cleage's outspoken political activism in the city, soon earned him a reputation as one of the foremost leaders of the black nationalist movement in Detroit. His tactics and pronouncements readily earned him the vilification of the white community. To them, Cleage was once quoted as saying, "When we take over, don't worry. We'll treat you like you treated us."

Shrine of the Black Madonna Thrived

In the years after the riots, Shrine membership swelled to the thousands, and the organization was soon able to establish several groundbreaking programs. A communal living center, where members were able to pool their resources and become active participants in the Shrine's social service outreach programs, was one such experiment. Cleage dreamed of economic self-sufficiency for the African-American community, and the Shrine set up a neighborhood supermarket with competitive prices as an example of such economic independence. The Shrine also established a bookstore to promote the works of African-American authors and the Black Nationalist movement.

Cleage's political battles with the Detroit school administration to hire more African-American teachers and initiate a curriculum beneficial to the district's growing majority of African-American students evolved into even more ambitious goals. Cleage developed a political action group called Black Slate Inc in 1973. Shrine members campaigned heavily to elect African-American city council members, city and county judges, and state representatives by distributing their "Black Slate" literature across the city. Their efforts were considered crucial to the 1973 election of the city's first African-American mayor, Coleman Young. They also supported the successful candidacies of such people as Bernard Kilpatrick, who served on the Wayne County Commission and in the Wayne County Executive's Office; and Carolyn Cheeks Kilpatrick, who served in the Michigan and U. S. House of Representatives, and as the Congressional Black Caucus chairperson; and Wayne County Circuit Court Judge Cynthia D. Stephens, who served on the State Bar of Michigan Board of Commissioners.

Barbara-Rose Collins remembered Cleage as an early mentor in her political career. An early member of the Shrine, Collins was working in an office when her discussions about her dissatisfaction with her children's schooling led Shrine leaders to suggest that she herself run for a seat on the school board. From there Collins was elected to a city council seat, and by the mid-1990s, she was representing Michigan's 13th Congressional District in Washington, DC. Collins remembered Cleage's advice during her time as a state representative to Keith Dye of the *Michigan Chronicle*; she had asked Cleage about the best way to assess a proposed bill. His advice, she said, was to ask herself, "Is it good for Black people? Is it good for poor people?"

Remained Focused on Community

The era of black militancy, for both Detroit and the rest of urban America, waned as the civil rights struggles of the 1960s seemed to be making strides. Gains made by African Americans—for better housing, schools, and employment opportunities—were celebrated by some as a positive step towards integration. More militant adherents, such as the Black Panther Party and the Black Liberation Army, had become targets of an FBI campaign to negate their effectiveness. By the 1990s, official membership in Detroit's Shrine of the Black Madonna had declined considerably, though similar shrines had been established in such cities as Houston, Texas, and Atlanta, Georgia. In 1999, the Shrine expanded to Calhoun Falls, South Carolina, with the establishment of a farm called Beulah Land.

Cleage, who had renamed himself Jaramogi Abebe Agyeman in the 1970s, remained active with his church and in the black community. By the 1990s the *Detroit Free Press* cited Cleage and his church for helping alter the political landscape of the city. "He wasn't just an important figure around Detroit," the Reverend Will Herzfeld told the newspaper. "He was a pretty important national figure during the black power movement and the subsequent rise of black theology and its subsequent connection to black power. He was right out front."

Esteemed for his early efforts, Cleage pressed onward, seeking out ways to help blacks even to his dying day. While visiting his church's newly formed farm, Beulah Land, in Calhoun Falls, in Abbeville County, South Carolina, Cleage died on February 20, 2000, at the age of 88. Cleage had been overseeing the growth on the nearly 3,000-acre farm, which he had envisioned as a vehicle to serve and feed the needy.

Heart disease ended his own ability to help, but Cleage's inspiration continued. At his funeral service in Detroit, attended by nearly 500, people spoke of his leadership, activism, and vision. Former U.S. Representative, Barbara-Rose Collins noted that he "didn't just change live, he transformed lives," as quoted by Darren A. Nichols of the *Detroit News*. The Second Holy Patriarch of the Shrine of the Black Madonna Menelik Kimathi added: "For what he was able to do, we stand in awe."

The Shrine of the Black Madonna continued his work with such projects as the development a private board-ing school for boys at Beulah Land; the provision of cultural, educational, recreational, and social services through community service centers in Atlanta, Houston, and Detroit; and the 2005 establishment of the Dr. Albert B. Cleage, Sr. Memorial Health Center, a non-profit healthcare organization in Detroit in honor of his father. Even the political networks and strategies he started in the 1970s continued to influence politics, especially in Detroit. On his birthday each year, the Shrine of the Black Madonna celebrated its founder; in 2007 the celebration included a showing of two documentary films featuring Cleage ministering at the height of his power: *The Black Eye* (1968) and *Black Christian Nationalism* (1972). From all the continuing activity, it seems his work in not yet done.

Selected writings

Books

The Black Messiah, Sheed & Ward, 1968.
Black Christian Nationalism: New Directions for the Black Church, Morrow, 1972.

Sources

Books

Chafets, Ze'ev, *Devil's Night: And Other True Tales of Detroit*, Vintage Books, 1990.
Melton, J. Gordon, *Religious Leaders of America*, Gale, 1991, pp. 7-8.
Theoharis, Jeanne, and Komozi Woodard, *Freedom North: Black Freedom Struggles Outside the South*, Palgrave, 2003, pp. 153-75.
Ward, Hiley S., *Prophet of the Black Nation*, Pilgrim Press, 1969.
Williams, Juan, and Quinton Dixie, *This Far by Faith*, William Morrow, 2003.

Periodicals

Chicago Tribune, February 28, 2000, p. 7.
Detroit Free Press, June 3, 1990, p. F1; July 18, 1993, p. J7; February 21, 2000, p. B1; February 27, 2000, p. C2.
Detroit News, February 22, 2000, p. D2.
Michigan Chronicle, February 23, 2000, p. 2; March 1, 2000, p. C7; March 13, 2002, p. A1; July 11-17, 2004, p. A5; June 10-16, 2007, p. A14.
New York Times, February 27, 2000, p. 49.
Pittsburgh Post-Gazette, February 28, 2000, p. D5.

On-line

Shrine of the Black Madonna Cultural Center and Bookstore, www.shrinebookstore.com (September 4, 2007).

—Carol Brennan and Sara Pendergast

Keyshia Cole

1983—

Vocalist

Cole, Keyshia, photograph. Fitzroy Barrett/Landov.

The young R&B vocalist Keyshia Cole "sings love stories that could almost be war stories," wrote Kelefa Sanneh of the *New York Times.* The Oakland, California-raised songstress broke through to national prominence with her 2005 debut album, *The Way It Is,* and thanks to the rough, down-to-earth edge in her voice she was hailed in some quarters as a potential successor to R&B superstar Mary J. Blige. Chuck Arnold of *People* opined that "[a]t its best, Cole's debut recalls the raw emotion, gritty realism and street beats of Blige's landmark first album, 1992's *What's the 411?.*" The honest quality of Cole's music wasn't manufactured by music-industry marketers; she wrote many of her own songs and they drew directly on the experiences of her own troubled past.

Escaped Rough Beginnings

Cole was born on October 24, 1983 (some sources say 1981). She grew up in foster care in Oakland after having been adopted by Yvonne Cole, a friend of hip-hop icon Tupac Shakur. "I went through a lot as a young girl," she recalled to Sonia Murray of the *Atlanta Journal-Constitution.* "That's why I'm so serious and determined to make it in this business. So I can help young ladies in general; but especially those in foster care, who I know need help finding jobs, and just getting their goals in line."

Setting her sights early on a music career, she talked Oakland rapper MC Hammer into giving her a backup vocal slot and a chance to record with him while she was still a pre-teen, according to her official Web site biography. By the end of her teens she had broken into the Bay Area's hip-hop and R&B scenes, appearing on recordings by rapper Messy Marv ("Nubian Queen") and Tony! Toni! Toné! sideman Dwayne Wiggins (the soundtrack for the film *Me and Mrs. Jones*). It was a romantic breakup, Cole recalled on her Web site, that led her to make the move to Los Angeles and its bigger music industry: shortly after catching her boyfriend with another woman, she jumped into her car and made the nine-hour drive south.

Her track record and her songwriting talent quickly set her apart from the crowd of other aspiring stars, and she was signed to the A&M label by its president, Ron

At a Glance . . .

Born on October 24, 1983 (some sources say 1981); raised in Oakland, CA, by foster mother, Yvonne Cole.

Career: Singer, 1995–.

Award: *Vibe* Next Award, 2005; ASCAP Award, for single "Love," 2007.

Addresses: *Agent*—c/o A&M Records, 2220 Colorado Ave., Santa Monica, CA 90404. *Web*—www.keyshia-cole.com.

Fair. A duet with Eve on the soundtrack of the film *Barbershop 2,* "Never," helped give her exposure, and some top production talent was lined up for her first solo effort, titled *The Way It Is:* R&B singer DaRon from the group 112, rapper Chink Santana, and above all superstar hip-hop artist Kanye West, with whom Cole toured as an opening act. "He's like my brother. He knows exactly what he wants," Cole told *Jet.* "He goes exactly for what he wants; he's definitely music motivated; he loves to use live instruments. Touring as the opening act was a lot of fun and I learned the ropes of being on tour."

Album Opened Strong

A promotional mixtape called "Team Invasion Presents Keyshia Cole," featuring unreleased duos with Remy Ma and Ghostface, helped build a buzz around Cole's upcoming album release, and *The Way It Is* was released in the spring of 2005, with "I Changed My Mind" as the first single. Produced by West, the track featured edgy handclaps in its rhythm track. Cole co-composed the no-nonsense lyrics, which, she told *Jet,* were "about the things you're trying to accomplish in life and dealing with somebody, a significant other, who comes in between that, especially with their ways. I want to be an example for young girls in following your goals and dreams and making it happen and checking him out later if you have to."

The album's third and fourth singles, "I Should Have Cheated" and "Love," put Cole at the top of the heap of emerging artists in the R&B field. "I Should Have Cheated" was a typically unsentimental Cole track in which she addressed a suspicious lover, telling him in no uncertain terms that if she was going to be constantly accused of unfaithfulness, she should have gone ahead and done something that would have justified the accusations. "That song has a lot of emotion, because

I feel every girl and every guy can relate to that issue," she told *Jet.* The video for "Love" featured an appearance by male R&B heartthrob Tyrese. The song was drawn directly on Cole's own experiences: after being told by a romantic interest that he wasn't ready for a committed relationship, she saw him dining in a restaurant with an obviously steady girlfriend. Cole's reaction, she recalled on her Web site, was to pick up her pen: "I just wrote about it, it came out really quick. After I wrote the song, I went to the studio about 4 in the morning, and by 5 or 6 I was done with the song and that's what you hear."

Reviews for *The Way It Is* were positive: Janet Tzou of *Entertainment Weekly,* for example, wrote that "Cole's street-savvy Oakland, Calif., upbringing gives her vocals depth and her songs a genuine, lived-in feel." Both "I Should Have Cheated" and "Love" cracked the top ten in *Billboard* magazine's R&B singles chart, and the album was certified platinum for sales of one million copies in February of 2006. Estimated sales by the summer of 2006 were close to two million, an impressive performance for a debut by any standard, and especially rare in an era of declining CD sales.

Turned to TV

One factor that aided Cole's breakout was her distinctive visual image: she was, in the words of Malcolm Venable of the Norfolk *Virginian Pilot,* "a budding queen of the hair weave" who "dismisses the notion of inconspicuousness entirely, opting for mounds of electric Kool-Aid red locks, often with a blond stripe running smack dab in the center." Another was an attempt by the BET cable television channel to capitalize on Cole's down-to-earth appeal: she was featured in a six-episode reality-show series, also called *The Way It Is,* that focused not only on the experiences of a young star trying to make it in the music business but also on Cole's own troubled upbringing.

That program premiered in July of 2006 and was renewed for a second season in 2007, by which time Cole's future in the music business looked bright. She had a solo tour in the summer of 2006 under her belt, and was in demand for guest appearances on recordings by other artists including rapper/producer Jazze Pha. In 2007 Cole released a new single, "Let It Go," and eyes and ears in the music industry were awaiting her second release, *Just Like You.*

Selected works

Recordings

The Way It Is, A&M, 2005 (includes singles "Love" and "I Should Have Cheated").
Just Like You, forthcoming 2007.

Television

The Way It Is, BET, 2006–.

Sources

Periodicals

Atlanta Journal-Constitution, June 8, 2005, p. E1.
Entertainment Weekly, July 8, 2005, p. 69.
Fresno Bee, July 28, 2006, p. E6.
Houston Chronicle, January 31, 2006, p. 3.
Jet, March 6, 2006, p. 24.
New York Times, September 4, 2005, p. AR22.
People, August 1, 2005, p. 40.
Virginian Pilot (Norfolk), April 4, 2006, p. E2.

On-line

Keyshia Cole, www.keyshiacole.com (July 15, 2007).
"Keyshia Cole," *All Music,* www.allmusic.com/cg/
amg.dll?p=amg&searchlink=KEYSHIA | COLE&sql-
=11:axfixq8aldhe~T0 (July 15, 2007).

—James M. Manheim

Common

1972—

Rap musician, author, actor, businessman

Common, photograph. Reuters/Phil McCarten/Landov.

Rapper Common is not a common rapper. Composing music that comments on such broad-ranging themes as "the hereafter, weather phenomena, the power of imagination, male-female relations, competition between males for women, marijuana, the process of creating hip-hop, commercialism in the music, adulthood, street life and leaving it, competition in the music, contagion, Black intellectual tradition and its liberationist ethic, cellular technology, Chicago race/class stratification, gang violence and its aftereffects, drug dealing, manhood, Egyptian burial practices, Moorish secret societies, and fandom," as listed by Harry Allen in the *Village Voice,* Common set himself apart as an artist, as a "conscious" rapper. Common grew beyond the boundaries of the music industry to become a "brand" in popular culture. After winning accolades for his music, achieving success in acting, landing a Gap ad, writing children's books, introducing a line of Italian hats, and starting a charitable foundation by 2007, Common looked beyond the personal satisfaction of his success, telling Marti Parham of *Jet* that "I know my purpose as an artist is even bigger now and I can utilize this platform for bigger things to really help make change." His commitment to change, both in himself and in the world, has endeared him to a growing fan base.

Drawn to Music as a Child

Born in Chicago on March 13, 1972, Common was named Lonnie Rashid Lynn after his father, Lonnie Lynn. He grew up on the south side of Chicago in an economically diverse Black neighborhood called Avalon Park with his mother, Mahalia Ann Hines, a teacher for the Chicago Public Schools; his stepfather, Ralph Hines; and his grandmother.

Two major passions of his early years were basketball and rap. As a young teen, he worked one season as a ball boy for the Chicago Bulls. His love of hip-hop began in the early eighties with a trip to visit his cousin in Cincinnati. When he returned to Chicago, he began, break-dancing, emceeing, and writing rap songs. In 1986, while attending Luther South High School, a Christian (Lutheran) school on Chicago's South Side, he formed his first rap group, called CDR for group members Corey, Dion, and Rashid. Dion, a friend of Common's from the fourth grade at Faulkner Elementary School, later became rapper and producer NO

At a Glance . . .

Born Lonnie Rashid Lynn on March 13, 1972, in Chicago, IL; parents Mahalia Ann Hines and Lonnie Lynn; children: Omoye Assata Lynn. *Education*: Attended Southern A&M University.

Career: Rap artist, 1991–; actor, 2006–; Common Ground Foundation, founder, 2006.

Awards: Grammy Award, for "Love of My Life," 2003; MTV Video Awards, for "Testify" and Best Hip Hop Video, 2006.

Addresses: *Web*—www.common-music.com.

I.D., and continued to work with Common on stage and in the studio after both had started to perform independently.

While Common continued to perform through high school and after, he also continued his education. After high school, he studied at Southern A&M in the College of Business for two years. But then in 1991, Relativity Records, which had begun to move into hip-hop from a straight rock line-up, offered him a contract, and Common decided to stop attending college to become a full-time performer.

Made a Name for Himself

Lonnie Rashid Lynn began recording under the name Common Sense. The title of his first album, *Can I Borrow a Dollar?*, produced on Relativity's label in 1992, was an allusion to his place as a Chicago rapper on the hip-hop scene. The title seemed to ask if there was room in hip-hop for rappers who were not from the East or West Coast. Common has always had a strong sense of place, and he gives much credit to his early experiences in Chicago as having been an important influence on his musical style. In the area around 87th Street and Stony Island, the neighborhood in which he grew up, Blacks with middle class aspirations, working-class Blacks, and young gang members lived side by side. In a fall 2000 letter to the *Chicago Sun-Times*, he said, "That area kind of shaped me. It taught me…to be real with myself and to be real with people. It taught me to speak the truth."

Common dropped "Sense" from his moniker after a conflict came up in 1994. Though Common's lyrics represent his own version of common sense, another group—a California-based reggae group going by the same name—challenged his right to call himself "Common Sense." Faced with a lawsuit, he shortened his performance name to simply Common.

Common provoked controversy in the hip-hop community for his allegorical song from his second album *Resurrection*, "I Used to Love H.E.R." The song describes his relationship with a girl that he met when he was 10, a funny, fresh, creative girl. She moved to L.A. after a few years and got involved with a negative scene, including some folks who, as the song says, "told her if she got an image and a gimmick that she could make money, and she did it like a dummy." Common says that even though he sees her being dragged through the sewer, he hasn't given up on her. He's going to try to help her turn herself around because, as the song's last line reveals, "…who I'm talkin' 'bout y'all is hip-hop." West Coast rapper Ice Cube took Common's attack on West Coast rap as a personal affront and came back with a cut on his album with Mac10, *West Side Slaughterhouse*. Common responded with another rap single. Apparently fearful of a rap war of words that might lead to physical violence, Louis Farrakhan of the Nation of Islam called the two together at a conference in 1997, and the two rappers declared a truce.

However, the target of Common's criticism wasn't Ice Cube or any one rapper, but his view of the dangerous state of hip-hop because of the tendency for rappers to bend to the will of commercialism and produce tracks that will sell, without regard for the ideas that they put forth. In a Thanksgiving message published in the *Chicago Sun-Times* in 2000, Common commented on the positive turn he saw hip-hop taking, stating, "I'm definitely grateful that I'm seeing a lot of hip-hop artists out there doing stuff for the community. I'm grateful that I see artists taking a stand in their music. They're saying important things that can affect some lives." As his words indicate, Common sees contemporary hip-hop as a vehicle for conveying messages of importance at the same time that it is generating good music and entertaining its audience. It is his vision that makes him stand out from other rappers. At the same time, his musicality, his blending of multiple musical traditions, and his creative poeticism make his fans want to hear what he has to say.

Developed a Signature Style

Common moved to Brooklyn early in his career to have greater access to the music industry, but he retained his Chicago-based version of reality. Music reviewers and fans generally find Common's raps more wide-ranging and thoughtful than most other rap artists. In an article in the *Minneapolis Star-Tribune*, Britt Robson said, "Common's most noteworthy contribution to hip-hop has been his definition of 'keeping it real.' The phrase, often used by gangsta rappers to justify their grisly themes, has devolved into a lazy cliché…Common's reality is braver, broader, and more down to earth."

One way that Common has "kept it real" is by rapping about some uncommon themes. His 1997 album, *One*

Day It'll All Make Sense, included the song "Retrospect for Life," about parenthood and abortion. It also featured rapper Lauryn Hill, and was recorded when both Hill and Common were expecting the birth of their first children. In fact, they shared the same due date for their children, August of 1997. The song's last line comments on the emotional price tag of abortion: "315 dollars ain't worth your soul." On the same album, in the song "G.O.D." which also featured artists Cee-Loo of the Goodie Mob, Common comments on world religions, rapping about the Koran and the Bible and concluding, "Who am I or they to say to who you pray ain't right?" Other albums include raps about how it feels to come home and find your place has been robbed, and a series of raps by his father, Lonnie Lynn, called "Pop's Raps."

Common's early albums sold well. His third album, *One Day It'll All Make Sense*, sold a respectable 435,000 units. However, in 1998, MCA heard a rumor that Common was not happy with Relativity Records. MCA had already signed artists with a similar vision and style, Mos Def and Roots. MCA executives began talking to Common, and MCA bought out his contract that December. Common was given free artistic license on the album. The resulting album, released under Common's imprint, Madame Zenobia, was well received, selling enough units to go gold. The *Village Voice*'s reviewer described it as "an honorable and beautiful continuation of Common's longtime project of bridging the life of the street and the life of the mind."

Although he had yet to break into mainstream popularity Common had developed a solid reputation among fans of hip-hop for his thoughtful lyrics and creative rhymes. *The Source*, a hip-hop magazine, has described him as "Chicago's lyrical warrior." While his songs offer biting and clever commentaries on contemporary topics, they are definitely not sermons. He told Soren Baker, a *Los Angeles Times* writer, that rap, while it needs to be socially conscious, needs to stay true to its tradition of word play and creativity. "I believe in balance," he said. "If you're going to educate people, then you've got to entertain them too."

Common's own education, both formal and informal, is a consistent influence on his music. As his social consciousness expanded, his ideas are reflected in his songs' themes and lyrics. And as his knowledge of music expands, his records show the influence of a wider bandwidth of musical styles. His album, *Like Water for Chocolate* (the title of which is taken from a highly acclaimed novel by Laura Esquivel), released in March of 2000, is a good example of this interplay. One track on the album is a result of an educational journey that Common took. In 1997, he read a biography of Assata Shakur, a former Black Panther accused and convicted of being involved in the killing of a New Jersey policeman, an event that happened the year before Common was born. Shakur escaped from prison and fled to Cuba in 1979, where she has lived

ever since. Common penned a rap to her, "A Song For Assata," and went to visit her in Cuba to add her voice to the song.

The album also reflected Common's musical growth. After the release of *Resurrection*, his 1994 album, Common decided to study more music theory. At the same time, he continued his informal musical education, listing to a wide range of artists including John Coltrane, Curtis Mayfield, Herbie Hancock, and Miles Davis. Many tracks on *Like Water for Chocolate* pay homage to the rich tapestry of African-American musical tradition. The first track, "Time Travelling," is a tribute to the legendary Nigerian musician Fela Kuti. It features his son, drummer Femi Kuti, and contemporary jazz trumpeter, Ray Hargrove. Other tracks reflect strong influences of R&B, of jazz, and of James Brown's driving guitar work. While the album is solidly in the genre of rap, it includes a wider range of music than mainstream hip-hop albums typically neglect. The album's cover also makes a statement: it's a black and white photo, taken by photographer Gordon Parks, of a well-dressed African-American woman in the 1950s drinking from a water fountain marked "Colored Only." The single, "The Light," from the album earned Common his first Grammy nomination for best rap solo performance in 2001.

Marched to His Own Beat

After breaking through to mainstream popularity, Common did not feel compelled to stick with the same formula for success. His next album, *Electric Circus,* was much anticipated by fans and critics alike. The album—on which he experimented with rock music inspired by the likes of Jimi Hendrix, Joni Mitchell, and Pink Floyd—disappointed, even though it included what National Public Radio review Will Hermes called a "10-minute gospel space jam." Described by critics with such terms as "sprawling" and "adventurous," the album sold poorly.

Yet the following year, Common rebounded, winning his first Grammy Award, for his song with Erykah Badu "Love of My Life (An Ode to Hip Hop)," for the *Brown Sugar* movie soundtrack. He followed that success in 2005 with the release of *Be*. Produced by Kanye West, the album debuted at the top of the Billboard R&B and Hip-Hop Album charts. *Rolling Stone* listed it among the top 50 albums of the year. Describing the 1970s samplings the album included, a *Vanity Fair* review noted that the album had "a classic sound that perfectly suits Common." Common appreciated the positive attention. "When you create your art, your music, you want people to say this is a timeless piece of work," he told *Jet* contributor Marti Yarbrough. "And for the critics to come out and say that from the beginning is just like a testament to my work." The album garnered four Grammy nominations and won two MTV Video Awards.

Common collaborated with West for his next album, *Finding Forever,* which West touted as the best rap album of the year even before its release, according to Lorainne Ali of *Newsweek.* It debuted at the number one position on the Billboard 200 chart. The theme of the album returned to Common's core impulse as an artist: to convey significant messages. "The impact of a conscious artist is necessary, and it ripples through the world," he told Brakkton Booker for a report on *Weekend All Things Considered.* "And it's people with platinum plaques that are forgotten. And in fact, that's why I named my album 'Finding Forever' because that's what I was thinking about. What did I want to contribute to this world that would live beyond my physical existence?"

Common's appeal broadened beyond the music industry. His children's book *I Like You, But I Love Me* was nominated for an NAACP Image Award in 2006. In 2007 he appeared in advertisements for The Gap and Converse Red. He began acting, landing parts in such films as *Smokin' Aces* with Jeremy Piven, Ben Affleck, and Ray Liotta; *American Gangster* with Denzel Washington; *The Nightwatchman* with Keanu Reeves; and *Wanted* with Morgan Freeman and Angelina Jolie. About Common's transition from music to film, Piven told Ali that "A lot of rappers' acting cadences are a couple clicks off, [b]ut Common's right there in the pocket. He's a natural." Common moved beyond the entertainment industry with such ventures as a line of fashionable hats called Soji, and the establishment of the Common Ground Foundation, through which he aimed to provide underprivileged children with health education and to help fight poverty. With such wide-ranging activities, Common established himself among the most eclectic representatives of the hip-hop generation.

Selected discography

Albums

Can I Borrow A Dollar?, Relativity, 1992.
Resurrection, Relativity, 1994.
One Day It'll All Make Sense, Relativity, 1997.
Like Water for Chocolate, Madame Zenobia/MCA, 2000.
Electric Circus, Geffen, 2002.
Be, Universal, 2005.
Finding Forever, Geffen, 2007.

Books

The Mirror and Me, HipHop Schoolhouse, 2004.
I Like You, But I Love Me, HipHop Schoolhouse, 2006.

M.E. Mixed Emotions, HipHop Schoolhouse, forthcoming.

Films

Smokin' Aces, 2006.
American Gangster, 2007.
The Nightwatchman, 2008.
Wanted, 2008.

Sources

Periodicals

Billboard, Feburary 19, 2000, p. 25.
Chicago Reader, October 10, 1997.
Chicago Sun-Times, November 23, 2000, p. 9.
Jet, June 27, 2005, p. 54.
Los Angeles Times, March 19, 2000, Calendar p. 5.
Rolling Stone, December 29, 2005-January 12, 2006, p. 106.
Source, March 2000.
Star Tribune (Minneapolis, MN), November 10, 2000, Freetime section, p. 3.
Vanity Fair, November 2005, p. 306.
Village Voice, November 4, 1997, p. 70; April 12-18, 2000, p. 146.

On-line

"Biography: Common," *Billboard.com,* /www.billboard.com/bbcom/bio/index.jsp?pid=246651 (September 6, 2007).
Biography Resource Center, www.galenet.com/servlet/BioRC.
Common, www.common-music.com (September 6, 2007).
"Music: Common," *MSNBC: Newsweek,* www.msnbc.msn.com/id/16240601/site/newsweek (September 6, 2007).
Pop Matters Columns, www.popmatters.com.
Pound Magazine, www.pound.com.
Westword, http://westword.com.

Other

"Common: 'Conscious Sound, Uncommon Success,'" *National Public Radio: Weekend All Things Considered,* August 11, 2007.
Additional material for this profile was obtained from an interview with *Contemporary Black Biography,* July 31, 2001.

—Rory Donnelly and Sara Pendergast

Andy Cooper

1898-1941

Baseball player

If Andy Cooper were playing baseball today, he'd be a superstar. Known for blazing left-hand pitches that dazzled fans and dizzied opponents, the Texas-born pitcher racked up impressive statistics during two decades of professional play. He was in the top ten in his league for career wins, shutouts, and strikeouts, and pitched for a career record 116 wins to 57 losses. In today's Major League Baseball, Cooper would have celebrity status, endorsement deals, and a very fat bank account. But Cooper played ball back when racial segregation was still the law, black children were not allowed to attend schools with white children, and public facilities were divided into "white" and "colored." America's favorite pastime was not immune to these divisions. Cooper, whose talents on the mound rate as legendary, played for the Negro Leagues. He pitched his last game a decade before Jackie Robinson broke the color barrier of professional baseball. The Negro Leagues received very little media coverage, and when Cooper died in 1941, he was nearly erased from baseball history. Then in the late 1980s, a baseball historian began to unearth and compile Negro League records. What he discovered about Cooper drew the interest of the Baseball Hall of Fame and, in 2006, the pitcher known as "Lefty" was enshrined in baseball's most esteemed institution.

Racked up Wins with Wide Range of Pitches

Andrew Lewis Cooper was born on April 24, 1898, in Waco, Texas, into a family with strong baseball inclina-

tions. His brother Daltie Cooper also grew up to play baseball for the Negro Leagues. In 1920, Cooper began his baseball career as a pitcher for the Detroit Star, one of the charter members of the Negro National League. His first two years with the team were unimpressive with twice as many losses as wins. However, beginning with the 1922 season, Cooper bounced back. Playing in the long-defunct Mack Park on the city's east side, he racked up six consecutive winning seasons for a total of 72 wins and just 30 losses. The wins were more impressive considering the ballpark's construction. "In that era, hitting dominated and Detroit's ballpark was certainly tailored to the hitters," Negro League historian James Riley told the Web site of Major League Baseball.

Other pitchers may have faltered, but the six-foot-two, 220-pound Cooper, who earned the nickname "Lefty" for his left-handed throws, thrived in the offense-friendly environment. Pitching in up to four games per week, Cooper perfected his technique. He was known for mixing up his pitches, sometimes lightning fast, other times deceptively slow. He was a master at technically tricky pitches, applying just the right amount of control and spin to produce curveballs, screwballs, sliders, and changeups. His repertoire of pitches often left batters standing at home plate. In fact, in four of his seasons with Detroit, Cooper had an earned-run average (ERA) of less than three. That is, less than three batters per game who faced Cooper managed to hit the ball and make a run. Though baseball measurements have changed since the days of the Negro Leagues, Cooper's ERA still stands out.

At a Glance . . .

Born on April 24, 1898, in Waco, TX; died on June 3, 1941, in Waco, TX; children: Andy Cooper Jr.

Career: Negro Leagues baseball player: pitcher, Detroit Stars, 1920-27, 1930; pitcher, Kansas City Monarchs, 1928-29; pitcher-manager, Kansas City Monarchs, mid-1930s-40.

Awards: Negro National League, championship pennant, with the Kansas City Monarchs, 1929; Negro American League, championship pennant, with the Kansas City Monarchs, 1937, 1939, 1940.

In the Negro Leagues, games were normally played in a five-game series. "The team would play a Saturday game, a doubleheader Sunday, then Monday and Tuesday," Dick Clark, the baseball historian who rediscovered Cooper, told the *Detroit Free Press*. Cooper, who was also renowned for his stamina, normally started two of those five and then came in as relief pitcher for one or two more. As relief pitcher, he racked up the record for the most saves in a single season in Negro League history. A save is defined when a relief pitcher enters a game in which his team is leading by a small margin. If the pitcher maintains the lead until a win, he is credited with a save. Though save averages in modern professional baseball can top 50, Cooper's record of 29 was astonishing back in the 1920s.

Moved from Championships to Obscurity to Legend

Cooper's achievements in Detroit made him the Stars' all-time leader in every pitching category and prompted Clark to tell the *Detroit Free Press*, "In my estimation, [Cooper was] the greatest black pitcher ever to pitch for Detroit—that's for the Stars or the Tigers," referring to today's pennant-winning Detroit Tigers. Cooper's skills made him well-known in Detroit's black community which regularly packed Mack Park's 15,000 seats to see him pitch. His talent also drew the interest of the Kansas City Monarchs, one of the best teams in the Negro National League. They the left-handed whiz so badly that in 1927 they gave Detroit five players in exchange for Cooper. Their trade paid off. As soon as Cooper took the mound for the Monarchs, he started racking up wins. In 1929, he led the team to the Negro National League championships. The pennant capped off a season record of 62 wins, 17 losses, the best overall single-season record in Negro League history.

In 1930 a car wreck kept Cooper off the field for a year. By the time he returned, various factors including

the Great Depression had caused the Negro National League to disband. By the mid-1930s, Cooper rejoined the Monarchs which had become an independent team, traveling across the Midwest to compete against other independents. Off-season Cooper played in Cuba, Latin American, Japan, and the Philippines. In 1937, the Monarchs became charter members of the newly formed Negro American League, and Cooper became the team manager. That same year, Cooper took the pitcher's mound once again, pitching 17 innings in the league's first ever championship series. The Monarchs won the pennant. Cooper coached the team to two more championship wins in 1937 and 1940 before falling seriously ill. By late 1940, he was back in Waco, Texas, under the care of his mother. The following year, on June 3rd, Cooper died of heart failure.

Cooper's only son, Andy Jr., was 11 years old at the time of his father's death. But for a summer spent traveling as a batboy with the Monarchs, he knew little of his father. As Cooper's other relatives began to pass away, so too did Cooper's memory. By the 1980s, his legacy was buried amid yellowing copies of the few old newspapers which once tracked Negro League statistics. Cooper was all but lost to history. Then stepped in Clark. Through countless hours of volunteer research, the baseball historian reconstructed the arc of Cooper's career and Lefty's astonishing baseball accomplishments. Over two decades later, the National Baseball Hall of Fame commissioned a Special Committee on the Negro Leagues. Relying on Clark's meticulous data, they chose Cooper and 16 other players out of a pool of 94 to join the 18 Negro Leaguers already inducted into the Hall of Fame. In front of some 11,000 attendees at the July 30, 2006, induction ceremony, Andy Cooper Jr. read the inscription on his father's plaque. Buck O'Neill, a 94-year-old veteran of the Negro Leagues and a first baseman with the Monarchs under Cooper, oversaw the ceremony as grand ambassador. Adding a human side to Cooper's statistical memory, O'Neill recalled in a conversation with Andy Jr. that Cooper was a father figure to the Monarchs players, treating them to dinners on the road and explaining the finer points of the game to them. "He was an outstanding human being," O'Neil told the *Detroit Free Press*. "And it felt so good when he finally made it." Baseball history, unsullied by modern media and celebrity players, has finally declared that Cooper was indeed a superstar after all.

Sources

Periodicals

Detroit Free Press, July 23, 2006; July 31, 2006. *Jet*, March 20, 2006, p. 47.

On-line

"Andy Cooper," *National Baseball Hall of Fame and*

Museum, www.baseballhalloffame.org/hofers/detail.jsp?playerId=506629 (August 12, 2007).

"Andy Cooper Jr. Remembers Hall of Fame Father," *National Baseball Hall of Fame and Museum,* http://209.23.71.87/hof_weekend/2006/cooper_andy.htm (August 12, 2007).

"Southpaw Piled Up the Victories," *Major League Baseball,* http://mlb.mlb.com/news/article.jsp?ymd=20060217&content_id=1313719&vkey=news_mlb&fext=.jsp&c_id=mlb (August 12, 2007).

—Candace LaBalle

Michael C. Dawson

1951—

Political scientist

In 2002 Michael C. Dawson, one of the nation's leading political scientists, left the University of Chicago—where he was founding director of the Center for the Study of Race, Politics, and Culture—for Harvard University, home to some of the foremost African-American scholars. Just three years later Dawson was back at Chicago, his Harvard colleagues having dispersed to other universities. His moves were symptomatic of the intense competition among the country's prestigious universities to attract this new breed of groundbreaking black scholars. Dawson's interests in American politics, democratic theory, and the politics of race led him to apply social and cognitive scientific data and decision theory to political movements and ideologies and to individual political decisions.

Formulated a Black Political Science

Born on October 21, 1951, Michael C. Dawson grew up in Chicago's Hyde Park and South Shore neighborhoods. He attended the University of Chicago Laboratory Schools. Although he came from a politically sophisticated family, his great uncle William L. Dawson having served as a Democratic congressman, Michael Dawson spent nine years as an engineer and programmer in California's Silicon Valley before pursuing an academic career. By the time he had earned his doctorate from Harvard in 1986, he was formulating the basic questions of his academic research. In the preface to his 2001 book, *Black Visions: The Roots of Contemporary African-American Political Ideologies,* Dawson defined one of these questions: "What

motivates individuals to adopt their suite of political preferences?"

At the University of Michigan, where he began his academic career in 1986, Dawson was co-principal investigator of the 1988 National Black Election Study. The following year Dawson and his colleagues published a now classic paper in which they argued that black American political views formed a coherent belief system based on racial identity.

In *Behind the Mule: Race and Class in African-American Politics* Dawson argued that the social and political identity of American blacks could be found "behind the mule," in the historical legacy of racial and economic oppression. Based on data from his studies, as well as the 1984-85 National Black Election Panel Study, Dawson concluded that blacks based their political choices on the belief that what was best for their racial group was best for them as individuals. He found that the majority of blacks were left-leaning Democrats and that the economically disadvantaged generally supported black nationalism and the redistribution of wealth. It was this latter assertion that garnered a great deal of pre-publication publicity for *Behind the Mule.*

Surveyed Black Political Opinions

While at the University of Chicago, Dawson was a principal investigator for the 1993-1994 National Black Politics Study. It was the first national survey of the ideological and political views of black Americans. The study made national headlines with its revelations

At a Glance . . .

Born Michael C. Dawson on October 21, 1951, in Chicago, IL; married Alice Furumoto. *Education:* University of California, Berkeley, BA, 1982; Harvard University, MA, 1985, PhD, political science, 1986.

Career: University of Michigan, Ann Arbor, assistant professor, 1986-90, associate professor of political science and African-American studies, 1990-92; University of Chicago, Chicago, IL, Department of Political Science, associate professor, 1992-97, founding director of the Center for the Study of Race, Politics, and Culture, 1996-02, professor, 1997-01, department chair, 1998-01, William R. Kenan, Jr. Professor of Political Science and the College, 2001-02, John D. MacArthur Distinguished Service Professor of Political Science and the College, 2005-; Harvard University, Cambridge, MA, professor of government and Afro-American studies, 2002-05; consultant to the *Washington Post,* Kaiser Family Foundation, MacArthur Foundation, and the National Association for the Advancement of Colored People.

Memberships: American Academy of Arts and Sciences, fellow; Center for Advanced Study of the Behavioral Sciences, Stanford University, fellow; Phi Beta Kappa.

Awards: National Conference of Black Political Scientists, Book of the Year Award for *Behind the* Mule, 1995, Best Book Award for *Black Visions,* 2002; Illinois Humanities Council, award for innovative programming for the Trading Fours Jazz Conference, 2001; American Political Science Association, Best Book Award on ideology, theory, and intellectual history and Ralph Bunche Award for *Black Visions,* 2002.

Addresses: *Office*—Pick Hall, 419, 5828 S. University Ave., Chicago, IL 60637.

that blacks were becoming increasingly disillusioned and radicalized.

With Lawrence Bobo of Harvard, Dawson conducted the 2000 Presidential Election Study, which found that more than 90% of blacks voted against President George W. Bush, more than 92% believed that the he did not represent their interests, and 20% believed that

he actively opposed their interests. Dawson was a frequently quoted source on the racial aspects of the Florida voting irregularities in 2000.

In *Black Visions* Dawson examined six historically important black American ideologies: radical egalitarianism or black liberalism, disillusioned black liberalism, black Marxism, black conservatism, black feminism, and black nationalism. He concluded: "the levels of political pessimism and racial division *should* be found shocking by concerned citizens...What should not seem surprising is that at the turn of the century African Americans continue to believe that American democracy is broken."

Studied Reactions to Hurricane Katrina

Harvard had been trying to recruit Dawson for several years and they offered his wife, Alice Furumoto-Dawson, an epidemiology position at the Harvard School of Public Health. Their move was finalized just prior to the exodus from Harvard of several prominent black scholars—Cornel West, K. Anthony Appiah, and Lawrence Bobo and his wife Marcyliena Morgan—due to conflicts with the controversial then-president Lawrence Summers.

Bobo's departure for Stanford University was particularly hard for Dawson. Between 2000 and 2004 the two had collaborated on six public opinion studies of America's racial divisions. The results of their studies are considered to be the richest source of data available on the subject. They were also collaborating on a book and in 2004 they launched a new peer-reviewed journal, the *Du Bois Review: Social Science Research on Race.*

Dawson took a leave of absence from Harvard in 2004-05. His decision to then return to Chicago drew the attention of the academic community. He told the *Chicago Sun-Times,* "Four of the people I thought I'd be working with are no longer at Harvard. The research environment at Harvard is radically different than when I accepted the job." Summers was also a factor in Dawson's decision to return to Chicago. He told the *Boston Globe:* "I certainly haven't agreed with the tenor of the comments he made on women in science.... They seemed to me to be consistent with the outlook that has led to what, for me, has been a less than congenial research environment." Dawson was referring to Summers' public suggestion that women were genetically inferior to men in math and science.

Dawson's return to Chicago was seen as a victory for the university. His wife was offered a fellowship at the University of Chicago's Center for Interdisciplinary Health Disparities Research, which studied early-onset breast cancer in black women. Dawson and his colleagues launched the "2005 Racial Attitudes and the Katrina Disaster Study." They found that 70% of blacks—but only 33% of whites—believed that the federal government should spend whatever was required to rebuild people's homes. Likewise 89% of blacks—but only 56% of whites—believed that blacks were trapped by the hurricane because they did not have the resources to escape. Black New Orleans residents were far more likely than whites to believe that the disaster was as much the fault of the government as of nature. In the spring of 2006 Dawson co-taught an undergraduate course, "Hurricane Katrina and American Politics." As of 2007 Dawson was being sought after as a commentator on Barack Obama's bid for the Democratic presidential nomination.

Selected writings

Books

(With Ernest J. Wilson III) "Paradigms and Paradoxes: Political Science and the Study of African-American Politics," in *Political Science: Looking to the Future,* Vol. 1, William Crotty, ed., Northwestern University Press, 1991, pp. 189-234.

Behind the Mule: Race and Class in African-American Politics, Princeton University Press, 1994.

"Globalization, the Racial Divide, and a New Citizenship," in *The New Majority: Toward a Popular Progressive Politics,* Theda Skocpol and Stan Greenberg, eds., Yale University Press, 1997, pp. 264-278.

"Dis Beat Disrupts: Rap, Ideology, and Black Political Opinion," in *The Cultural Territories of Race: White and Black Boundaries,* Michèle Lamont, ed., University of Chicago Press, 1999, pp. 318-342.

"Slowly Coming to Grips with the Effects of the American Racial Order on American Policy Preferences," in *Racialized Politics: The Debate About Racism in America*, David O. Sears, Jim Sidanius, and Lawrence Bobo, eds., University of Chicago Press, 1999.

Black Visions: The Roots of Contemporary African-American Political Ideologies, University of Chicago Press, 2001.

Periodicals

(With Richard L. Allen and Ronald E. Brown) "A Schema-Based Approach to Modeling an African-American Racial Belief System," *American Political Science Review,* Vol. 83, No. 2, June 1989, pp. 421-441.

(With Cathy J. Cohen) "Neighborhood Poverty and African American Politics," *American Political Science Review*, Vol. 87, No. 2, 1993, pp. 286-302.

"A Black Counterpublic? Economic Earthquakes, Racial Agenda(s), and Black Politics," *Public Culture,* Vol. 7, 1994, pp. 195-223.

(With Lawrence Bobo and Devon Johnson) "Enduring Witness: Through the Eyes of Black America," *Public Perspective,* Vol. 12, No. 3, May/June 2001, pp. 13-16.

"Progressive Blues," *Boston Review,* Summer 2004.

"After the Deluge: Publics and Publicity in Katrina's Wake," *Du Bois Review,* Vol. 3, No. 1, Spring 2006.

(With Cathy J. Cohen and Melissa Harris-Lacewell) "Studying the Politics of Hurricane Katrina," *News from the Center for the Study of Race, Politics and Culture at the University of Chicago,* Fall 2006, p. 4.

Sources

Books

"Dawson, Michael C.," in *American Political Scientists: A Dictionary,* Glenn H. Utter and Charles Lockhart, eds., Greenwood Press, 2001.

Periodicals

Black Issues in Higher Education, February 28, 2002, p. 17.

Boston Globe, April 6, 2005.

Chicago Sun-Times, April 6, 2005.

Chicago Tribune, January 29, 2002; April 6, 2005.

Contemporary Sociology, March 2003, pp. 219-221.

Journal of Blacks in Higher Education, Spring 2005, p. 23.

On-line

"Kathleen Dunn: June 7, 2007," *Wisconsin Public Radio,* www.wpr.org/webcasting/ideas_audioarchives.cfm?Code=dun (September 7, 2007).

"Michael C. Dawson," *Contemporary Authors On-line,* http://galenet.galegroup.com/servlet/BioRC (September 7, 2007).

"Michael Dawson Returning to the University Faculty," *University of Chicago Chronicle,* http://chronicle.uchicago.edu/050414/dawson.shtml (September 7, 2007).

"Prominent Poli Sci Professor Leaves Harvard, Returns to U of C," *Medill Chicago News Service—Northwestern University,* http://mesh.medill.northwestern.edu/mnschicago/archives/2005/04/dawson_prominen.html (September 7, 2007).

—Margaret Alic

Taye Diggs

1972—

Actor

A Broadway veteran who came to popular attention with his role as the handsome young Jamaican in the successful 1998 film *How Stella Got Her Groove Back*, Taye Diggs became part of a new generation of African-American leading men to enjoy impressive Hollywood success while steering clear of negative typecasting. Diggs, along with actors such as Larenz Tate and Djimon Hounsou, benefited from a spate of popular films in the late 1990s and early 2000s, like *Stella*, whose themes rested upon color-blind hopes, dreams, and sorrows, but just happened to feature a cast of color. Though Diggs's film debut made him a household name, he was already well known to New York theatergoers, especially after appearing in the original cast of the acclaimed Broadway musical *Rent* in 1996. His popularity continued over the next decade as he appeared in films and even started a contemporary dance company. His 2007 casting in *Private Practice,* a spin-off of ABC's *Grey's Anatomy,* signaled that his star continued to rise.

Bestowed with the first name of "Scott" when he was born in Rochester, New York, in 1972, Diggs was the oldest of five children in his family. "Taye" supplanted

Diggs, Taye, photograph. Robert Pitts/Landov.

his real name following the habit of one of his uncles, who used to call him "Scot-tay." As a teenager, he was thin, awkward, and on the short side. "I was a large geek," *Ebony* magazine reported him as saying. "I remember going home and praying to God and saying, 'I want to be good-looking. I want to have a girlfriend. I want girls to like me.'" To improve his physique, Diggs took modern dance classes and lifted weights. His mother convinced him to attend the local performing arts high school, where, he said, "I came into my own," the *Ebony* article quoted him as saying. "If you wore glasses or tight pants, you were still accepted. It was pleasant. It was not only the jocks who got the girls."

Acted on Broadway

After earning a degree in theater from Syracuse University in 1993, Diggs moved to New York City, where he was fortunate to land an understudy role in a major Broadway production. As an understudy, an inexperienced actor shadows a colleague, learning the lines and stage cues of the role, in the event that an emergency replacement is necessary. Diggs then took the unusual

At a Glance . . .

Born Scott Diggs on January 2, 1972, in Rochester, NY; married Idina Menzel, 2003. *Education*: Syracuse University, BFA, 1993.

Career: Actor, 1990s–; Tokyo Disneyland, performer, 1990s; dre.dance, co-founder and artistic director, 2004–.

Addresses: *Web*—www.dredance.com.

step of moving to Japan, where he found work as a performer at Tokyo Disneyland in its "Caribbeanland" shows. When he returned to the United States, he landed a role in a planned Broadway rock opera called *Rent*.

Rent debuted in early 1996 and won immediate, enthusiastic reviews for its musical portrayal of life, love, and death among a group of modern-day bohemians in New York's hip East Village neighborhood. Based in part on the Puccini opera *La Bohème*, *Rent* also achieved a certain tragic notoriety due to the sudden death of its creator, Jonathan Larson, just weeks before it opened. Centered around a group of struggling artists, *Rent* touched upon heroin addiction and the specter of AIDS, and won the Tony Award for best Broadway musical that year.

In *Rent*, Diggs was cast as Benjamin, once a denizen of the East Village scene himself. Benny, however, turned on his friends when he achieved some measure of financial success, and is now the despised landlord of the building where many of the characters live. At one point he padlocks the building, while also trying to eject a group of homeless people squatting in the building next door. "Sparked by a young, intensely vibrant cast…and sustained by a glittering, inventive score, the work finds a transfixing brightness in characters living in the shadow of AIDS," asserted critic Ben Brantley of the *New York Times*.

Film Brought Fame

Diggs's career trajectory climbed steadily after the success of *Rent*. He appeared in guest spots on *Law and Order* and *New York Undercover*, and in 1997 was cast as Adrian "Sugar" Hill in the CBS daytime drama *The Guiding Light*. But the actor was still appearing in *Rent* when he auditioned for and won his first-ever film role: the screen adaptation of the 1996 Terry McMillan novel, *How Stella Got Her Groove Back*. The upcoming project came close on the heels of *Waiting to Exhale*, the successful film version of another of McMillan's acclaimed novels. *Stella*'s plot

revolved around an overworked single professional woman whose vacation romance with a much younger man evolves into something more serious. As producer of *Stella*, McMillan reportedly wanted Ralph Lauren model Tyson Beckford for the male lead, but Diggs's combination of looks and professional stage experience won him the role instead.

As *Stella* opens, Bassett's character is lured to Jamaica by a friend for a much-needed vacation. A hardworking San Francisco stockbroker, Stella is also the divorced mother of an 11-year-old boy and thoroughly dejected by the dating scene. At the luxury resort she meets Diggs's character, the handsome, charming Winston Shakespeare. Just 20 years old, Winston is a native of the island and has vague plans to enter medical school soon. A romance develops, despite the age difference. When the vacation ends, the relationship continues, and Diggs soon moves into Stella's posh Marin County home. It becomes apparent, however, that in some ways he has more in common with Stella's son, who enjoys having a new friend to play video games with him.

"Diggs imbues Winston with an easy grace and dignity," opined Stephen Holden in the *New York Times*. "But his performance is too soft-spoken and embellished with too many vacant smiles for his character to emerge as anything more than a misty romantic fantasy. Even when he loses his temper, Winston is impossibly, reassuringly nice." Despite the flaws in the on-screen character, Diggs won notoriety for his role in the film because of a particularly revealing shower scene. "I didn't know what was going to be shown in the nude and I really didn't care," he told *Newsweek* reporter Allison Samuels. "I wanted the role so bad it didn't matter what I had to do to get it."

Honed Skills with Various Character Studies

In 1999, Diggs appeared in a number of other well-received films. He was part of the ensemble cast of *Go*, a comic and violent *Pulp Fiction*-style film. In it, he played Marcus, whom several of the characters meet on a Las Vegas jaunt that is one of three interrelated plots in the movie. The work follows the adventures of a hapless supermarket cashier who becomes involved in a drug deal; her best friend is then held hostage, and her English co-worker from the supermarket finds himself in Las Vegas, "in which the smoothly appealing Taye Diggs plays a major role," wrote *New York Times* film critic Janet Maslin, who called the film "a jaundiced comedy of manners that toys with who may or may not be gay, and has a white character tell a black one that 'color's just a state of mind.'"

The Wood, which opened in the summer of 1999, offered Diggs another appealing big-screen character study. The film's title is the nickname for a middle-class

African-American suburb of Los Angeles, Inglewood, and its plot follows the 13-year friendship of three men who meet as teens there in the mid-1980s. Told in flashback, *The Wood* opens as Diggs's character, Roland, is suffering from a case of pre-wedding jitters so severe that he flees to the home of an ex-girlfriend and becomes quite drunk. His longtime friends, played by Omar Epps and Richard T. Jones, track him down and attempt to get him to the altar.

Roland, however, becomes sick in the car, and they return to the ex-girlfriend's home to wash themselves off with a garden hose. "The desperate last-minute cleanup resonates with the threesome's adolescent adventures, none especially harrowing," wrote the *New York Times*'s Holden. "They include being stopped by the police in a car in which one person is carrying a gun, finding themselves in the back of a grocery store while it's being robbed and of course, pitching inept lines at girls who adamantly stand their ground."

Later in 1999, Diggs appeared in the title role of *The Best Man*, another African-American-themed comedy, and a film produced by Spike Lee. Diggs was cast as Harper Stewart, a Chicago writer whose debut novel, *Unfinished Business*, is about to be published. Terrific sales and celebrity status are assured for the book and its author, because Oprah Winfrey has selected it as one of her book-club titles. Prior to this, however, Harper must first endure the New York City wedding of his friend, a former college athlete (Morris Chestnut) and notorious womanizer now coming to terms with the permanence of his upcoming wedding vows. In the pre-nuptial festivities, Harper rekindles a flirtation with bridesmaid Jordan, played by actress Nia Long, who was the inspiration for one of the characters in *Unfinished Business*.

Adding to this drama, Diggs's character is also trying to keep the groom from discovering that he once had a fling with the bride-to-be—also recounted in the forthcoming novel—and struggles to remain faithful to his girlfriend back in Chicago, despite Jordan's lure. Maslin, giving *The Best Man* a positive review in her *New York Times* column, called it "another demonstration that current movies about upscale black characters have much more traditional values than ones about catty white teen-agers."

Retained Footing on Stage

Diggs returned to Broadway in the spring of 2000 when cast in *The Wild Party*. Set in the 1920s, the musical revolves around a group of vaudeville performers living it up during an economic boom. Toni Collette, Mandy Patinkin, and Eartha Kitt were also in Virginia Theater production. "He thus returns to the New York stage something of an established heartthrob, and audiences may be surprised to discover (again) what a beautiful voice he has, what a natural, un-Hollywood presence," wrote Jesse Green in the *New York Times Magazine*. Diggs's girlfriend at the time, Idina Menzel, also appeared in the musical. The two met as cast members of *Rent*—at one point, Menzel's spirited character, a performance artist, moons the hated landlord Benjamin. Diggs married Menzel in 2003.

Diggs assured his feet would remain on stage by forming a contemporary dance company in 2004 with high school friend and professional choreographer Andrew Palermo. "Nobody knows that between singing, acting and dancing, I enjoy dance the most," Diggs told Lola Ogunnaike of the *New York Times,* explaining that he had fallen in love with dance in high school and continued to take lessons over the years. From its premiere performance at the Joffrey Ballet School's annual gala, the company, known as dre.dance, has garnered praise from dance critics. The company has offered seasons of contemporary dance as well as classes and workshops. Reviewing the company's show "pre.view" in 2006 for the *New York Times*, Roslyn Sulcas noted how unusual it was for an actor of some renown like Diggs to open a dance company. But she concluded after seeing his choreography that "he has every right to be taken seriously in his new venture." After offering two full seasons of new, contemporary work with dances that blended modern aesthetics and vigorous athleticism, the company had developed what Joy Goodwin of the *New York Sun* called its "own discernible style," which intimated that it would have "an intriguing future." As his own company thrived, Diggs helped highlight the richness of African-American modern dance history as the host of the PBS program *Dancing in the Light,* a part of the Great Performances series in 2007 which featured works by such choreographers as Asadata Dafora, Katherine Dunham, and Donald McKayle.

As Diggs sought out more stage opportunities—he landed his first dramatic role on stage in 2005 in Charles Fuller's Pulitzer-prize-winning *A Soldier's Play*—he maintained steady work on screen. Notably he starred in *Drum*, a film about South African journalists working for *Drum* magazine during apartheid, which won Africa's top film prize in 2005. Along with a slew of films, including *Brown Sugar, Chicago, Basic, Cake, Slow Burn,* and the film adaptation of *Rent,* Diggs continued to make a name for himself as a television actor. He quickly graduated from parts on various series to starring roles. He starred in two short-lived television series: *Kevin Hill,* about a playboy who takes on the responsibility of raising an infant, and *Daybreak,* in which he starred as a detective who is trying to solve a crime as he keeps reliving the same day. Though these series ended quickly due to poor ratings, Diggs landed a part in *Private Practice,* the ABC spin-off of the popular *Grey's Anatomy* show that viewers and critics eagerly awaited for the fall 2007 season. In it Diggs featured prominently as Dr. Sam Bennett in an ensemble cast including Kate Walsh playing Addison Montgomery from *Grey's Anatomy*.

No matter the medium, Diggs possessed a unique versatility, giving him myriad career options. His appeal stemmed from "What Diggs does best," explained critic Ken Parish Perkins for the *Chicago Defender.* "Whether he's on stage, in TV or in a film," Diggs makes "nearly every word he delivers count, as though he really, truly, cross-his-heart-hope-to-die means it." His appeal enabled Diggs to remain, after a more than a decade of work, a rising star.

Selected works

Films

How Stella Got Her Groove Back, 1998.
The Wood, 1999.
The Best Man, 1999.
House on Haunted Hill, 1999.
The Way of the Gun, 2000.
Brown Sugar, 2002.
Chicago, 2002.
Basic, 2003.
Drum, 2004.
Cake, 2005.
Slow Burn, 2005.
Rent, 2005.

Plays

Carousel, Broadway, 1994.
Chicago, 1996.
Rent, Broadway, 1996.
A Soldier's Play, 2005.

Television

Guiding Light, 1996-97.

Ally McBeal, 2001.
Kevin Hill, 2004.
Will & Grace, 2006.
Day Break, 2007.
Grey's Anatomy, 2007.
Private Practice, 2007.

Sources

Periodicals

Chicago Defender, November 17-19, 2007, p. 12.
Ebony, December 1998, pp. 108-114; January 2000, p. 100.
Entertainment Weekly, April 16, 1999, p. 36.
Essence, October 1999, p. 70.
New York Times, February 14, 1996; August 14, 1998, p. B9; April 9, 1999; July 16, 1999; October 22, 1999, p. B26; March 19, 2000, p. AR13.
New York Times Magazine, February 13, 2000; February 6, 2006, p. E5.
Newsweek, August 24, 1998, pp. 58-59.
People, September 7, 1998, p. 40; May 10, 1999, p. 125.
Sacramento Observer, June 14-20, 2007, p. E7.

On-line

"Diggstown—An Afternoon with Rising Star Taye Diggs," *Filmcritic.com*, www.filmcritic.com/misc/emporium.nsf/reviews/Diggstown—An-afternoon-with-rising-star-Taye-Diggs (August 27, 2007).
dre.dance, www.dredance.com (August 29, 2007).

—Carol Brennan and Sara Pendergast

Luisa Dias Diogo

1958—

Politician

Luisa Dias Diogo came of age in a time of liberating revolution and devastating civil war in the African nation of Mozambique. Though she saw her homeland ravaged by war, natural disasters, governmental corruption, disease, and bitter poverty, Diogo did not become hopeless or resigned. Instead, she studied economics and went to work in the government's Ministry of Planning and Finance, where she could have a direct influence on her country's economy. Diogo's hard work, resourcefulness, and hard-headed business sense enabled her to advance rapidly in the ministry, as she introduced many creative economic programs to help relieve poverty and improve conditions in the newly-independent nation. She became not only Mozambique's first female Minister of Finance, but, in 2004, at the age of 45, was appointed the country's first female Prime Minister.

Having earned a position of so much power, Diogo was keenly aware of a sense of responsibility to the citizens she represented, especially to the women, who did much of the work to create and sustain the community and often had little voice in its government. Along with working to rebuild a healthy economy in Mozambique, she has become an international ambassador, working with the United Nations and the World Bank to build bridges of understanding and support between the developing nations of Africa and the rest of the world.

Luisa Dias Diogo was born on April 11, 1958, in the Mágoè district in Tete province in the central inland area of Mozambique. She was the third of eight children born to Luis João Diogo and Laura Atanásia

Dias. At the time of young Luisa's birth, Mozambique had been a colony under the domination of Portugal for over 200 years. The African residents of the area had experienced slavery, economic exploitation, and racist political suppression at the hands of their European conquerors. By the late 1950s, an independence movement had formed, initiated by farmers, who began organizing in order to keep control of the food they produced. Mozambique's freedom fighters faced more than two decades of opposition before their nation would finally be independent.

Grew Up Amid Revolution and Civil War

Until she was 12 years old, Diogo attended the Dona Maria Primary School in Tete City. Then she went to Tete Commercial School for two years before entering the Maputo Commercial Institute for high school. She was attending high school in 1975 when Mozambique became an independent state. One of the major organizations in the fight for self-rule had been the Front for Liberation of Mozambique (FRELIMO), which formed a new government. FRELIMO was a socialist party which believed in government control of many industries and resources and attempted to modernize Mozambican society by outlawing some traditional practices.

Soon another powerful faction arose to challenge FRELIMO's changes. The National Resistance movement of Mozambique (RENAMO) was made up of a variety of groups who opposed FRELIMO. These included traditionalists, who were offended by the government's new liberal rules about religion and the status of women. Also involved in RENAMO were white Mozambicans, many of whom had fled the country after the war of independence, and conservatives from neighboring countries who feared that the fight for liberty might spread across their borders. RENAMO grew rapidly and soon the newly independent nation was embroiled in a bitter civil war that raged from 1975 until 1992. Before it ended, over a million Mozambican citizens would be killed.

In addition to its political problems, the newly forming nation faced other serious challenges. Mozambique was an agricultural society, deeply affected by the extremes of weather that are common in southeastern Africa. During the early years of independence, the country suffered severe damage from floods, which destroyed food crops, leaving much of the population in extreme poverty. During the 1980s, a new terror became a part of daily life in Mozambique as doctors discovered a deadly virus they called Acquired Immune Deficiency Syndrome (AIDS), which was sweeping the African continent south of the Sahara Desert.

Studied Economics in College

During the late 1970s, as Mozambique tasted independence and endured continued fighting, disease, and

poverty, Luisa Dias Diogo entered college at Eduardo Mondlane University, a college in the capital city of Maputo which had recently been renamed to honor one of the heroes of the revolution. The excitement of liberation, coupled with the urgent needs of the new state had created unprecedented opportunities for young people, even women, who wished to serve their country. Diogo took advantage of this new atmosphere to study economics.

The economy of Mozambique had suffered greatly from decades of colonialism and cycles of drought and flood. Seventy percent of Mozambicans lived in extreme poverty. The civil war was still raging, killing hundreds of thousands, damaging roads and bridges with explosives, and leaving the land filled with hidden bombs called land mines. The nation was deeply in debt to other nations and to international organizations such as the International Monetary Fund. Just as often happens with individuals, poverty among nations can lead to a cycle of indebtedness, where the economies of poor nations become increasingly dependent on loans that they are never able to repay.

In 1980, during her second year of college, Diogo went to work at the Ministry of Planning and Finance. Her passionate enthusiasm for her country's well-being and her administrative skills led to quick promotion. By 1989, she had become director of the Budget Department with the important responsibilities of managing the nation's investments, state treasury, and defense budget. While working hard to stabilize her country's economy, Diogo continued her own training, earning a master's degree in economics from the University of London in 1992.

In 1993, after ably managing Mozambique's budget for several years, Diogo left her work in the government to take a job with the World Bank, an international financial institution with ties to the United Nations. Officially titled the International Bank for Reconstruction and Development, the World Bank provides grants, loans, and financial advice to developing nations. From 1993 to 1994, Diogo worked as the Bank's program officer for Mozambique, helping carry out economic relief programs and making many international connections that would serve her well in her later career.

Became Minister of Finance

The civil war in Mozambique ended in 1992, and in 1994, a new election put a FREMILO government in place. The new president, Joaquim Chissano, offered Diogo a job in his government as deputy finance minister. She accepted the appointment and left the World Bank to devote herself to helping create the new government's financial development plan.

Seventeen years of civil war had had devastating effects on most aspects of Mozambican society. The country's infrastructure, that is, roads, bridges, power, and communication systems, had been demolished. Seventy percent of the education system and 60 percent of the health system had been destroyed during the conflict, and the nation faced a dire shortage of food and medical supplies. Diogo, as part of Mozambique's new government, began to work steadily to repair the damage and reform the economy in order to reduce poverty.

To help launch this new program of economic development, Diogo sought financial aid from the World Bank, the International Monetary Fund, and individual wealthy nations, such as the United Kingdom. She worked hard to obtain the aid in the form of grants rather than loans, hoping to stop the cycle of increasing debt in Mozambique. The contacts she had made while working with the World Bank helped her in raising the money her country needed, and, with the funds she raised, she began making improvements in agriculture, health, and telecommunications.

By 2000, Diogo's efforts led to her appointment as minister of finance. Though no woman had ever held the post before, Diogo was not afraid to take on the job. She knew from her own experience that women could do far more than men believed they could. She often told the story of how her grandfather, a respected man who made many decisions, regularly (and privately) asked her grandmother's advice on important matters.

Appointed First Female Prime Minister

In February 2004, President Chisanno appointed Diogo to be his prime minister. In Mozambique's parliamentary system of government, the president is elected, then appoints a chief minister to help govern. Diogo took on the important post of prime minister while keeping her job as minister of finance until the national elections in December. In the December 2004 elections, a new president, Armando Guebuza, was elected, and Diogo devoted herself to her new job as Mozambique's first female prime minister. In 2004, just before she left the Ministry of Planning and Finance, she was named Finance Minister of the Year by *The Banker*, a world famous financial journal.

One of her first priorities as head of the government was combating the spread of the AIDS virus. When Diogo took office in 2004, 1.4 million of Mozambique's 18 million citizens had AIDS, with 500 new cases reported every day. By July 2004, Diogo had set up an AIDS emergency program to increase education about the disease and provide financial support and medical assistance for people with AIDS and their families.

She also committed to improving education, literacy, and health care and promised to actively recruit more teachers and health workers. And she pledged to eliminate corruption within the government. Diogo believed that citizens in a democratic society had the right to ensure that the government lived up to their expectations. To oversee her government's progress, she set up a citizens' consulting group called the "Poverty Observatory."

Under Diogo's administration, living conditions in Mozambique have steadily improved. The country's chaotic economy has stabilized, and, since 1994, when Diogo became deputy finance minister, has shown a steady growth of eight percent per year. She has led reform of government bureaucracy and streamlined customs procedures to increase imports. She has also fulfilled her promises to rebuild Mozambique's infrastructure and prioritize health and education. Though the nation still suffers from extreme poverty, climate extremes, and the devastation of the AIDS epidemic, Diogo regards the problems with a typically female practicality. Speaking to Lucy Fleming in a BBC News interview, Diogo said that she approaches her job "like a Mozambican woman who has to create a meal for a large family, often without ingredients."

Diogo skills as an economist and a leader have attracted international attention, and she is frequently called upon to work in world forums as a representative of poor developing nations and as an African. In 2003, she worked with the World Bank to develop a joint project to fight HIV/AIDS, and in 2004 she was the only prime minister invited to meet with the general directors of the United Nations about the issues of developing nations. In 2005 she co chaired a 15-member United Nations panel charged with coordinating UN projects for humanitarian aid, economic development, and the environment. In February 2007, she was invited to be the keynote speaker at the 30th session of the International Fund for Agricultural Development. Her practical, competent approach to leadership in her country as well as in international forums has prompted both international political analysts and many Mozambican citizens to predict that Diogo will become president of Mozambique one day.

Sources

Periodicals

Banker, January 5, 2004, p. 26, July 2, 2004, p.121-2.
Global Information Network (New York), April 13, 2007, p.1.
New York Beacon, March 9-March 15, 2006, p.9.
Seattle Times, November 20, 2005, p. A.24.
UN Chronicle, March-May 2006, p. 56.

On-line

"Blazing a Trail for Africa's Women," *BBC News Website,* http://news.bbc.co.uk/1/hi/world/africa/4428434.stmBy (September 10, 2007).

"First Female Prime Minister in Mozambique," *afrol News,* www.afrol.com/articles/11288 (September 10, 2007).

"Interview with Honorable Luisa Dias Diogo," *Winne,* www.winne.com/topinterviews/diogo.html (September 10, 2007).

"Keynote Address by H.E. Dr. Luísa Dias Diogo, Prime Minister of the Republic of Mozambique to the 30th Session of IFAD's Governing Council," *International Fund of Agricultural Development,* www.ifad.org/events/gc/30/speech/mozambique.htm (September 10, 2007).

"Listen to the Voices of Mozambique," *Rural Poverty Portal,* www.ruralpovertyportal.org/english/regions/africa/moz/voices.htm (September 10, 2007).

"Luisa Diogo," *Biography Resource Center Online,* http://galenet.galegroup.com/servlet/BioRC (September 10, 2007).

"Luisa Diogo," *Notable Biographies,* www.notable-biographies.com/news/Ca-Ge/Diogo-Luisa.html (September 10, 2007).

"Luisa Diogo," *Time in Partnership With CNN,* www.time.com/time/magazine/article/0,9171,993968,00.html (September 10, 2007).

"Mozambique, Personnalites, Femmes : Luisa Dias Diogo, Première Femme Premier Ministre Du Mozambique," *Quid.fr,* www.quid.fr/zoom/index.php/2007/03/27/237-mozambique-personnalites-femmes-luisa-dias-diogo-premiere-femme-premier-ministre-du-mozambique (September 10, 2007).

"Mozambique: Luisa Diogo, New Prime Minister," *Regional Economic Development and Integration News Features: Southern African Research and Documentation Centre,* www.sardc.net/Editorial/Newsfeature/04110204.htm (September 10, 2007).

—Tina Gianoulis

Margie Eugene-Richard

1941—

Environmental and community activist

When Margie Eugene-Richard was a child in the rural community of Belltown, Louisiana, she loved to play in the beautiful countryside and follow her father and grandfather around as they worked on their small farm, growing corn and peas and tending the pomegranate trees. She was only ten years old when the petroleum refining plants moved into her town, and she watched in horror as her beautiful home became part of an industrial area that would soon be nicknamed Cancer Alley. Toxic emissions and frequent fires and explosions not only made life unpleasant in the mostly African-American neighborhoods surrounding the plants, but they also caused a wide variety of severe health problems.

As conditions in her hometown grew progressively worse, Eugene-Richard began to fight back. Inspired by her parents' example of community service, she organized her neighbors and confronted the oil company that had made their homes unlivable. After many years of struggle, the residents of the community known as Old Diamond won their fight and Shell Oil paid for their relocation to a safer area. However, the struggle for environmental justice was far from over, and Margie Eugene-Richard has continued to work for the rights of poor people and people of color to a safe and healthy environment.

Grew Up in Historic Community

Margie Eugene-Richard was born on December 21, 1941, in the historic Southern city of New Orleans. She grew up in the tiny, close-knit African-American community of Belltown, the fourth generation of her family to live on the fertile strip of land beside the Mississippi River between New Orleans and Baton Rouge. Her father, Theodore D. Eugene, was a farmer and skilled laborer, and her mother, Mabel Smith, worked in the home and as a cook in a local restaurant. Theodore Eugene had attended college at the historically black Xavier University in New Orleans until his father's death forced him to quit school to take over the family farm and care for his younger brothers. Even though he did not graduate from college, he became a community leader, offering support and counsel to those who needed it and becoming one of the first black sheriff's deputies in the area. He would make sure that his two daughters received the education that he had not been able to complete.

As a young child, Margie Eugene-Richard spent as much time as she could outdoors, trailing after her father and grandfather as they tended the fields, orchard, and animals on their small farm. She especially loved caring for the family's horses and watching the ships on the river as they sailed to and from the port of New Orleans. Though the Eugenes did not own much land, they made productive use of what they did own, growing vegetables, melons, and fruit trees to provide food for the family and to sell in the French market in New Orleans. However, when young Margie was ten years old, things began to change in the town where her family had lived for more than a hundred years.

The African-American communities of Belltown and Wattstown were sometimes also called Old Diamond, after the Diamond Plantation that had been located

through the mid 1950s. Inspired by Bethune's achievements and by her respect for her own health teacher, Eugene-Richard decided to become a health and physical education teacher. After graduating from high school, she attended Grambling State University, a historically black college in northern Louisiana, where she majored in health and physical education and minored in social studies.

After earning her bachelor's degree in 1965, Eugene-Richard returned home to Wattstown to teach at her old high school. She married Peter Richard, her childhood sweetheart, and devoted herself to her family and her community. Through her long career at Mary McLeod Bethune High School, she taught health, phys ed, and history. She especially loved making history come alive for her students by taking them on field trips and teaching, not just the dates of battles and the names of presidents and kings, but the history of ordinary people.

In addition to being an educator and mentor to her students, Eugene-Richard took an active role in her community. She taught community enrichment courses in such subjects as substance abuse prevention and treatment and how to turn a hobby into a home business. She also taught parenting classes and, following her divorce from Peter Richard, she helped her neighbors through their own divorces.

Became Environmental Activist

As the years passed, the oil refining industry surrounding the small African-American community of Wattstown, also known as Old Diamond, grew larger and larger, and the danger and toxicity grew along with it. The stink of poisonous gasses filled the air, and the health of local residents began to suffer, including Eugene-Richard's sister, who died at the age of forty-three from a rare condition called sarcoidosis. There were so many industrial accidents, explosions, and fires that, in the early 1970s, Eugene-Richards began sleeping in her clothes so that she could run away quickly in case of emergency. To add even more distress to the situation, Shell hired very few black workers, so that local community members did not even benefit from the plant in that way. Many residents had moved away, but many others could not afford to move, especially since no one would want to buy their houses because of the conditions caused by the huge refinery.

In 1988 an explosion at the refining plant caused the deaths of seven workers and released a cloud of toxins into the surrounding community. Margie Eugene-Richard decided it was time to fight back. The Eugene family had long been caring and active members of their tiny community, so, it seemed natural to Eugene-Richard to take a leadership role to fight the mighty oil company that was poisoning their home. In 1989, she founded a community group called Concerned Citizens of Norco, whose goal was to force the Shell Oil

there during the days of slavery. In 1811, Diamond Plantation had been the site of one of the largest known slave revolts. After the end of slavery and the plantation system, many freed blacks remained in the area. Their descendents, bound to the land by deep historical roots, formed tightly knit African-American communities, where they farmed and built businesses and schools. Beginning in the 1920s, the Royal Dutch (later Shell) Oil Company began constructing oil refineries in the area. The company name, New Orleans Refining Company, or Norco, eventually became the official name of the town. The refining company continued to expand, and, in the early 1950s, Shell Oil began buying up property in the town of Belltown. The mostly African-American residents had little choice except to sell their homes at the low prices offered by the oil company and move to Wattstown, a half mile down the road.

Returned Home to Teach

Margie Eugene-Richard attended Mary McLeod Bethune High School in Wattstown. She had great admiration for Bethune, who was a well-known African-American educator and activist from the early 1900s

Company to relocate the remaining citizens of Wattstown, paying fair market value for their homes and giving financial support the a new community far away from the refinery's toxic emissions.

Working with others in her community, Eugene-Richard enlisted the help of national environmental organizations and other activists. A state-wide group called the Louisiana Bucket Brigade helped the citizens of Wattstown measure the air pollution in their neighborhood, and Eugene-Richard installed a web camera on her home to broadcast the visible emissions that were released by the nearby plant. In doing this work, the Concerned Citizens of Norco became a part of a much larger national movement for environmental justice.

The environmental justice movement works to publicize the fact that a disproportionate number of people of color live in areas that are polluted by industry. Environmental justice activists point out that factories, mines, and other industries that emit toxic waste are almost never located near wealthy white neighborhoods, but near neighborhoods where poor people of color live. The *Secure Tunnel* website cites the startling statistic that, "Seventy-one percent of African Americans live in counties that don't meet federal air pollution standards." As part of this movement, Eugene-Richard began not only working for her own community, but also to support other communities seeking safer living conditions and more fair environmental policies.

Won Battle with Shell Oil

Concerned Citizens of Norco kept applying pressure to Shell Oil. In 1999, Eugene-Richard helped found a national activist group called the National Black Environmental Justice Network. She spoke before Congress, pointing out that the Civil Rights Act of 1964 authorized them to legislate racially fair environmental laws. She traveled to Geneva, Switzerland to testify before the United Nations Human Rights Commission, and she went South Africa to speak at the World Conference Against Racism in Durban and the World Summit on Sustainable Development in Johannesburg.

Finally, the hard work of the CCN began to pay off. By 2000, the company promised to reduce the level of the refinery's emissions, and in 2002, they finally agreed to relocate the three hundred families who still lived in the Old Diamond neighborhood. As Eugene-Richard and her group had demanded, Shell agreed to pay market value for their homes and give financial support to a new community a safe distance from the plant.

Though she had achieved the goal that she and her neighbors had set in 1989, Eugene-Richard has continued to work for environmental justice, advising other communities on strategies and tactics to fight polluters in their own neighborhoods. When hurricane Katrina struck the gulf coast in 2005, she worked to help victims of the storm and to publicize the environmental effects of the disaster, which, once again, most severely affected poor communities of color. One of her many future goals is the establishment of a New Orleans hospital to study illnesses caused by environmental pollution.

Eugene-Richard has also continued to set personal goals. Always a deeply religious person, she had taught Bible school classes since the age of twelve, and later in her life she felt called to enter the ministry. In 1996, a year after she retired from teaching, she enrolled in the School of Urban Mission, a Bible college in nearby Gretna, Louisiana, where she earned her two-year certificate in theology. From her new home in Destrehan, Louisiana, she continues her work in her community, in her church, and in the environmental justice movement.

Sources

Periodicals

E, March-April 2006, p. 31.
OnEarth, Winter 2006, p. 10.
Wall Street Journal, April 19, 2004, p. B4.

On-line

"Diamond, Louisiana," *Guardian*, www.guardian.co.uk/usa/story/0,,1070021,00.html (August 7, 2007).
"First African American Wins 2004 Goldman Environmental Prize," *Environmental Justice Resource Center*, www.ejrc.cau.edu/GoldmanEnvAwardEJ.htm (August 7, 2007).
"Margie Eugene-Richard," *Goldman Environmental Prize*, www.goldmanprize.org/node/100 (August 7, 2007).
"Margie E. Richard: Pollution Fighter," *AARP the Magazine*, www.aarpmagazine.org/people/impact_awards_rich.html (August 7, 2007).
"Norco Profile: Community Group: Concerned Citizens of Norco," *Louisiana Bucket Brigade*, www.labucketbrigade.org/communities/norco/profile/index.shtml (August 7, 2007).
"Oppression in the Air: The Threat of Environmental Racism," *Louisiana Weekly*, www.louisianaweekly.com/weekly/news/articlegate.pl?20010910e (August 7, 2007).

Other

Information for this profile was obtained through an interview with Margie Eugene-Richard on June 21, 2007.

—Tina Gianoulis

Isaac Newton Farris, Jr.

1962—

President and CEO of The King Center

Farris, Isaac Newton, photograph. AP Images.

In September of 2005 Isaac Newton Farris, Jr., was named president and chief executive officer (CEO) of the Martin Luther King Jr. Center for Non-Violent Social Change, commonly known as The King Center. The nephew of Dr. King, Farris had spent the previous five years as chief operating officer (COO) of the center. Established in 1968 by Coretta Scott King as a "living memorial dedicated to the advancement of the legacy" of Dr. King, the center came to include the Freedom Hall Complex, the Ebenezer Baptist Church, Dr. King's birth home, and Dr. and Mrs. King's crypt. The King Center drew nearly one million visitors annually, making it the most visited cultural and tourist attraction in the southeast United States. As head of the center, Farris directed its activities and often acted as spokesperson for the King family.

Raised in the King Family Tradition

Born on April 13, 1962, in Atlanta, Georgia, Isaac Newton Farris was not quite six when Martin Luther King, Jr., was slain. His memories of his uncle were as a playmate. Only later did he come to appreciate the significance of Dr. King's contributions to American society. Nevertheless Farris grew up at the very center of the Civil Rights Movement, nurtured by the activism of the extended King and Farris families. His mother, Christine King Farris, Dr. King's oldest sibling, was a professor of education at her alma mater Spelman College in Atlanta. Isaac Newton Farris, Sr., was an entrepreneur, the owner of Farris Color Visions in Atlanta, and the author of *Scenes of Black Atlanta: A Pictorial Guide.* Like his uncle before him, Farris attended Morehouse College in Atlanta. He graduated in 1985 with a major in pre-law. His younger sister, Angela Farris-Watkins, attended Spelman and eventually joined her mother on the Spelman faculty as a psychology professor.

Following graduation Farris went to work for his cousin, Martin Luther King III, Dr. King's eldest son and a commissioner of Fulton County, which encompassed the Atlanta metropolitan area. Farris functioned as King's campaign manager and chief of staff until 1995 when he was named COO of The King Center.

The King Center opened at its present location, within Atlanta's Martin Luther King, Jr., National Historic

Site, in 1980 at a cost of $8 million. The nonprofit organization regularly employed King family members and was perpetually short on cash. Dexter Scott King, Dr. King's youngest son, was elected president and CEO in 1994 and proceeded to cut programs and staffing.

Appointed CEO in Family Coup

In August of 2005 The King Center board voted Dexter King out and Martin Luther King III became chairman of the board. One month later, however, Dexter appointed eight new board members. They voted him back in as chairman and Farris as president and CEO. Farris also joined the board, which included his mother as vice chair. In a press release announcing Farris's appointment, quoted in the *Atlanta Inquirer*, Dexter King said: "the Center's board election of Isaac Newton Farris as president and chief executive officer will strengthen our capacity to act more effectively. Isaac brings an insightful understanding of my father's teachings, combined with knowledge of The King Center's history and a vision for its unique potential. We expect significant progress in the Center's development under his leadership." Meanwhile Martin and Bernice King accused Dexter of abusing his power, and Farris was forced to counter media reports that the King family lived off the funds raised by the center. He pointed out that only he and Dexter received salaries, reportedly in the mid-$100,000 range.

The direction and future of The King Center had been the focus of a long-standing dispute among Dr. King's children. Following the death of Coretta Scott King in February of 2006, the board was faced with making their own decisions rather than simply carrying out Mrs. King's wishes. Although founded to promote King's legacy of nonviolent social transformation, the organization had been strongly criticized for not living up to its promise and, in fact, for not doing very much at all.

In February of 2005 the National Park Service (NPS) had reported that the center required $11 million in structural and mechanical repairs to meet city and state building codes. Isaac Farris, along with Dexter King and his sister Yolanda, board member Andrew Young, and Georgia Congressman John Lewis, favored turning over the maintenance and control of the buildings and grounds to the NPS, which was already contributing about $1 million annually to the center. Martin Luther King III and Bernice King feared that the center would lose its independence. As of 2007, although discussions were still ongoing, it appeared less likely that the NPS would take over The King Center.

Strove to Maintain King's Legacy

In April of 2007 Farris learned for the first time of a folder containing notes, letters, and speeches written by Dr. King that were about to be auctioned off. As a representative of the King estate Farris blocked the sale. The family had recently sold a large collection of King's papers to the city of Atlanta for $32 million, which in turn donated the collection to Morehouse College where a civil and human rights museum was being proposed. Farris told the *Atlanta Journal-Constitution:* "We are going to get the papers...I believe we will be calling Morehouse and telling them that we are sending over 25 additional documents." Farris told *Contemporary Black Biography* that, although the center and the family had at times been criticized for claiming ownership of King's writings and correspondence, "Everything that we do he did. He copyrighted everything during his lifetime. Everything we're doing he put in motion. Everything else he put into the movement. He gave away a lot. His private papers were for the family to have and we keep them housed at Morehouse."

Farris told *CBB* that the major focus of his work was to redirect the activities of The King Center back to its original purpose as an educational and policy-formulating institution. "We are not a frontline activist organization. Because of their memories of my uncle, people often push us in activist directions, such as voter registration drives. However direct confrontation is the last step; we are part of the actual policy formation. Our model would be the Brookings Institute and other think tanks. No other organization can bring the unique perspective that we can."

The major undertakings of the center under Farris included maintaining its archives, the single largest collection documenting the U.S. Civil Rights Movement and an important resource for scholars. Farris collaborated with Stanford University on the King Papers Project–a projected 14-volume collection of Dr. King's writings, of which five volumes had been published as of 2007. The center was also collaborating with the U.S. Department of Education on the development of a non-violence educational curriculum. As of 2007, the curriculum had been completed through the fifth grade and was being extended through the high-school level. Farris worked with individual states to assure that the Dr. Martin Luther King, Jr. national holiday was celebrated appropriately as a day of service. To that end, the center worked with the U.S. Congress in 1998 to change the wording of the law creating the holiday. Farris also continued to work with various groups on non-violent conflict resolution and planned to reintroduce the Scholar Intern Program, whereby students earned college credit working on projects at the King Center. Speaking of his work at the center, Farris told *CBB*: "We are at a crucial point."

Sources

Periodicals

Atlanta Inquirer, January 7, 2006, p. 1.
Atlanta Journal-Constitution, April 5, 2007.
Atlanta Tribune, July 2007, p. 25.
Chicago Defender, March 3-6, 2006, p. 6.
New York Times, April 4, 2007, p. A9.
Seattle Times, January 20, 1997, B4.

On-line

The King Center, www.thekingcenter.org (August 12, 2007).
"King Center Sold to the Federal Government?" *National Newspaper Publishers Association, Inc.,* www.blackpressusa.com/News/Article.asp?SID=3& Title=Hot+Stories&NewsID=6074 (April 23, 2007).

Other

Additional information for this profile was obtained through an interview with Isaac Newton Farris, Jr., on August 10, 2007.

—Margaret Alic

Arthur A. Fletcher

1924-2005

Federal government official

Arthur A. Fletcher was eulogized as the "father of affirmative action" in tributes that followed his death in July of 2005. A moderate Republican who had served as an advisor to three U.S. presidents and chaired the Federal Commission on Civil Rights, Fletcher achieved his most lasting impact back in the early 1970s as the Labor Department responsible for new federal guidelines that required companies bidding on government contracts to prove they had an ethnically diverse workforce. This strategy finally compelled employers to hire more minorities in order to continue to win financially lucrative government contracts, and the lifelong Republican did not underestimate the power of the dollar as an equalizing force in America. "It's not about social justice," Fletcher once told an Illinois church group, according to his *New York Times* obituary. "Social justice is nice, but I've got something in my pocket that can buy all the social justice I need."

Fletcher was born in 1924 at Camp Huachuca, later known as Fort Huachuca, a U.S. Army base on Arizona's border with Mexico. At the time, his father Andrew was serving with one of the all-black cavalry regiments that had patrolled the region since the end of the U.S. Civil War. His mother, Edna, worked as a live-in housekeeper, though she was a trained nurse and had a teaching degree; because of institutional racism, she was unable to find a job in either profession in any of the Western states where the family lived during Fletcher's childhood.

Inspired by Mary McLeod Bethune

Fletcher did not apply himself to his schoolwork with much gusto in his early years. By the time he reached his high-school years, Fletcher had attended 17 different schools, mostly located near the military bases where his father had been stationed. One day when civil rights and education pioneer Mary McLeod Bethune visited his Oklahoma City middle school, however, Fletcher's life changed. She told the assembled students that she had been an advisor to presidents, and then said, according to an interview with Fletcher that appeared in a 1991 issue of *Ebony,* "I know that I am talking to someone in this auditorium who is going to grow up and advise a president of the United States, too." As Fletcher recalled, "I was a D-plus/C-minus student but when she spoke, her spiritual electricity held me in the palm of her hands and I got excited and thought, wouldn't it be great if I was the person carrying that message?"

Another influential figure for Fletcher was his Junction City, Kansas, high school teacher, who suggested he try out for the football team. He proved a talented athlete—aided by his height and bulk—and won an athletic scholarship to Washburn College in Topeka. He later served in the U.S. Army at the height of World War II as part of the "Red Ball Express" transportation line that aided a joint Allied advance across France. Once the war ended, he signed with the Los Angeles Rams as a defensive end, and played a few seasons in

At a Glance . . .

Born Arthur Allan Fletcher on December 22, 1924, in Camp Huachuca, AZ; died on July 12, 2005, in Washington, DC; son of Andrew (a U.S. Army officer) and Edna (a nurse and domestic worker; maiden name, Miller) Fletcher; married Mary Harden (died 1961); married Ayesha Bernyce Hassan-Fletcher (a White House aide), 1964; children: (from first marriage) Phyllis Palmer, Sylvia Austin, Arthur Jr., Paul. Phillip. *Education:* Washburn College, B.A., 1950; post-graduate work at Kansas State University and San Francisco State College; earned law degree from La-Salle University. *Politics:* Republican. *Military service:* U.S. Army during World War II.

Career: Los Angeles Rams, professional football player (defensive end), 1950-54; Baltimore Colts, professional football player (defensive end), 1954-55; Kansas Highway Commission, assistant public relations director, 1954-57; Kansas State Republican Central Committee, vice-chair, 1954-56; Topeka, KS, car dealership owner, 1956-(?); Washburn University, assistant football coach, (?)-1958; Aerojet-General Corporation, management control coordinator; White House Domestic Committee on the Elimination of Economic Discrimination, chair, and Assistant Secretary of Labor for wage and labor standards, 1969-71; United Negro College Fund, executive director, 1971-73; U.S. deputy assistant for urban affairs, mid-1970s; U.S. Federal Commission on Civil Rights, chair, 1990-93; University of Denver, College of Business Administration, Director of Institute for Social Policy, 1992-94; corporate consultant, 1994-(?); Republican presidential candidate, 1996.

the early 1950s before being traded to the 1954 Baltimore Colts, where he became that team's first African-American member.

Back in Kansas, Fletcher was a supporter of the civil rights movement and personally donated funds to bring a racial-discrimination lawsuit before the courts. That case became *Brown v. the Board of Education of Topeka,* a landmark decision by the U.S. Supreme Court that outlawed separate schools for blacks and whites in America. He was also drawn into local Republican Party politics when he helped a gubernatorial candidate canvass black neighborhoods in the state.

When the candidate won, Fletcher was made assistant public relations director for the Kansas Highway Commission. At the time, there was a major federal initiative underway to build an interstate highway system, and Fletcher began to see firsthand how the government bidding process worked. Such contracts meant lucrative, often-long term jobs for the companies who won them, and would later become the cornerstone of the first federal affirmative-action policies.

Endured Years of Discrimination

Fletcher lost his government job in 1957 when a new governor took office in Kansas, and he was soon forced to leave the state anyway when his efforts to establish a car-dealership business were thwarted—perhaps the result of his involvement in the *Brown v. the Board of Education* case. With his wife, Mary, and a growing brood that would number five children, he moved to Sacramento, California, where he found a job as a management-control coordinator with an aerospace company. The Fletchers, however, became the target of harassment, and endured rocks being thrown through their windows, in the all-white neighborhood where they had managed to find a house. They moved on to the ostensibly more liberal community of Berkeley, where Fletcher worked for a tire company and ran a restaurant, but his wife committed suicide in 1961, a tragedy those who knew her attributed to the stress of being denied housing once again in a largely white part of the city.

Fletcher remained active in local Republican politics, and for a time held a post with the party in the California state assembly as chair of its advisory commission on civil rights. In 1967, he relocated his family to Washington State and the Pasco-Kennewick-Richland area, where he established a community self-help program for the desperately poor black migrant workers who lived at the edge of town and had been unable to secure government welfare benefits. This successful job-training program caught the eye of federal policy-makers, as did Fletcher's increasing profile in the Republican Party. In 1968, he won the primary as a candidate for lieutenant governor, but the ticket lost in Washington State's general election.

In 1969, a newly elected Republican president, Richard M. Nixon, found a place in Washington for Fletcher in his cabinet. Nixon appointed him to serve as Assistant Secretary of Labor for wage and labor standards, and also made him chairperson of the White House Domestic Committee on the Elimination of Economic Discrimination. This was the body that helped put in place the first affirmative-action policies in the federal government, and Fletcher authored the template for this with a document that became known as the Revised Philadelphia Plan. Under its terms, a plan adopted by the city of Philadelphia to force construction trade unions with government contracts to hire and train more minorities was altered to meet federal guidelines with a rule that decreed any company submitting a bid for a government contract must hire a certain minority of minority workers; it also called for minimum quotas for any labor union benefiting from the bid.

Fletcher's role in the U.S. Department of Labor's successful implementation of this was not unusual, given his credentials and long history of activism, but the fact that such a major turning point occurred during Nixon's presidency was a surprise. Nixon was a conservative California Republican who would later be forced out of the White House in disgrace in 1974, but his election to a first term in 1968 was viewed as a potential reversal for some of the recent gains made in the U.S. civil rights movement up to that point. The Nixon Administration did little to dispel the perception that it was hostile toward minorities, which made the Labor Department's implementation of the newly renamed "Compulsory Preferential Treatment" plan all the more remarkable. Fletcher was interviewed by the *New York Times* in 1971—an article whose headline reflected the tenor of the times with the title "A Hard-Driving Black Official"—in which he admitted that "the black community expects so little from this Administration" it enabled him and other civil-rights advocates within it "a chance to go a long way."

Coined Famous UNCF Slogan

Fletcher resigned, however, not long after that article appeared, though he had said that his new position as executive director of the United Negro College Fund (UNCF) would be concurrent with his Labor Department job. His superiors evidently felt differently, and then his relatively brief tenure as UNCF head was stymied as well by policy-makers and decision-makers there who objected to his Republican leanings. He is credited, however, with coining the UNCF's enduring slogan, "A mind is a terrible thing to waste," before leaving the post in 1973.

Fletcher returned to Washington under Nixon's successor, Gerald R. Ford, to serve as deputy assistant for urban affairs in the mid-1970s. A few years later, when Republican Ronald Reagan was elected to the White House, Fletcher was invited to serve in some capacity but his request for direct access to the Oval Office was denied, and he refused the offer. He later caused somewhat of a stir when he called Reagan "the worst president for civil rights in this century," according to the *Ebony* article.

In 1990, Fletcher accepted a job offer from Reagan's successor, George H.W. Bush, as chair of the Federal Commission on Civil Rights. His three-year tenure was notable for his support of a civil rights bill in Congress, which Bush vetoed twice against Fletcher's advice, and Fletcher was also snubbed by senior administration officials and the more conservative Republican Party leadership ranks. He was the top civil rights official in Washington, but one year his name did not appear on a list of invitees to the White House dinner in honor of Black History Month; an invitation was quickly issued, but President Bush was reportedly outraged at the slight against the esteemed Fletcher.

Urged Businesses to Diversify, Educate

After leaving the Commission, Fletcher headed the Institute for Social Policy at the University of Denver's College of Business Administration, and made a brief run as a contender for the 1996 Republican Party presidential nomination. He spent the final years of his career as a consultant to corporations and their executives explaining why affirmative action was vital to the health of their companies and the future of the nation. "Companies that ignore diversity will struggle to flourish in the global marketplace during the 21st century," he told *Fortune*'s Eryn Brown in 2000. "According to Department of Labor statistics, the pool of talent that will supply the next generation of employees, managers, and executives will soon be dominated by women and ethnic minorities. They will be hard to ignore."

Despite the legal challenges and growing public perception of affirmative action as an irrelevant relic of a previous age, Fletcher was still a firm supporter of the idea behind it. He spoke in favor of federal initiatives like the "Community Reinvestment Act, which prods banks to make loans in low-income neighborhoods," he said in the *Fortune* interview. "Look, every minority individual will not reach the executive suite or even thrive in a corporate environment. But the CRA provides entrepreneurial-minded residents in poor areas an opportunity to join the mainstream economy by being upfront, out-front, participants in the economic revival of their own neighborhoods."

Sources

Periodicals

Colorado Business, November 1997, p. SS8.
Ebony, July 1991, p. 19.
Fortune, March 6, 2000, p. 76.
New York Times, December 2, 1971, p. 52; July 14, 2005.

—Carol Brennan

Ann Gregory

1912-1990

Amateur golfer

Ann Gregory began playing competitive golf during the 1940s, a time of war, when the absence of men opened up opportunities for women to excel in many fields. She was a devoted and self-possessed player who won hundreds of tournaments, both in the United States and abroad. Although almost all golfers of the time were wealthy and white, Gregory was neither intimidated nor defiant. With calm confidence and unfailing politeness, she quietly broke down racial barriers, both in her home city of Gary, Indiana, and nationally, as she became the first African American woman to enter a U.S. Golf Association championship tournament. Though she experienced many incidents of racism and discrimination, Gregory impressed almost everyone she met with her warmth, humor, and grace, making many friends in both the black and the white golf circuits. She continued to play competitively right up to her death, winning a gold medal in the U.S. Senior Olympics at the age 76.

Left the Segregated South

Gregory was born Ann Moore on July 25, 1912, in the eastern Mississippi city of Aberdeen, a port on the Tombigbee River. Her parents, Henry and Myra Moore, died when she was still a young child. Gregory was then raised by a white family in Aberdeen. However, the Mississippi of the early 1900s was only two generations removed from the days of slavery, and young Ann Moore was not brought into the white family like a daughter, but made to work as a servant and often treated poorly. With few other options, she remained with the family, working as a maid, until she married in 1938.

When her husband, Leroy Percy Gregory, wanted to go north to look for work, Ann Gregory eagerly took the opportunity to leave her bad experiences in the South behind. The couple moved to Gary, Indiana, where Percy went to work in the steel mills and Ann worked as a caterer at the University Club. Both the Gregorys were athletic, and Ann soon began playing tennis, winning the Gary city tennis championship. Percy enjoyed playing golf and had begun teaching Ann to play when the start of World War II cut their lessons short. Shortly after the birth of their only daughter, Jo-Ann, in 1942, Percy Gregory entered the U.S. Navy and spent several years overseas.

Took Up Golf

Left alone with her baby, Gregory continued to pursue her interest in golf, honing her skills and taking lessons from a local African-American golf professional named Calvin Ingram. By the time her husband returned home at the war's end, Ann Gregory had begun entering amateur golfing competitions.

As the second half of the twentieth century began, a majority of U.S. public institutions, organizations, and sporting events were still racially segregated. This was especially apparent in sports like golf, which required expensive, well-maintained grass courses for play, so were most often confined to the country clubs of the upper classes. Even the public golf course in Gary was

At a Glance . . .

Born Ann Moore on July 25, 1912, in Aberdeen, MS; died 1990, in Gary, IN; married Leroy Percy Gregory, 1938 (died 1989); children: Jo-Ann.

Career: Amateur tournament golfer, 1950-89.

Selected memberships: Chicago Women's Golf Association; Community Chest; United Fund; Gary, Indiana Public Library, Board of Directors.

Awards: U.S. Senior Olympics, golf, gold medal, 1989.

segregated, with only a small nine-hole course open to black players, while white players were permitted to use a full eighteen-hole course. In 1925, black golfers had come together to form the United States Colored Golfers Association (later called the United Golfers Association or UGA). The UGA held black-only tournaments for both men and women, creating a place for competitive African American golfers to meet and play.

Gregory played in many UGA tournaments and soon began winning. Her successes attracted the notice of George S. May, a successful white Chicago businessman and well-known golf promoter. May owned an exclusive Illinois country club called the Tam O'Shanter, and, in 1947, he invited the new African-American champion to compete in one of his tournaments. In her 1992 book *The Illustrated History of Women's Golf*, Rhonda Glenn quotes Gregory's description of her first experience playing golf at an all-white club, "The galleries were just beautiful to me, but I was lonely. For a whole week I didn't see any black people. My neighbors drove up from Gary to see me play the final round and, when I saw them, that's the only time I felt funny. It just did something to me to see my black friends among all those white people, and I cried."

Broke Color Barriers

Though breaking the color barrier was frightening and painful, Gregory's love of golf along with a strong sense of justice urged her forward. She enjoyed the challenge of competition, so she continued to look for new places to test her skill. In 1950, Ann Gregory entered seven black golf tournaments and won six, including the National UGA tourney in Washington, D.C. The next logical step was to enter the competitions sponsored by the U.S. Golf Association, an amateur golfer's group that had been founded in 1894. Centered in various country clubs, the USGA was a segregated white organization.

During the mid-1950s, the civil rights movement was growing stronger and an increasing number of African Americans were no longer willing to accept second-class citizenship. In 1956, the same year that Dr. Martin Luther King, Jr. organized a boycott of the bus system in Montgomery, Alabama, the Chicago Women's Golf Association became the first black organization to join the USGA, in large part so that one of its members, Ann Gregory, could begin to compete in USGA tournaments. On September 17, 1956, Gregory entered in the USGA Women's Amateur Championship in Indianapolis, Indiana, becoming the first African-America woman to play in any USGA tournament.

Gregory continued to play in USGA tournaments throughout the next three decades. She approached the game with dedication, cordiality, and humor and made many friends among the other golfers. In spite of this, she frequently encountered prejudice and discrimination, such as not being permitted to stay in white hotels with the other golfers. In 1959, at a tournament in Bethesda, Maryland, the local tournament committee voted to exclude her from the players' dinner, and, during a 1963 competition, a white golfer mistook her for a maid. Gregory remained unruffled in the face of such examples of ignorance and bigotry, offering a friendly smile, then devoting her energy to winning. "Racism works best when you let it affect your mind," she said, according to Rhonda Glenn. "It was better for me to remember that the flaw was in the racist, not in me. For all the ugliness, I've gotten nice things three times over. I can't think ugly of anybody."

While paving the way for black golfers nationally, Gregory also continued to break barriers at home. During the 1960s, she entered Gary's segregated public golf course, stating that she was a taxpayer and intended to play on the white-only eighteen-hole course. She played her round without incident, and soon other African American golfers left the black nine-hole course to join her. She also devoted much time and energy to supporting her community with charity work and became the first black member of Gary's Public Library board.

Ann Gregory continued to compete in amateur golf tournaments throughout the United States and abroad. Her courage and grace provided inspiration to a new generation of African-American women golfers, beginning with pioneering golf professionals like Althea Gibson and Renee Powell and continuing into the twenty-first century with such successful players as Robin Aikens and LaRee Sugg. Gregory also provided an example of aging with vigor by continuing to play competitive golf into her seventies. In 1989, at the age of 76, she won the gold medal for golf at the U.S. Senior Olympics, defeating a field of golfers over the age of 49. She died in 1990. A decade later the Urban

Chamber of Commerce of Las Vegas launched an annual Ann Gregory Memorial Scholarship Golf Tournament to honor Gregory's achievements.

Sources

Books

Glenn, Rhonda, *The Illustrated History of Women's Golf,* Taylor Trade Publishing, Boulder, Colorado, 1991.

McDaniel, Pete, *Uneven Lies: The Heroic Story of African Americans in Golf,* American Golfer, 2000.

Sinnette, Calvin H., *Forbidden Fairways: African Americans and the Game of Golf,* Thomson Gale, 1998.

Periodicals

Black Enterprise, August 1992, September 1999.

Sentinel (Los Angeles, California), February 17, 2000, p. B3.

Sports Illustrated, May 20, 1991, pp. 16-20.

On-line

"Ann Gregory," *AfroGolf.com,* www.afrogolf.com/ ANNGREGORY.HTML (August 8, 2007).

"Black Golf History," *Golfblogger,* www.golfblogger. com/index.php/golf/comments/black_golf_history/ (August 8, 2007).

"African Americans and Golf, A Brief History," *African American Registry,* www.aaregistry.com/ african_american_history/2160/AfricanAmericans_ and_golf_a_brief_history (August 8, 2007).

"Pioneer Gregory Broke Color Barriers," *USGA,* www.usga.org/news/2005/february/gregory.html (August 10, 2007).

—Tina Gianoulis

Bob Herbert

1945—

Journalist

Bob Herbert has often been called "the conscience of the *New York Times*." As an op-ed columnist for the nation's most celebrated newspaper since 1993, Herbert has repeatedly called attention to matters of race, social injustice, and the widening gap between rich and poor. An unapologetic liberal, Herbert has been one of the sharpest and most consistent critics of President George W. Bush and his policies, including the war in Iraq. Over the past two decades, he has been one of the most prominent black journalists in America.

Bob Herbert was born on March 7, 1945, in Brooklyn, New York, and grew up in the New York suburb of Montclair, New Jersey. His parents owned a couple of upholstery shops, and during his youth, Herbert felt destined to go into the family business. At the same time, the Herbert household was politically engaged, and the hot issues of the day were a regular topic of conversation around the family dinner table. A voracious reader from an early age, Herbert was reading newspapers by the time he was five years old. He also liked the classics. He was smitten by Dickens at an age when most kids are just dipping their toes into comic books. He read *Oliver Twist* when he was nine.

During the buildup to the Vietnam War, Herbert was drafted into the armed forces and sent to Korea. Returning home from the War, Herbert decided that he wanted to pursue a career as a writer, though he was not certain about what kind of writer he wanted to be. He contacted the *Newark Star-Ledger,* and to his surprised he was offered a job as a reporter in 1970. He gladly accepted the offer, which he called "a gift

from the gods" in a *New York Times* "Meet the Columnist" video interview years later.

Herbert instantly fell in love with his new journalism career. At the *Star-Ledger*, he had the opportunity to cover a number of big stories, which caught the attention of editors at the *New York Daily News*. He was offered a job there in 1976, bringing him into the nation's most important media market. Herbert arrived at the *Daily News* during an exciting time in local politics—and in political journalism in general, with Watergate still fresh in the public's memory—and he quickly earned a strong reputation for his reporting on issues playing out at City Hall. In 1981 he was promoted to City Hall bureau chief, and two years later he was named city editor. Herbert became a columnist, as well as a member of the editorial board, at the *Daily News* in 1985, the job for which he first gained national attention. That attention eventually led to a series of television jobs. In 1990 Herbert became a founding panelist on *Sunday Edition,* a talk show on New York's CBS affiliate WCBS. He also became a host of the weekly New York public television talk show *Hotline* around that time.

Meanwhile, Herbert found time to complete his education. While covering important stories and issues, he took classes at Empire State College—part of the State University of New York system—graduating with a journalism degree in 1988. Since then, he has put in time on the other side of the lectern, teaching journalism classes at Brooklyn College and the Columbia University Graduate School of Journalism. Herbert reached a national market in the early 1990s. His success in the nation's largest local broadcast market led to a three-year stint as a national television correspondent at NBC news, beginning in 1991. This job included, among other spots, regular appearances on the *Today Show* and *NBC Nightly News.* All the while, he continued writing his *Daily News* column. Ultimately, Herbert's national television exposure resulted in an offer to become an op-ed columnist at the *New York Times,* one of the most sought-after positions for a political journalist in the English-speaking world. He accepted the job, becoming the first African American op-ed columnist in the history of the *Times* in 1993. That year, Herbert chaired the Pulitzer Prize jury for spot news reporting.

Since 1993, Herbert's column, covering politics, urban affairs and social trends, has appeared in the *Times* twice a week. He continues to make frequent guest television appearances on national issues shows. In 2005, Henry Holt and Co. published a collection of Herbert's columns. The book, titled *Promises Betrayed: Waking Up from the American Dream,* touches on many of Herbert's favorite themes from his two decades as a noted columnist, including racism, poverty, criminal justice, and the foibles of the Bush administration. However, he balances his criticism with portraits of ordinary Americans accomplishing great things, and retaining hope for the future of their country. In her commentary on the book, Marian Wright Edelman, founder and president of the Children's Defense Fund, wrote that Herbert's voice "consistently reminds America of where we still fall short of the ideals of the nation we want to be and can become."

Herbert gets his column ideas from a variety of sources. Perhaps the biggest is from the newspaper. He reads several papers every day. Other ideas come from a broad range of contacts developed over the years, from government bureaucrats to educators to military officials. In addition, tips arrived from every corner of society. In recent years, much of Herbert's prose has been harsh criticism of President George W. Bush and his administration. Herbert has been a leading critic of the conduct of and justification for the war in Iraq. He has also voiced loud displeasure regarding Bush's fiscal and economic policies, particularly tax cuts which Herbert says disproportionately benefit the wealthy, and the administration's perceived failure to address issues that affect the poor, such as access to health care.

While Herbert's reputation has to some degree been built on a willingness to be critical, and not just of conservatives but of individuals of all political stripes when he senses hypocrisy, his writing reflects a surprising optimism about Americans and their collective future. As he said in a 2005 interview with the *Progressive* magazine, "It is easy, as a journalist, to be enclosed in an ivory tower and to look down at the masses. It is also easy in this business to become cynical. But when I go out into the streets and neighborhoods and speak to people, I am overwhelmed by what they have to say. The more you talk to ordinary men and women and kids, the less cynical you become because they are speaking with a sense of openness and honesty. They still have a sense of optimism and a sense of hope about their lives."

Selected writings

Books

Promises Betrayed: Waking Up from the American Dream, Henry Holt and Co., 2005.

Sources

Books

Promises Betrayed: Waking Up from the American Dream, Henry Holt and Co., 2005.

Periodicals

Progressive, August 1995, p. 36.

On-line

"Columnist Biography: Bob Herbert," *New York Times,* www.nytimes.com/ref/opinion/HERBERT-BIO.html (July 1, 2007).

"Columnist Bob Herbert Views the American Dream: But Can It Still Be Found?" *BuzzFlash,* www.buzzflash.com/interviews/05/05/int05018.html (July 1, 2007).

"Meet the Columnists: Bob Herbert," *TimesSelect,* http://select.nytimes.com/packages/khtml/2005/09/19/opinion/20050919_HERBERT_FEATURE.html (July 1, 2007).

"Poynter Fellowship Biographies, 2006-07," *Yale University,* www.yale.edu/opa/campus/poynter/2006_2007.html (July 1, 2007).

—Bob Jacobson

Oliver W. Hill

1907-2007

Lawyer

Hill, Oliver W., photograph. Ralph Morse/Time Life Pictures/Getty Images.

As a young man Oliver W. Hill realized that the legal system offered the most effective way to achieve an equal footing for African Americans in American society. He went to law school and blazed a trail virtually unparalleled in the history of the civil rights movement. In 1948, Hill became the first African American elected to the Richmond City Council since Reconstruction. Hill was applauded as "one of the pioneer civil rights lawyers of our age" by Ronald L. Plesser in 1994. Plesser, the section chair of the Individual Rights and Responsibilities, was announcing Hill's selection as the recipient of that year's Thurgood Marshall Award from the American Bar Association. "His lifetime commitment to achieving equal rights through law positively affected the direction of the entire nation at a crucial time in our history."

Fascinated with Impact of Laws

Born Oliver White Hill in Richmond, Virginia, on May 1, 1907, Hill had an early fascination with the role of law in society as it related to African Americans. While at Howard University, he and other students realized there was no hope of attaining equal rights through the U.S. Congress. That branch of government clung to the 1896 Supreme Court decision in *Plessy vs. Ferguson*, a case that stated that the provision of "separate but equal" facilities for African Americans did not violate the Thirteenth and Fourteenth amendments, amendments which outlawed slavery after the Civil War.

The *Plessy vs. Ferguson* decision led to the creation of Jim Crow laws, which institutionalized racial separation in schools, public facilities and transportation. "So our only hope was to go back through the courts and get the courts to reinterpret and correct the mistake made in 1896," Hill said at a program celebrating the 40th anniversary of *Brown vs. Board of Education*, and excerpted in *Human Rights*. "And that is the reason I went to law school." While attending the Howard University School of Law, Hill became friends with a fellow student, Thurgood Marshall, who would become the lead attorney in the *Brown* case and a future Supreme Court Justice. The two friends both graduated in 1993; Marshall was the top law student in their graduating class, Hill the second.

At a Glance . . .

Born Oliver White Hill on May 1, 1907, in Richmond, VA; died on August 5, 2007, Richmond, VA; son of Olivia Lewis White-Hill and William Henry White II; married Beresenia Walker, September 5, 1934; children: Oliver White Hill, Jr. *Education*: Howard University, AB, 1931; Howard University School of Law, JD, 1933.

Career: Attorney, Roanoke, Virginia, 1934-36; law practice, Richmond, Virginia, 1939-61; elected to Richmond City Council, 1948-50; worked on *Davis vs. County School Board of Prince Edward County* (Virginia), one of the five cases the Supreme Court combined into their 1954 decision of *Brown vs. Board of Education*, 1951-54; named to committee on government contract compliance, 1952; FHA, assistant to commissioner, 1961-66; partner and founder, Hill, Tucker & Marsh, 1966-1998.

Memberships: NAACP.

Selected awards: Chicago Defender Merit Award, 1948; Howard University Alumni Award, 1950; Omega Man of the Year, Omega Psi Phi, 1957; National Bar Association, Lawyer of the Year, 1959; Judicial Council of National Bar Association, 1979; NAACP Legal Defense and Educational Fund, The Simple Justice Award, 1986; American Bar Association, Pro Bono Publico Award, 1993; The Justice Thurgood Marshall Award, 1994; Oliver Hill Day in Roanoke, VA, 1995; Oliver Hill Courts Building in Richmond, VA, 1996; Presidential Medal of Freedom, 1999; NAACP, Springarn Award, 2005; University of Richmond Law School, Oliver W. Hill Social Justice Award, 2007.

Began Legal Career

Hill began his law practice in 1934 and was one of the few African-American lawyers in the South. By 1940 he had won his first civil rights case, which demanded black teachers receive pay equal to that of white teachers. Many of his cases were race related, and Hill was involved in litigation involving voting rights and equal access to housing and public facilities. In 1947 Hill ran for the Virginia House of Delegates, the lone African American in a field of 18 candidates seeking seven seats. Hill fell 190 votes short. "Had he been nominated and then elected in November," the *New York Times* reported at the time, "Mr. Hill would have been the first [black] to occupy a seat in the General Assembly since the session of 1889-1890."

The following year Hill sought political office again, this time as a candidate for the Richmond City Council. Hill's quest was successful and he became the first African American to be elected in Richmond in 52 years. Hill placed ninth in a field of 29 candidates for nine vacant seats and finished ahead of some white candidates. In a *New York Times* editorial, the election was hailed as "a good omen for the South." The article continued, "That the candidate is an educated person and a young man is especially important, for from the age of thirty-one, he can look forward to long years of service to his people and to his community as a whole."

In 1950, Hill lost his bid for reelection to the Richmond City Council and returned to his private law practice. In 1951 another council member resigned to take a job outside of Richmond, and the all-white council had to decide who would replace him. Hill was mentioned as a possible replacement, but his increasingly outspoken views against segregation had sparked opposition within the council and the white community. In a move that angered Richmond's 40,000 African Americans, the council chose a former white council member to fill the vacant seat.

Influential in Landmark Case

By this time, Hill was actively assisting the National Association for the Advancement of Colored People in their lawsuits against the state of Virginia. These lawsuits demanded improved educational facilities for African-American children. Hill eventually became the leading attorney in the case of *Davis vs. County School Board of Prince Edward County* (Virginia), which was initiated on behalf of black students protesting the poor conditions at their segregated school in Farmville, Virginia. It was one of five cases that the Supreme Court combined into their 1954 decision of *Brown vs. Board of Education*. That decision, which overturned *Plessy vs. Ferguson*, was the culmination of nearly 20 years of hard work.

"Two or three of us, including Thurgood Marshall, wanted to do something about segregation from the get-go in the 1930s," Hill recalled at the *Brown* symposium. "We had to educate judges and the white and black public as to what we were trying to do.... We were careful with our cases. We never carried a case to the Supreme Court that we didn't have well documented. Anything weak, we passed aside." The *Brown* decision, which integrated public schools throughout the United States, was a landmark case that helped to set the civil rights movement in motion. In overturning *Plessy vs. Ferguson*, the Supreme Court ruled that education was an essential element of modern life and that the doctrine of "separate but equal" was unconstitutional. Hill and his colleagues then went to work implementing the Court's decision, which was a difficult task because the state of Virginia had taken steps to dismantle the public school system rather than desegregate. Hill again took to the courtroom to ensure that the state's public school system would remain intact and become integrated. Forty years later, on the occasion of Hill's acceptance of the Marshall Award, James E. Coleman, Jr. of the American Bar Association remarked, "By using the courts, rather than physical resistance, to fight desegregation, Virginia made civil rights lawyers' work much more difficult….If the state's strategy had succeeded, desegregation would have taken much longer."

Devoted Life to Vision of Equality

Following his efforts to desegregate Virginia's public schools, Hill returned to private practice and established the law firm of Hill, Tucker & Marsh in 1966. He continued to work for civil rights causes throughout his career. In 1994, 40 years after the *Brown* decision, Hill lamented the state of race relations in America in a *Human Rights* interview, "I can't understand why Americans are willing to send their children—black and white—to foreign lands to fight, and sometimes die, to preserve the American concepts of freedom, democracy, and civil rights when at the same time these same Americans are unwilling to undergo an occasional inconvenience or suffer a slight financial loss to help break down racial barriers and racial discrimination in *this* country."

He actively continued his quest for civil rights until retiring in 1998. For his lifelong commitment to civil rights, Hill received numerous honors. In 1999 President Bill Clinton recognized Hill's tremendous achievements and service to the country by awarding him the Presidential Medal of Freedom. The NAACP presented Hill with its highest honor, the Springarn Award, in 2005. On his 100th birthday, Hill was awarded the first Oliver W. Hill Social Justice Award from the University of Richmond Law School. Hill died on August 5, 2007. Virginia Governor Timothy M. Kaine honored Hill by ordering flags lowered to half-staff throughout the state and that his body would lie in state with a public memorial service to celebrate his life. A memorial featuring Hill among the students of Farmville, whom he helped during their historic case of 1951, was scheduled to be placed on the grounds of the Virginia State Capitol in Richmond in 2008. At Hill's memorial service, according to the *Richmond Times-Dispatch,* Sen. Henry L. Marsh III praised the work of his former colleague, adding "We must keep his vision alive."

Sources

Books

Govenar, Alan, *Untold Glory: African Americans in Pursuit of Freedom, Opportunity, and Achievement,* Harlem Moon/Broadway Books, 2007.

Periodicals

Fort Worth Star-Telegram, August 6, 2007, p. B6.
Human Rights, Spring 1994, p. 12; Summer 1994, p. 6.
Life, September 27, 1948, p. 47.
New Republic, April 9, 1951, p. 7.
Newsday, August 6, 2007, p. A38.
New York Times, August 7, 1947, p. 23; June 10, 1948, p. 16; June 12, 1948, p. 14; October 1, 1948, p. 22; June 15, 1950, p. 27; January 11, 1952, p. 13; August 11, 1955, p. 43.
Richmond Times-Dispatch, August 6, 2007, p. A1, A6.
Washington Post, August 7, 2007, p. A12.
Virginian Pilot, August 13, 2007, p. A1.

—Brian Escamilla and Sara Pendergast

Jennifer Hudson

1981—

Singer, actress

Hudson, Jennifer, photograph. J.H. Saunders/Landov.

Jennifer Hudson's infamous ousting from the 2004 finals of the talent-search television series *American Idol* became one of the most controversial events in the history of the show, but the Chicago native rebounded admirably two years later as the hottest new singer and film star thanks to her lead role in *Dreamgirls,* the movie version of the hit Broadway musical. Remarkably, the musical adaptation was Hudson's big-screen debut, and for it she earned near-universal accolades as well an Academy Award. "I have never worked with anyone in my entire career with as much raw talent and openness as Jennifer," the movie's writer/director, Bill Condon, enthused to *Vogue* writer Andre Leon Talley. "She came to the project with such confidence. She said, 'It may take me a while, but I'll get it.' She had never acted or danced before, and she got it."

Came from Family of Singers

Hudson was born in Chicago on September 12, 1981, the last of three children of Samuel Samson, a bus driver who died when she was in her teens, and Darnell Hudson. Her mother encouraged her daughter's childhood ambition to become a singer, which seemed natural given that she came from a long line of musical talents herself, including Hudson's maternal grandmother, Julia Kate Hudson, who was a standout in the church choir. "Jennifer has that dynamic voice, just like my mother," Darnell Hudson told *Essence* writer Cori Murray. "She always seemed to know how to put emphasis in certain places. When my mother sang, you could feel her, and Jennifer has that same quality."

Seven-year-old Hudson made her church choir debut as a soloist but was nerve-wracked enough to forget the lyrics. She developed a novel way of combating stage fright: "Till this day it shocks me when I'm at a mic and open my eyes and people are standing up," she said in an interview with *Los Angeles Magazine*'s Mary Melton. "Until I was 19, I sang with my eyes closed." Following high school, she left her home in the Chicago community of Englewood to attend college at Langston University, Oklahoma's only historically black college, but later returned and took classes at Kennedy-King College. She appeared in community

At a Glance . . .

Born Jennifer Kate Hudson on September 12, 1981, in Chicago, IL; daughter of Samuel Samson (a bus driver) and Darnell Hudson. *Education:* Attended Langston University and Kennedy-King College. *Religion:* Baptist.

Career: Actress and singer. Worked at Burger King, and on a Disney cruise ship, 2003; appeared on *American Idol,* 2004.

Awards: Academy Award for Best Performance by an Actress in a Supporting Role, Golden Globe Best Performance by an Actress in a Supporting Role in a Motion Picture, Hollywood Foreign Press Association, Screen Actors Guild Award for Best Supporting Actress, NAACP Image Award for Best Supporting Actress in a Movie, and BAFTA Award for Actress in a Supporting Role, all 2007, all for *Dreamgirls.*

Addresses: *Agent*–William Morris Agency, 151 El Camino Dr., Beverly Hills, CA 90212.

of morning talk shows and entertainment programs, and displayed some good-natured optimism. "I've learned that America loves me," she told *People* magazine. "It feels good to be stopped by people telling me, 'You should still be on the show.'" Over the next few months, she appeared on a concert tour with former *American Idol* contestants, delivering the standard cover tunes to her first real audiences. "I'd say, 'Lord, if I don't get another chance, thank you for this—at least I got to taste it,'" she recalled in *Essence.*

Hudson moved to the Los Angeles area for a few months in an attempt to establish herself, and was one of 783 female vocalists who tried out for the role of Effie White, the lead role in *Dreamgirls,* a hit Broadway musical that was in the planning stages for a film adaptation. Its story was loosely based on that of the Supremes, a 1960s trio of three Detroit women who rose to fame as protégés of local record producer Berry Gordy, owner of the Motown label. The Supremes' strongest vocalist was Florence Ballard, but she was replaced as the frontwoman by a slimmer, lighter-skinned Diana Ross, who became a major star and went on to successful dual careers as a solo recording artist and actress. Hudson was called back several times to sing again for the movie version's director, Bill Condon—whose last work was the immensely successful film adaptation of the Broadway musical *Chicago*—and finally ended the anxiety-ridden process by given them her rendition of *Dreamgirls'* showstopper "And I'm Telling You (I'm Not Going)." Hudson won the role of the character based on Ballard.

Made Screen Debut

Hudson's screen debut in *Dreamgirls* was greeted by effusive reviews for her performance even before the movie premiered in December of 2006. She starred alongside high-wattage R&B/pop diva Beyoncé Knowles as Deena Jones, the Diana Ross-type character, and Anika Noni Rose as Lorrell Robinson, the third member of the trio. *Ray* star Jamie Foxx played Curtis Taylor Jr., the manager who grooms them to stardom, with Eddie Murphy as a famous funk star who gives the Dreamettes their first real break when he puts them in his stage line-up. Fans and critics alike raved over Hudson's mid-film number, "And I'm Telling You," which serves as Effie's farewell, with *Entertainment Weekly*'s Owen Gleiberman calling it a "grandly shattering...piece of musical acting." David Denby, writing in the *New Yorker,* even mentioned Hudson's own near-career-ending moment in his review. "Hudson, the young singer who was voted off 'American Idol' for the same reasons that Effie gets tossed out of the group here, begins quietly and reaches a pitch of wailing defiance that goes on forever," he wrote of "And I'm Telling You." "As a piece of singing, this performance is intentionally over the top—exciting but almost scary in its intensity."

The cast and crew of *Dreamgirls* were nominated for eight Academy Awards, and Hudson took home one of

theater productions, worked at Burger King, and finally landed her first professional job in 2003 on a Disney cruise ship, where she performed as Calliope the Head Muse.

Voted Off American Idol

Hudson's mother encouraged her to travel to Atlanta, Georgia, where tryouts were being held for the third season of *American Idol.* She sang an *a cappella* version of "Share Your Love with Me," an Aretha Franklin song, and made the cut for the show. As the show's weekly episodes unfolded in early 2004, she and two other young African-American women she was teamed with were pegged as potential winners, though Hudson endured some characteristically caustic comments from judge Simon Cowell after her performances, some even addressed to her choice of outfit. Viewer voting results—a controversial practice on the perennially popular talent showcase—remained somewhat slim once she became one of a dozen finalists, and on April 21, 2004, Hudson was eliminated from *American Idol* as the season's seventh-place finisher.

Hudson's *Idol* fans were stunned by her ouster, and the show's Web-site chat rooms exploded with comments in her favor. Even celebrity judge Elton John made a controversial remark suggesting racial bias in the voting tallies. Following the ejection, Hudson made the rounds

the film's two Oscars, for Best Supporting Actress. She even became one of just three African-American women who were not fashion models ever to appear on the cover of the U.S. edition of *Vogue*, after Oprah Winfrey and Halle Berry. *American Idol*'s most famous failure was also celebrated as a style icon and new role model for her curvy figure, which dozens of the world's top designers were suddenly eager to dress. Hudson was delighted with the new dresses, but pointed out to journalist Lola Ogunnaike of the *New York Times*, "I'm the size of the average girl. My theory is that we're not too big, they're too small."

Selected works

Films

Dreamgirls, 2006.

Meet the Browns, 2008.
Winged Creatures, 2008.

Sources

Periodicals

Entertainment Weekly, December 22, 2006, p. 54.
Essence, March 2007, p. 129.
Los Angeles Magazine, January 2007, p. 34.
New Yorker, December 25, 2006, p. 150.
New York Times, February 25, 2007.
People, May 10, 2004, p. 22.
Vogue, March 2007, p. 542

—Carol Brennan

Samuel L. Jackson

1948—

Actor

"I never get tired of acting because I have a passion for it," Samuel L. Jackson declared to Paul B. Cohen of the *L.A. Village View*. "Every time I have an opportunity to do it, I will do it." Despite occasional encounters with the implicit racist attitude of Hollywood, he has managed to get cast "color-blind" more often than many of his black colleagues. His versatility and professionalism have been Jackson's keys to survival. As Phillip Noyce, director of *Patriot Games*, told the *New York Times*, "Sam has a remarkable connection with the cinema audience."

Jackson, Samuel L., photograph. AP/Wide World Photos.

consisted mostly of low-profile character parts until his award-winning performance in Spike Lee's *Jungle Fever* in 1991 moved him to the top of casting directors' lists. He went on to appear in increasingly varied features with two goals in mind—stretching his range and returning to stage, the arena in which he got his start.

Hooked on Acting at an Early Age

Jackson was born on December 21, 1948, and grew up in Chattanooga, Tennessee, with his mother, grandparents, and his aunt, who was a schoolteacher. His urge to perform emerged while he was still quite young. "As a kid I loved *Treasure Island*," he informed Jean Oppenheimer of the *L.A. Village View*. "My favorite pirate movie was *The Crimson Pirate* with Burt Lancaster. When I was a kid we played pirates in our neighborhood, not sissy stuff like Captain Hook but serious pirates." He also participated in rowdy neighborhood recreations of favorite westerns, substituting bicycles for the horses. When he was not pretending to be a high sea rogue, he acted in his aunt's school plays. However, he did not seriously participate in the theater world until he was in college.

Likewise, Jackson is much beloved by those who enjoy live drama. Unlike film work—which tends to offer little immediate reward for the actor—Jackson has acknowledged to Cohen that "theater is such a healthy exchange of energy between the audience and the actors." He added that he can *sense* audience members "sitting forward, sighing, or getting carried along with the momentum of what we're doing, so it's very invigorating."

Jackson spent years investing that energy in role after role, finally gaining widespread public notice in the early 1990s. His lengthy resume of film appearances

At a Glance . . .

Born December 21, 1948, in Chattanooga, TN; married LaTanya Richardson, an actress, c. 1981; children: Zoe. *Education*: Received Dramatic Arts degree from Morehouse College, Atlanta, GA, 1972.

Career: Actor, 1972–.

Awards: Cannes Film Festival, Best Supporting Actor, and New York Film Critics award, for *Jungle Fever*, 1991; BAFTA (British Academy) Film Award for Best Supporting Actor, for *Pulp Fiction*, 1995; Independent Spirit Awards, 1995, 1998; Image Award, Outstanding Supporting Actor in a Motion Picture, for *A Time to Kill*, 1997; Berlin International Film Festival, Silver Berlin Bear for Best Actor, for *Jackie Brown*, 1998; Acapulco Black Film Festival, Black Film Award, 1998; Acapulco Black Film Festival, Career Achievement Award, 1999; Hasty Pudding Theatricals, Man of the Year, 1999; star on the Hollywood Walk of Fame, 2000; Image Award, Outstanding Actor in a Motion Picture, for *Coach Carter*, 2006.

Addresses: *Agent*—c/o International Creative Management, 8942 Wilshire Blvd., Beverly Hills, CA 90211; c/o Addis-Weschler & Associates, 5 South Carillo, #300, Los Angeles, CA 90048.

Jackson attended Morehouse College in Atlanta, Georgia, but in order to major in theater he had to take all his theater classes at the college's sister school, Spelman. There he met LaTanya Richardson, an actress whom he would later marry; there too, he made his adult performance debut in the darkly satirical Weill-Brecht classic, *The Three Penny Opera*, making up for his lack of singing acumen with his acting skills. Meanwhile, offstage he was becoming radicalized by the burgeoning black liberation movement of the early 1970s. Student anger at the lack of African American studies and the institution's control by a white governing body caused him to participate in an action that involved locking a few Morehouse trustees—including Rev. Martin Luther King, Sr.—in a room until the insurgents' demands were met. For their involvement, Jackson and some of his comrades were briefly suspended.

Focusing on what would soon become his career, Jackson helped start the Just Us theater company in Atlanta, but he and Richardson ultimately left for New York City in 1976. "All I know is, we pulled into [Greenwich] Village at night, and everyone on the street looked really bizarre," Jackson told Michael Angeli of the *New York Times*. "We were going to live with some friends on Barrow Street. What we didn't realize was that it was Halloween, and we were in the middle of a parade." Though he did not begin his own parade of acting roles until some years later, he did start working in the theater almost immediately.

Theater Work Led to Films

For the next several years, Jackson appeared in various plays. Film work was sometimes offered, as when he appeared in 1981's *Ragtime*, but it was when he was appearing onstage in *A Soldier's Play* the same year that he began making real connections. He befriended actor Morgan Freeman, who greatly encouraged him, and met a young film student named Spike Lee, who came backstage to introduce himself. Jackson recollected to the *New York Times*. "He told me he was a Morehouse alumnus, that he was at NYU [New York University] film school, da-da-da. He was going to, um, be a filmmaker. He said when he started to make films, he would love for me to be in his movies. It was, like, I had my dream, and he had his—a surplus of reality there, you know what I mean?"

Lee's dream came true, and Jackson appeared in several of the writer/director's films, including *School Daze* in 1988, and the following year's *Do the Right Thing*. Jackson observed that Lee's tendency to use the same actors in different films lent an *esprit de corps* to the productions. "Bill Nunn, Giancarlo [Esposito]—we knew each other from Morehouse, where we did plays together. There's something to be said for the ensemble feeling, for getting to know other actors and having a feeling for working with them," Jackson explained to Angeli. "And doing Spike's films, that was the one thing we all had to look forward to *every* year—knowing we were going to get together again. Same crew, same actors," he continued. Jackson also landed character roles in features by other directors; in the late 1980s to early 1990s, Jackson worked in *The Exorcist III, Coming to America, Sea of Love* and Martin Scorsese's *Goodfellas*. But Lee was the creative force behind the film that made Jackson's reputation, *Jungle Fever*.

In that 1991 production, Jackson played Gator, the crack-addicted brother of Flipper Purify, played by Wesley Snipes. This character hit home because Jackson himself was a recovering crack addict. He brought an explosive charisma and unpredictability to the portrayal; Peter Travers of *Rolling Stone* called him "a blistering actor in an unforgettable role." When the film debuted at the Cannes film festival, the judges named Jackson the best supporting actor. The award was a double honor because the Cannes judging had never before extended to that category. Besides winning at Cannes, Jackson also received a New York Film Critics award.

A few months after *Jungle Fever*'s release, Jackson was surprised to find that his increased visibility and all the acclaim made some filmmakers think he was unavailable except at high salaries. He emphasized to Williams that he was "not out of anyone's range yet." Nonetheless, he proceeded to take small roles in such offbeat films as *Juice* and *True Romance*, among others. When Jackson was sent the script for the thriller *White Sands*, he assumed he was being considered for the part of the villain—a role eventually bagged by Mickey Rourke.

"Then they call me back and say no, you're Meeker, the FBI agent. What? I had to go back and read it again," Jackson admitted to *Premiere*'s Veronica Chambers. "And I like the guy [Meeker] a lot. He's not obviously bad or obviously good. It was a stretch from Gator to that character. And I really would like to display the fact that I have that range." The film's director, Roger Donaldson, praised Jackson to Chambers, saying "He's got enormous resources as an actor. He's extremely talented technically. Sam can do something one take, then go back and build on it. He's spontaneous, but he's well trained.... And he's a nice guy."

Expanded His Range

Hollywood did not need to be persuaded about Jackson's willingness to take on different genres. He shared above-the-title billing in two broad comedies, *Amos & Andrew* and *National Lampoon's Loaded Weapon I*. Unfortunately, critics trashed both 1993 films. *Entertainment Weekly*'s review of *Amos & Andrew,* for example, consisted largely of career advice for the actor. Their reviewer wondered, "did Samuel L. Jackson really have to follow up his mesmerizing, out-on-the-edge performance as a homeless crack addict [in *Jungle Fever*] with *National Lampoon's Loaded Weapon I* and the imbecilic mistaken-identity farce *Amos & Andrew*?" The unequivocal pan concluded by urging the actor to "call your agent—and fire him."

Despite such misfires, Jackson continued working regularly in the 1990s, appearing as a technician in the box-office hit *Jurassic Park*—one of the top-selling movies of all time—as one of Harrison Ford's allies in *Patriot Games*, and in an ensemble role in *Menace II Society*. *Patriot Games* director Noyce told the *New York Times* that Jackson, despite having his performance severely edited, "made so much out of so little that the audience imagined he had a greater participation than he actually did."

In 1994, Jackson was cast as a killer in writer-director Quentin Tarantino's *Pulp Fiction*, an ultraviolent thriller boasting what Jackson described to Cohen as "one of the best scripts I've read in a couple of years." The plumb role contained "four to five page [long] speeches...and that's something you don't normally do in a film," though he had done so on stage. Jackson had earlier appeared in such prestigious New York productions as August Wilson's two acclaimed pieces, *The Piano Lesson* and *Two Trains Running*. His appreciation for the dialogues Wilson had written was obvious. Speaking to Cohen, Jackson reflected, "August writes three-hour plays, and when I was doing *Piano Lesson*—I was the original [protagonist] Boy Willie before [actor] Charles Dutton did it—that character talks for about two hours and ten minutes in a three-hour play...."

Despite the plethora of motion picture work he obtained in the 1990s, Jackson pined to appear onstage again. Once he did, he was pleasantly surprised to find a new environment in regards to many playwrights. In a *New York Times* interview, Jackson observed that "the black acting community is relatively small. Especially in New York theater. The funny thing is that when they used to cast black roles, everybody from age 20 to 50 was called because they had no idea what kind of black person they wanted for the role. That kind of let you know that they sort of didn't have a clue as to who these people are."

Though Jackson assumed he would have to maintain himself in New York City for theatrical roles, he was pleasantly surprised at the opportunity to be in the 1993 working-class play *Distant Fires* in Los Angeles. "Everybody's very concerned about the production as a whole and not about their own performances," he enthused to Cohen. He similarly told *Premiere*'s Chambers "I always want to get back to theater to make sure that I'm still an actor. You have to convince people who are actually sitting there looking at you that you're doing what you're doing, without all the trappings of reality around you."

Action Movies and Beyond

Despite his love for the stage, Jackson has spent his career since the 1990s appearing in films...dozens and dozens of films. Jackson's ability to take on all kinds of roles with equal credibility, from hero to villain, from star to supporting actor, made it easy for him to find work. The majority of that work has been in action-packed drama. He teamed up with fellow *Pulp Fiction* star Bruce Willis in *Die Hard: With a Vengeance* (1995), played Carl Lee Hailey, the father who murdered two white rednecks who brutally raped his daughter in *A Time To Kill* (1996), and he teamed up again with Quentin Tarantino in *Jackie Brown* (1997), an adaptation of author Elmore Leonard's book, *Rum Punch*.

Jackson's run of action dramas continued well into the 2000s. In 2002, Jackson added to his action movie resume when he took the role of Mace Windu in *Star Wars: Episode II—Attack of the Clones,* and reprised the role *Episode III—Revenge of the Sith* (2005). Other notable films of the 2000s included *XXX* (2002) and its sequel *XXX: State of the Union* (2005), and *S.W.A.T.* (2003.), an update of the 1970s television series of the same name which quickly became a box-office hit. Perhaps the most notorious of his recent pics was *Snakes on a Plane* (2006), a movie about poisonous snakes loose on a plane which Jackson reportedly committed to solely on the outrageous nature of movie title. When movie producers threatened to change the name to the innocuous *Pacific Air 121*, Jackson joined outraged internet fans lobbying to keep the movie's title—and its gratuitous violence. The movie was a huge hit.

Jackson's range has always extended beyond action movies, however. In 1997, he starred and co-produced *Eve's Bayou*. The independent film won raves from critics and encouraged Jackson to take on other production roles, as he did with *The 51st State* (2001) and *Cleaner* (2007). Jackson also played a prominent role in *The Red Violin*, a serious Canadian film that explored the 300-year history of a finely crafted instrument and the impact it had on the lives of those who owned it. In a very different vein, Jackson gave voice to Lucius Best, a man who becomes the superhero Frozone in the Disney animated feature *The Incredibles* (2004). Jackson took on the title role in *Coach Carter* (2005), the inspirational story of a high school basketball coach who insists that his players develop academic abilities to match their basketball prowess. In 2007, Jackson appeared in another sports-related, based-in-fact story, *Resurrecting the Champ,* when he played a homeless man who is rescued by a reporter (played by Josh Hartnett)—and turns out to be a former boxing champion who was thought to have died.

Entering his seventh decade, Jackson must be acknowledged as one of the most popular actors of the late twentieth century. In 2005, he had appeared in films whose gross receipts topped $30 billion, making him the highest grossing actor of all times, topping Harrison Ford. In 2000, he became 191st actor, and the seventh African American, to be given a star on the Hollywood Walk of Fame. For Jackson, however, the big thrill still remains the work of acting. He told a *Time* reporter that he goes to see every one of his films in a regular theater, sitting as an anonymous member of the audience. He noted, "Even during my theater years, I wished I could watch the plays I was in—while I was in them. I dig watching myself work." He also collects action figures of the characters he has portrayed in films.

Selected works

Films

Together for Days, 1972.
Ragtime, 1981.
Raw, 1987.
School Daze, 1988.
Sea of Love, 1989.
Do the Right Thing, 1989.
Mo' Better Blues, 1990.

Def by Temptation, 1990.
Goodfellas, 1991.
Jungle Fever, 1991.
Jumpin' at the Boneyard, 1992.
White Sands, 1992.
Patriot Games, 1992.
True Romance, 1993.
Menace II Society, 1993.
National Lampoon's Loaded Weapon I, 1993.
Amos & Andrew, 1993.
Jurassic Park, 1993.
Against the Wall, 1994.
Assault at West Point: The Court Martial of Johnson Whittaker, 1994.
Fresh, 1994.
Pulp Fiction, 1994.
Kiss of Death, 1995.
Die Hard: With A Vengeance, 1995.
Losing Isaiah, 1995.
A Time To Kill, 1996.
The Long Kiss Goodnight, 1997.
(And producer) *Eve's Bayou,* 1997.
187, 1997.
Jackie Brown, 1997.
Sphere, 1998.
The Negotiator, 1998.
The Red Violin, 1998.
Star Wars: Episode I - The Phantom Menace, 1999.
Deep Blue Sea, 1999.
Shaft, 2000.
Rules of Engagement, 2000.
Any Given Wednesday, 2000.
Unbreakable, 2000.
Changing Lanes, 2001.
The 51st State, 2001.
The Caveman's Valentine, 2001.
XXX, 2002.
Star Wars: Episode II - Attack of the Clones, 2002.
S.W.A.T., 2003.
The Incredibles, 2004.
Twisted, 2004.
In My Country, 2004.
Coach Carter, 2005.
XXX: State of the Union, 2005.
Star Wars: Episode III - Revenge of the Sith, 2005.
The Man, 2005.
Freedomland, 2006.
Snakes on a Plane, 2006.
Home of the Brave, 2006.
Black Snake Moan, 2006.
Resurrecting the Champ, 2007.
1408, 2007.
Cleaner, 2007.
Lakeview Terrace, forthcoming.
Jumper, forthcoming.
Iron Man, forthcoming.
The Spirit, forthcoming.

Plays

Mobile Theatre: The Mighty Gents, 1979.

Mother Courage and Her Children, 1980.
Home, 1981.
A Soldier's Play, 1981-83.
Ohio Tip-Off, 1983.
Native Speech, 1984.
The District Line, 1984-85.
Fences, 1985.
The Piano Lesson, 1987.
We: Part I-Sally/Part II-Prince, 1988.
Two Trains Running, 1989.
Burners Frolic, 1990.
Jonquil, 1990.
Distant Fires, 1993.

Television

The Displaced Person, 1977.
The Trial of the Moke, 1978.
Uncle Tom's Cabin, 1987.
Dead Man Out, 1989.
Also appeared as guest star and as himself in numerous television episodes.

Sources

Books

Dils, Tracey E., *Samuel L. Jackson,* Chelsea House, 2000.

Hudson, Jeff, *Samuel L. Jackson: The Unauthorised Biography,* Virgin Publishing, 2004.

Pendergast, Sara, and Tom Pendergast, eds., *International Dictionary of Films and Filmmakers,* Volume 3: *Actors and Actresses,* 4th ed., St. James Press, 2000.

Periodicals

Ebony, March 2006.

Entertainment Weekly, March 5, 1993, p. 42; February 18, 1994, pp. 102-3; November 25, 1994; March 5, 2004, p. 48; May 13, 2005, p. 64; September 23, 2005, p. 67.

Essence, April 1992, p. 48; May 1, 2002.

Interview, April 1992, p. 50.

Jet, March 9, 1998, p. 36; August 18, 2003, p. 60; January 17, 2005, p. 54; October 24, 2005, p. 48.

L.A. Village View, February 12, 1993, 11; December 3, 1993.

Los Angeles Times Magazine, June 11, 2000, pp. 12-15, 33-36.

New York Times, June 9, 1991; February 7, 1993; November 2, 1997.

People, January 24, 2005, p. 31; March 28, 2005, p. 30; September 19, 2005, p. 37.

Premiere, May 1992, p. 57; June 2002, pp. 70-71.

Rolling Stone, June 27, 1991, 75-76.

Sight and Sound, vol. 6, no. 12, 1996, pp. 7-8; November 2005, p. 68.

Time, August 14, 2006.

On-line

Samuel L. Jackson, www.samuelljackson.com (August 31, 2007).

—Simon Glickman, Ashyia N. Henderson, and Tom Pendergast

Je'Caryous Johnson

1977—

Stage producer, playwright

Chairman and chief executive officer of I'm Ready Productions, Je'Caryous Johnson has emerged as a major force in the world of popular African-American theater from his base in Houston, Texas. Producing, directing, and writing stage productions that toured all over the United States, Johnson and business partner Gary Guidry were on track to earn a projected $15 million in revenue from three shows mounted during the year 2007. But Johnson had his eye on even bigger things, with movie, television, and Broadway musical projects in the works. His ultimate goal was nothing less than a shift in the nature of African-American entertainment toward the positive themes his shows promoted. "I'm going to create a movement so great that it can shift the consciousness of a people," he told Eric Harrison of the *Houston Chronicle*. And no one who knew Johnson well was likely to underestimate him. "He just does not know the word 'impossible,'" his college instructor Sidney Berger recalled to Harrison.

Je'Caryous Johnson was born May 26, 1977, in Houston, Texas. Johnson's mother was single and 15 years old at the time, but his father remained involved in his life as a source of help he could count on if needed. Johnson grew up in northwest Houston's Studewood neighborhood. "I can say that we were poor, but as a kid you kind of don't know it," he told Troy Schulze of the *Houston Press*. "You make do with what you have. I couldn't have a moped, but I'd certainly take a bike and put a can on the back of it, so it sounded like a moped."

Johnson's imagination revealed itself in his gift for performing, displayed while he was still in elementary school at Houston's James D. Burrus Magnet School

for Fine Arts. He returned to the stage in high school, and his choice of theater as a career was cemented in 1996 when his play *Harlem Renaissance* won a nationwide contest in playwriting that was part of the National History Day Contest held at the Kennedy Center in Washington. The following year, Johnson performed for President Bill Clinton at the White House. After taking classes at Prairie View A&M University, Johnson enrolled at the University of Houston, where he majored in theater and fine arts.

At Houston, Johnson received a state-of-the-art education as nationally known playwrights and actors came to the prestigious program to teach classes. He was a star student who had the lead role in the William Hanley play *Slow Dance on the Killing Ground* while he was still an undergraduate. Outside of school he also encountered a different kind of stage production that, he told Schulze, "didn't really even have a plot. It just went off on these things, and at the end of the day everybody kind of found God and that was the end of it."

What Johnson had discovered was the African-American gospel musical, a homegrown inspirational form that evolved from the comic stage shows of the so-called chitlin' circuit. As he observed the direct emotional appeal and the uninhibited audience of the gospel musical, Johnson realized he was seeing something new, completely different from the classical dramas and experimental plays he was involved with at the university. The experience, he told Schulze, sparked "an internal battle...between my education and what I was viewing. They seemed to be in direct conflict with each other."

At a Glance . . .

Born on May 26, 1977, in Houston, TX. *Education:* Attended Prairie View A&M University; University of Houston, fine arts and theater, BA.

Career: Actor and playwright, 1990s; I'm Ready Productions, co-founder, 1998.

Awards: National History Day playwriting competition, Kennedy Center, Washington, DC, First place medal, 1996, for *Harlem Renaissance*; NAACP, Trailblazer award, 2006.

Addresses: *Office*—I'm Ready Productions, Inc., P.O. Box 10254, Houston, TX 77206. *Web*—www.imready. com.

Armed with positive reviews of his student work, Johnson headed for Hollywood—and bombed. "I thought I was the king of acting," he told Harrison. "You couldn't tell me anything. I may have been the king in Houston, but the only crown I had in Los Angeles was the Crown Royal bottle I had with me on the balcony as I tried to figure out why I couldn't get roles." After eight months he returned home and started a new theatrical company, I'm Ready Productions, with a slightly older uncle, Gary Guidry. The pair had high hopes for a musical Johnson had written at the University of Houston, *Heaven's Child: The Legacy of Emmett Till.* The full-length production traced the life of Emmett Till, the African-American teenager whose murder in Leflore County, Mississippi, galvanized the civil rights movement.

Johnson and Guidry maxed out their own credit cards to finance the show and then started in on relatives. Johnson's family believed in his dream, and a wide net of friends and acquaintances invested in the project. Johnson borrowed about $500,000 in total—and in 2000 *Heaven's Child* closed after just a week and a half on the road and a gross of $60,000. "We failed miserably," Johnson admitted to Margena A. Christian of *Jet.* "We made every conceivable mistake."

Encouraged by family support and by some positive reviews of the show, Johnson avoided the temptation to give up. He and Guidry bounced back in 2002 when Johnson met African-American romance novelist Michael Baisden and discussed the idea of turning Baisden's novel *Men Cry in the Dark* into a stage play. No one had ever attempted a similar project in an African-American theatrical world, and the gospel musicals of *Diary of a Mad Black Woman* creator Tyler Perry were demonstrating that a huge audience existed for live theater in African-American communities.

After veteran actor Richard Roundtree of *Shaft* fame signed on for the production, Johnson and Guidry were on their way. They built on their success with *Men Cry in the Dark* by adapting another Baisden novel, *The Maintenance Man,* in 2003, and continued with adaptations of Eric Jerome Dickey's *Friends and Lovers* and *Cheaters* in 2004 and 2005, respectively. By 2006, when they mounted *Casino aka Confessions,* they were approaching a total gross of $100 million. Performers such as Billy Dee Williams, Kelly Price, Brian McKnight, and Gerald Levert had appeared in their productions, which borrowed the direct emotional appeal and the audience involvement of earlier urban theater but aimed toward more realistic characters and detailed plots. "Don't forsake art for entertainment, and don't forsake entertainment for art, but create a perfect merger and a blend between the two," Johnson explained to Schulze in outlining his attitude toward theater in general.

Johnson became one of the African-American entertainment world's most eligible bachelors, and in 2006 he was the subject of an *Essence* magazine interview in which he discussed his experiences with "gold diggers"—women who were only after his growing fortune. By 2007 (at which time he was still single) the growth of his career was gaining wide notice. A top-rank screen actress, Vivica A. Fox, worked with Johnson to develop a vehicle called *Whatever She Wants* in which she starred (as a woman named Vivian Wolf) and alternated between stepping into her character and directly addressing the audience. Fox and Johnson discussed turning *Whatever She Wants* into a film, and Johnson was branching out into fiction as well; he adapted his play *Men, Money & Gold Diggers,* which also featured Fox, into a novel and planned to make it into a film as well. Television productions and a Broadway musical based on the film *The Five Heartbeats* were in the works as well. "Everything is kind of pouring in at the same time from every direction, from Hollywood to New York," Johnson told Harrison.

Yet Johnson was aiming at something more than simple stardom. Though mostly divorced from their roots in the gospel musical, Johnson's productions never lost their positive, moral tone, and he hoped to exert a beneficial influence on young people. "I'm done with romantic plays," he explained to Christian. "Next we need to do something to reel in the kids. Parents don't understand their kids." Whatever future plans Johnson came up with, they would surely be approached fearlessly. "I believe we're at the point where things are about to change for black, white, and indifferent, and we're on the edge," he told Schulze. "Can't wait to jump off the cliff."

Selected works

Plays

Heaven's Child: The Legacy of Emmett Till, 2000.
Men Cry in the Dark, 2002.
The Maintenance Man, 2003.

Friends and Lovers, 2004.
Cheaters, 2005.
Casino aka Confessions, 2006.
Whatever She Wants, 2006.
Men, Money & Gold Diggers, 2007 (also adapted into novel).

Sources

Periodicals

Black Enterprise, August 2005, p. 48.
Essence, June 2006.
Grand Rapids Press (Grand Rapids, MI), April 28, 2005, p. 20; May 6, 2007, p. C10.
Houston Chronicle, May 6, 2007, p. 12.
Houston Press, June 14, 2007.
Jet, May 29, 2006, p. 60.

On-line

"About IRP," *I'm Ready Productions,* www.imready.com (July 15, 2007).

—James M. Manheim

Denise Kaigler

1962—

Executive

Denise Kaigler is the embodiment of the American Dream. Reared in a single-parent home and plagued by poverty through college, Kaigler worked hard to succeed. She had no choice. With no one to fall back on financially, Kaigler had to rely on herself. She put herself through college by working two jobs. From there, through hard work, determination, and integrity, she moved up to become one of the most powerful people—black or white, male or female—in the billion-dollar sportswear industry. Though much press has been given to the fact that Kaigler is an African-American woman in a boardroom composed mainly of white men, she has admitted to very few incidents where she felt discriminated against due to her sex or skin color. She told the *Black Sports Network*, "If my race or my gender puts me in a position to standout, if those things called for me to run faster, talk louder and work harder, then it's never been a burden."

Learned to Overcome Adversity

Born Denise Moore in Huntington, West Virginia, on June 26, 1962, Kaigler was raised with her two sisters in a poverty-stricken neighborhood of Washington, D.C., by her single mother, Diane Moore. Although Diane Moore struggled financially, she offered her children steadfast emotional and mental support. Moore also served as a good role model for her children; she managed to earn a 1978 fellowship to MIT and eventually landed a job with NASA. Kaigler drew inspiration from her mother's determination in the face of hardship. After graduating from Laurel High

School in Laurel, Maryland, Kaigler headed to Boston with a dream of graduating from Emerson College, a prestigious communication arts school.

After being admitted to Emerson, Kaigler made some financial missteps, including choosing to live in on-campus housing. "That was foolish of me because it was too expensive, but I wanted to feel the experience of being around my peers and classmates," Kaigler told the *Los Angeles Sentinel*. Although she had worked part-time in the Dean's office and at Filene's department store, she was unable to pay an outstanding university bill and faced expulsion. She appealed fruit-lessly to the mercy of the administrators. "Even though my grades were good, they said 'no way,'" she recalled to the *Black Sports Network*. To pay the bill, she took on additional work. She earned enough to pay the bill by working three part-time jobs and went on to graduate with her class in 1985. She has often cited that incident in reflecting upon her success. "The experience was the most difficult in my life, but it made me strong, resilient, self-reliant, confident and a true believer that if you work hard and truly believe, you can achieve anything," she told the *Network Journal*.

After a brief stint as a press aide to a Boston city councilman right out of college, Kaigler hit the road with $100 dollars in her pocket and the companion-ship of her cat Shadow. She landed in Columbus, Georgia, where she became an on-air reporter with the NBC affiliate WLTZ-TV. She soon returned to Boston and another on-air reporting job for WHDH-TV, also an NBC affiliate. "I had a lot of dreams then about reporting from the White House and chasing the big

At a Glance . . .

Born Denise Moore on June 26, 1962, in Huntington, WV; married Joseph Kaigler; children: Joseph Jr. and Danielle. *Education:* Emerson College, BA, journalism, 1985.

Career: Boston City Council, press aide, Boston, MA, 1985; WLTZ-TV, television reporter, Columbus, GA, mid-1980s; WHDH-TV, television reporter, Boston, MA, mid-1980s; Boys & Girls Clubs of Boston, director of communications, Boston, MA, 1989-91; Reebok International Ltd., 1991–: media relations specialist, 1991; senior media relations specialist, 1992-94; corporate communications manager, 1994-97; director of global public relations, 1997-98; senior director of corporate communications,1998-2000; vice president of global communications and talent relations, 2000-04; senior vice president and chief communications officer, 2004-07; Reebok International, head of global corporate communications and corporate citizenship, 2007–; Adidas (Reebok parent company), head of U.S. corporate communications, 2007–.

Memberships: Public Relations Society of America, member; Boston Association of Black Communicators, member; Arthur W. Page Society, member; Boston Chamber of Commerce, board of directors; Sportsmen's Tennis Club of Boston, former board member.

Awards: *The Network Journal*, one of the "25 Most Influential Black Women in Business," 2004; *Women's Business Boston,* one of the "Woman to Watch," 2005; Magic 106.7 (Boston radio station), Exceptional Women in Business Award, 2005; Boston YWCA, named to the Academy of Women Achievers, 2005; Dimock Community Health Center, Mary Eliza Mahoney Award, 2005; Emerson College, Alumni Achievement Award, 2005; *Profiles in Diversity Journal,* one of the "Women Worth Watching," 2006; Western New England College, Honorary Doctor of Humane Letters, 2006.

Addresses: *Office*—Reebok International, 1895 J. W. Foster Blvd., Canton, MA 02021.

I didn't want my life to just be about my career." She left reporting in 1989 and took a job as communications director for the Boys & Girls Club of Boston. Meanwhile, she married lawyer Joseph Kaigler and went on to have two children, Joseph Jr. and Danielle.

Achieved Big Success in Corporate America

In 1991, at a fundraising event for the Boys & Girls Club, Kaigler approached the director of human resources for Reebok with the goal of seeking funding for the club. A few weeks later, she was shocked when the director contacted her about a job opening at Reebok. Within the year, Kaigler was working as a media relations specialist at the company's headquarters in Canton, Massachusetts. The move seemed fated as Kaigler quickly blossomed in her new corporate capacity. Within six months she was promoted to a senior position in media relations. Two years later, she was moved into the corporate department and promoted to communications manager, a position she held for three years. In 1997, she was promoted to director of global public relations, a high-profile role which kept her traveling all over the world as she oversaw Reebok's media relations activities in Europe, Asia, Latin America, Africa, and the Middle East. By the late 1990s, Kaigler had become senior director of corporate communications.

Though Kaigler's rise in the company was noteworthy, it was not until her next promotion that her career became newsworthy. In 2001, Kaigler was appointed vice president of global communications and talent relations. Her promotion to this newly created position made her the highest-ranking African American in Reebok. In this role, she oversaw both internal and external communications, was responsible for worldwide corporate and brand public and media relations, and served as the main corporate spokesperson. Kaigler excelled especially in talent relations, working with celebrity endorsers, such as Allen Iverson, 50 Cent, and Venus Williams, and creating and overseeing their product launch events. Though her role in talent relations took her all over the world including to Paris on the private jet of Jay-Z, to the Athens Olympics, and to dozens of glamorous parties, Kaigler kept her head. "I've not once considered myself a celebrity," she told the *Black Sports Network*. "I look at my job like anyone else looks at their job."

In 2004 Kaigler was promoted to senior vice president and chief communications officer of Reebok. The position, created expressly for her by Reebok CEO Paul Fireman, was in response to the need for a communication strategist at the upper management level. In a widely quoted press release on the promotion, Fireman called Kaigler, "a strong and effective leader, talented visionary and strategic partner." The position put Kaigler on the company's nine-member President's Council, making her one of the most powerful people in the company. When Adidas bought Reebok in 2005, Kaigler moved up again, becoming

story," she told the *Black Sports Network*. "But I then realized that the lifestyle that accompanies being a reporter is not conducive to having a stable family, and

head of global corporate communications and corporate citizenship for Reebok worldwide and corporate communications director for Adidas in the United States. As head of corporate citizenship, Kaigler oversees The Reebok Foundation, a role which has allowed her to give back to her roots. For years Kaigler has expressed a desire to help inner-city youth overcome the obstacles she once faced. Considering the incredible success she has achieved soaring over those hurdles, Kaigler is more than qualified to show kids, who like herself were given very little to start with, that it is still possible to reach the top.

Sources

Periodicals

Ebony, March 2005, p. 8; March 2007, p. 16.

Los Angeles Sentinel, November 10, 2004.
PR Week, November 1, 2004, p. 7.

On-line

"Denise Kaigler," *Network Journal,* www.tnj.com/ archives/2004/march_april2004/25women.php? id=112 (August 7, 2007).

"Denise Kaigler: Happiness & Success," *Black Sports Network,* www.blacksportsnetwork.com/articles/ features/kaigler_102506.asp (August 7, 2007).

"She's Denise Kaigler, Reebok's Sr. VP and Chief Communications Officer," *Sister 2 Sister,* www. s2smagazine.com/content/content.asp?issueid= 200503&listid=05 (August 7, 2007).

—Candace LaBalle

Rachel Boone Keith

1924-2007

Physician, activist

"Some people referred to my mother as the tiny dynamo because physically, she was very small, just over 4 feet 11 inches tall. But she had tremendous strength," Cecile Keith Brown told Cecil Angel and Cassandra Spratling of the *Detroit Free Press,* referring to her mother, Detroit physician Dr. Rachel Boone Keith. A pioneering African-American physician, Keith was an institution in the Detroit community. "Can you imagine what kind of spirit was needed?" Michigan governor Jennifer Granholm said of Keith's decision to earn a medical degree in the late 1940s, when few African Americans, and fewer women still, dreamed of entering the field. "Back in the day, that just wasn't done. This is a woman of steel."

Keith was born Rachel Hannah Celestine Boone in Monrovia, Liberia, on May 30, 1924. Her parents, Clinton C. Boone and Rachel Tharps Boone, were both Baptist ministers and had gone to Africa as missionaries and health-care workers; her father had already undertaken a missionary expedition to the Congo and had lost his first wife there when she became the victim of a venomous animal bite. When Rachel was three, the family returned to the United States and settled in Richmond, Virginia, where Keith attended the segregated Paul Lawrence Dunbar Elementary School and Armstrong High School. She graduated from high school at age 13, as class valedictorian, but her graduation year was shadowed by her mother's death from tuberculosis. Watching that wasting disease take its toll, Keith decided that she was going to become a doctor.

She had a role model: her aunt Bessie Tharps, in whose Rhode Island home Keith lived after her mother's death, had gotten a medical degree at Boston University in 1916 and also studied higher mathematics. Keith attended Houghton College in New York state, graduating second in her class in 1943, and then moved on to Boston University's medical school herself. She finished her degree in 1949 and was profiled in a *Boston Globe* article after receiving the highest score in history on one of the school's standard tests. She worked as a caregiver in the university's home medical service and was also featured in a *Look* magazine article about the program.

Keith interned at Harlem Hospital in New York City and worked at Coney Island Hospital in Brooklyn after earning her degree. She moved to Detroit in 1951 and joined the staff of Detroit Receiving Hospital (then Detroit General Hospital) as a resident in internal medicine, becoming only the second African-American woman to hold that position. Around this time she met Damon Keith, a lawyer and future judge. The friend who introduced them wondered whether the lawyer would be intimidated by the young doctor's high-flying career, but the two got along immediately.

"Her life was a by-product of how she was raised," Damon Keith recalled to *Detroit Free Press* columnist Desiree Cooper. "She was very religious. She was very strong, but not pushy or demanding. She saw her life as one of service." The two were married in 1953, lived in the same house for 43 years, and raised three daughters, Cecile, Debbie, and Gilda. Damon Keith became a major player in Michigan legal and political circles, and

At a Glance . . .

Born Rachel Hannah Celestine Boone on May 30, 1924, in Monrovia, Liberia; parents were Baptist medical missionaries; returned to U.S. at age 3; raised in Richmond, VA; married Damon J. Keith, a lawyer and later judge, 1953; children: Debbie, Gilda, Cecile; died January 4, 2007, in Detroit, MI. *Education:* Paul Lawrence Dunbar High School, Richmond, VA, valedictorian; Houghton College, BS, 1943; Boston University Medical School, MD, 1949. *Religion:* Missionary Baptist.

Career: Harlem Hospital, New York, NY, intern; Coney Island Hospital, Brooklyn, NY, staff physician,1949-51; Detroit General Hospital (now Detroit Receiving Hospital), internal medicine resident, 1951-53; private practice, Detroit, MI 1954-2005.

Selected memberships: NAACP; The Links; American Leprosy Mission; Detroit Science Center; and the Detroit Symphony Orchestra.

in among the demands of her practice and of raising a family, Rachel remained supportive of his career. Detroit physician Lorna Thomas recalled to Bailey that "Rachel was very, very quiet. Damon was always in the forefront. But if you could just get her off to the side, it was a delightful conversation."

Keith was part of the staff at several Detroit hospitals before opening her own private practice in the city's Conant Gardens neighborhood. Her generosity toward patients without resources was known throughout the city, and she was legendary for being a caring physician. "She gave each of her patients so much care and love that sometimes it got her in trouble," Brown told Angel and Spratling. "People knew if they were coming to see Dr. Keith, they were going to have to wait because she gave each one time and attention." Motivated by faith, she was reluctant to proclaim it. "She didn't carry her religion on her shoulders," Damon Keith told Cooper. "She acted everyday as a woman of faith."

Both Keiths were leaders in the large Detroit branch of the National Association for the Advancement of Colored People (NAACP), and Rachel Boone Keith in later life was active in many other organizations, serving on the boards of more than 20 medical bodies and 18 nonprofit organizations. The latter group included the Detroit Symphony Orchestra; Keith as a young person had been an enthusiastic classical pianist and singer.

Keith also became interested in reconnecting with her African origins, especially after she and her husband attended the World Peace Through Law conference held in Abidjan, Ivory Coast, in 1973. The two took the opportunity to travel to the area in Liberia where Keith was born, visiting a church her father had constructed there and meeting an old woman who remembered her as a baby. Keith actually considered returning to Liberia as a missionary herself. Her father wrote two books about his experiences in Africa, *Congo as I Saw It* and *Liberia as I Knew It,* rare documents that Keith worked to prepare for republication in modern editions. She finished only a month before her death. Keith was also a member of the African American Association of Liberia, the American Leprosy Mission, and the African Development Fund.

Old age hardly slowed Keith's activities. She retired from active practice only in 2005, and her daughter Gilda told Cooper that "[i]nto her 70s, she was still coming home at 10 p.m. and working six days a week." Despite her heavy schedule she was committed to her family life, and even as her daughters entered middle age she gathered them together for Sunday dinner and related the contents of the sermon she had heard that morning at Tabernacle Missionary Baptist Church, basing her remarks on notes she had taken. After her death on January 4, 2007, her funeral was attended by luminaries including Governor Granholm, Detroit Mayor Kwame Kilpatrick, and U.S. Representatives John Conyers and Carolyn Cheeks Kilpatrick. "Her pet peeve was pretentiousness," Gilda Keith recalled to Bailey.

Sources

Periodicals

Detroit Free Press, January 5, 2007, January 9, 2007, January 10, 2007.
Detroit News, January 5, 2007, p. B1.

On-line

"Rachel Keith," *History Makers,* www.thehistorymakers.org/biography/biography.asp?bioindex=973 (August 8, 2007).

—James M. Manheim

Gwendolyn Knight

1913-2005

Painter, sculptor

Though Gwendolyn Knight showed an artistic temperament from early childhood, her career as a professional artist blossomed relatively late in life. After dropping out of art school during the Great Depression, she met and married artist Jacob Lawrence, who became one of the leading figures of the Harlem Renaissance. She moved with him as he accepted teaching posts in North Carolina, Massachusetts, and Maine, and though she continued to work on her own art, Knight let her husband's career come first. "It wasn't necessary for me to have acclaim," she remarked in a *Callaloo* magazine interview with Charles H. Rowell quoted in the *New York Times*. "I just knew that I wanted to do it, so I did it whenever I could."

Knight did not begin publicly exhibiting her work until the 1970s. She became known for her fluid line and bold use of color. The pleasure that Knight took in painting was evident to her audience and to critics. As Seattle gallery owner Francine Seders noted in the *Seattle Times*, "I really liked the fact that she followed her own style and didn't worry about contemporary things." Remaining productive into her final years, Knight continued to produce works that remained fresh and indicated her consistent growth as an artist until her retirement in 2001.

Influenced by Harlem artists

Born on May 26, 1913, in Bridgetown, Barbados, in the West Indies, Knight immigrated to the United States at age seven. Her father had died when she was two, and she traveled to St. Louis, Missouri, with a

foster family. When she was 13, the family relocated to New York City. Knight finished high school in 1930, and enrolled at the Howard University School of Fine Arts in Washington, D.C. Her teachers recognized her talent and encouraged her to pursue her studies, but financial hardship during these years of the Depression forced her to drop out.

Knight moved back to Harlem and looked for work. With the help of Augusta Savage, a respected sculptor and teacher, she found employment through the Works Projects Administration (WPA). This arm of President Franklin D. Roosevelt's New Deal created jobs for millions of unemployed Americans; artists were put to work creating murals, paintings, and sculptures for public buildings, and were also employed in art education. At the same time, Knight continued her fine arts studies, taking classes at the Harlem Community Art Center. In Harlem Knight met Lawrence, who by then had already established a national reputation for his bold and moving paintings, in particular his series on the Great Migration of rural blacks to northern cities after World War I. The couple married in 1941.

As Lawrence's career flourished, Knight continued to paint for enjoyment rather than fame. She moved with her husband to Black Mountain College in Ashville, North Carolina; to Brandeis University, near Boston, Massachusetts; and to Skowhegan, Maine, where he taught at the Skowhegan School of Painting and Sculpture. The marriage was a happy one; Knight and Lawrence inspired, learned from, and supported each other in their creative endeavors. Knight did not experiment with the various artistic movements of the

At a Glance . . .

Born on May 26, 1913, in Bridgetown, Barbados, West Indies; died on February 18, 2005, in Seattle, WA; married Jacob Lawrence, 1941. *Education:* Howard University School of Fine Arts, 1931-33; New School for Social Research, 1960-66; Skowhegan School of Painting and Sculpture, 1968-70.

Career: Artist.

Awards: Caucus Centennial Medallion, Black Caucus; Centennial Award of Merit, Arizona State University, 1984; National Honor Award, Women's Caucus for Art; Pioneer Award, Twelfth Annual Artists' Salute to Black History Month, 1994; honorary degrees from University of Minnesota and Seattle University.

time, such as abstraction and expressionism, preferring to paint portraits of her friends, studies of dancers, and landscapes. As *New York Times* writer Christopher Lehmann-Haupt noted, these paintings were considered "companion pieces to her husband's work." Knight's images, according to Sheryl Conkelton in the catalog *Never Late for Heaven: The Art of Gwen Knight,* "are not a polemical record of a historical era, nor are they anxiously ambitious in their artistic reach; they simply and quietly render in paint what occupies the artist's mind. They are made to satisfy the artist in her own explorations, and it is the artist's openness to experience and learning as well as the modest intimacy of the works that are part of their great appeal."

Inspired by West African Art

In the early 1960s Knight and Lawrence lived in Nigeria, where Knight became fascinated by West Africa sculpture. She studied these works and met contemporary artists and artisans, observing their techniques. As the artist was quoted as commenting in *Contemporary Women Artists,* "It is not so much 'who has influenced one' as what kinds of art have intrigued and given pleasure and inspiration. For myself I would say West African sculpture because it is powerful and mystical; Asian drawings for their linear beauty and economy of means; and the impressionist school for its use of color and subtlety."

Among Knight's works from this time are "African Memories," a figurative painting influenced by the stylized motifs of Yoruba sculpture; and "Mask V," comprised of geometric motifs adopted by cubist painters. As a writer for *Contemporary Women Artists* observed, "This painting deftly fuses her African and impressionist influences."

In 1971 Knight and her husband moved to Seattle, Washington, where Lawrence was offered a tenured teaching position. Within a few years Knight began attracting critical attention in her own right. Her first solo exhibit, at the Seattle Art Museum, took place in 1976. She continued to exhibit in Seattle and other neighboring Washington venues, as well as in group shows in California, Florida, and Washington, D.C.. Critics admired her expert and fluid use of line, especially in her depictions of dancers and movement.

Through the 1990s Knight continued to develop her interest in the use of line and color, creating paintings, drawings, and monoprint portraits and figure studies. In the late 1990s, however, her work suddenly took a new direction. She began making quick, fluid sketches of animals, from memory, which she rendered as monoprints, silkscreen prints, and etchings. She continued exhibiting in group shows through the late 1990s, and in 2003 had a major retrospective show at the Tacoma (Washington) Art Museum, *Never Late for Heaven: The Art of Gwen Knight.* The artist died at her Seattle home in 2005, at age 91.

In 2007 the Seattle Art Museum opened the Gwendolyn Knight and Jacob Lawrence gallery in honor of the two artists and their contribution to the cultural life of the Seattle area. When Knight died she bequeathed several items to the museum and also funded a fellowship to support African-American art and artists. Her works are included in several other collections, including Hampton University; the Weisman Art Museum, University of Minnesota-Minneapolis; Museum of Modern Art, New York City; and the St. Louis Art Museum.

Selected works

Solo exhibitions

Seattle Art Museum, 1976.
Virginia Lacy Jones Gallery, Atlanta University Center (retrospective), 1988.
Francine Seders Gallery (Seattle, WA), 1994.
Never Late for Heaven: The Art of Gwen Knight, Tacoma Art Museum, 2003.

Sources

Books

Conkelton, Sheryl, *Never Late for Heaven: The Art of Gwen Knight,* University of Washington Press and Tacoma Art Museum, 2003.
Contemporary Women Artists, St. James Press, 1999.

Periodicals

New York Times, February 27, 2005, p. 1.40.

Seattle Post-Intelligencer, February 19, 2005, p. A1.
Seattle Times, February 19, 2005, p. A1.

On-line

"Gwendolyn Knight and Jacob Lawrence Gallery Created for Downtown Expansion Opening May 5," *Seattle Art Museum,* www.seattleartmuseum.org (July 10, 2007).

The Jacob and Gwen Knight Lawrence Virtual Resource Center, www.jacobandgwenlawrence.org/ (July 10, 2007).

"Jacob Lawrence and Gwendolyn Knight," *HistoryLink.org: The Online Encyclopedia of Washington State History,* www.historylink.org/essays/output.cfm?file_id=5120 (July 10, 2007).

—E. M. Shostak

Amel Larrieux

1973(?)—

Singer, songwriter, music producer

Growing up in New York's Greenwich Village during the 1970s, Amel Larrieux lived in an atmosphere of creativity, diversity, and acceptance. The child of a dynamic and creative mother, she was encouraged to develop her own creativity and to guard her independence. As an adult, Larrieux built a career as a successful singer songwriter and, with her husband Laru Larrieux, started her own record company. By holding on to the lessons of independence and artistic integrity she learned as a girl, she has managed the almost impossible feat of achieving commercial success without commercializing her sound, her image, or her life.

Born Amel Gottschild during the early 1970s, Larrieux grew up in the cultural and artistic center of New York City. Her mother, Brenda Dixon Gottschild, was a dancer, performance artist, poet, and critic, and young Amel grew up in an artists' apartment building in the bohemian neighborhood of Greenwich Village. Her home was filled with music, dance, books, and ideas, and she was surrounded by friends of all races and classes.

Growing up in this fertile atmosphere, Larrieux felt free to explore her own artistic talents. She danced, painted, wrote poetry, and read voraciously, developing a lifelong love of learning. The Gottschild home was also full of music, and Larrieux grew especially to love the work of singer-songwriters, such as John Lennon, Joni Mitchell, and Jimi Hendrix. It seemed to her there was great power in writing a song that could move others the way her favorite songwriters moved her.

Along with the knowledge she gained from books and the understanding she learned from her diverse neighbors, Larrieux gained strength from the example of the strong women in her family. Her grandmother had been a single parent who raised five children during the 1950s, and her mother had always been an independent career woman. With such women as her role models, Larrieux never doubted that she could accomplish great things.

When Larrieux was 12, her mother took a job teaching performance studies at Temple University in Philadelphia. They lived in Philadelphia for several years, and Larrieux attended a performing arts high school there. When she was 19, she moved back to New York and began working at a publishing company. However, music was still her first love, and she made a demonstration tape of a song she wrote in hopes of getting work as a singer. She soon met musician and rapper Bryce Wilson, who had formerly been part of the group Mantronix. She and Wilson began to perform together under the name Groove Theory. In 1995, Groove Theory released a self-titled album. One of the most successful tracks, "Tell Me," reached *Billboard Magazine's* top ten.

Larrieux performed with Wilson until 1999, when she signed a contract with Sony Records to produce her first solo album. The title of that album, *Infinite Possibilities*, reflects the sense of empowerment that Larrieux got from her own childhood and which she felt was vitally important for all children. Fulfilling her desire to be a songwriter, Larrieux wrote many of the songs on her debut album, including "Get Up," an

At a Glance . . .

Born March 8,1973(?) in New York, NY; married Laru Larrieux; children: Sky and Sanji-Rei.

Career: Groove Theory (musical group with Bryce Wilson), singer, 1991-99; solo performing artist, 2000–.

Addresses: *Office*—118A Fulton Street, Suite 332, New York, New York 10038.

anthem dedicated to working people, and "Even If," a touching love song to her baby daughter.

Though *Infinite Possibilities* was well-received, and Larrieux's music career was beginning to take off, she began to feel that her low-key style and her vision of making music that could create change in the world did not fit with a large commercial record companies like Sony. Larrieux also wanted to be part of all phases of the production of her albums, not only writing and performing the songs, but choosing the musical arrangements and engineering the sound. Though it was risky, she and her husband Laru Larrieux decided to form their own record company. They named it Bliss Life and set out to produce her next album.

Bravebird, Larrieux's second solo album, was released in 2004. Like *Infinite Possibilities, Bravebird* is a fusion of a wide range of genres, from rhythm and blues and soul to jazz, Middle Eastern, African, and Indian sounds. The album continues to demonstrate Larrieux's commitment to social issues. The title track tells the story of an African woman fleeing female genital mutilation, a cultural and religious rite practiced in many African and Middle Eastern countries and opposed by many human rights activists.

Larrieux wrote all of the songs on her third album *Morning,* released in 2006. Continuing in the rich fusion style that some critics have called "neo-soul," the album includes a tribute to working single parents like the singer's own grandmother and mother, the tender and jazzy "Weary." *Morning* was followed in 2007 by *Lovely Standards,* a reworking of classic jazz songs and show tunes.

Larrieux has worked hard to build a solid music career while remaining separate from the often artificial world of the music industry. Though she has received criticism for not fitting into either the celebrity image or the most commercially popular sound, she has gained respect both among her increasing number of fans and

in the entertainment industry. Her songs have been included in the soundtracks of such films as *Love Jones* (1997), *Down to Earth* (2001), and *Barbershop* (2002), and she has collaborated on albums with other groups, such as Sweetback and The Roots. In 2003 she received a Grammy nomination for Best R and B Performance by a Duo or Group for a duet of "Where Is the Love" with Stanley Clarke.

However, though her albums have been both popular and highly praised by critics, Larrieux does not especially enjoy the artificial atmosphere of the recording studio. She is happiest when performing in concert, where she can experience the exchange of energy between audience and performer. Larrieux is far more interested in touching other people with her music than in projecting a cool and stylish celebrity image, and her most important goal is translating and communicating feelings through her music.

Selected works

Albums

Infinite Possibilities, Sony Records, 2000.
Bravebird, Bliss Life, 2004.
Morning, Bliss Life, 2006.
Lovely Standards, Bliss Life, 2006.

Sources

Periodicals

Billboard, January 22, 2000, p.36; April 29, 2006, p. 40; June 24, 2006, p. 55.
Blackgirl Magazine, July-August 2004, p. 14.
Ebony, February 2004, p. 30.
People Weekly, May 15, 2006, p. 51.
Time, December 11, 1995, pp. 83-4.

On-line

"Amel Larrieux," *Bliss Life,* www.blisslife.com/artists_amelsbio.html (July 17, 2007).
"Amel Larrieux," *Sing365.com,* www.sing365.com/music/lyric.nsf/Amel-Larrieux-Biography/68C3-AD2969DB8FCF48256D2D000A1658 (July 17, 2007).
"Hip-Hop: Interview: Amel Larrieux," *1-42 Fueling Stimulus,* www.onefortytwo.com/MUSIC/hiphop/Interviews/AmelLarrieux.html (July 17, 2007).
"R & B and Hip-Hop: Back In The Groove: Brave Bird Amel Larrieux Soars with Another Eclectic Set," *Barnes and Noble,* http://music.barnesandnoble.com/features/interview.asp?NID=768182&z=y (July 17, 2007).

—Tina Gianoulis

Bobby Lashley

1976—

Professional wrestler

Lashley, Bobby, photograph. Bryan Bedder/Getty Images.

As a child growing up in poverty, Bobby Lashley was fascinated by the flamboyant, theatrical wrestling matches he watched on television, and he dreamed of someday becoming a famous professional wrestler. He became a dedicated amateur wrestler, developing the skill and discipline necessary to earn a number of prestigious amateur championships before entering the professional arena. A powerhouse in the "squared circle," as insiders call the professional wrestling ring, Lashley is a soft-spoken and even-tempered athlete who has gained a reputation for congeniality among his fans and colleagues. He is also a devoted father, determined to offer support and guidance, not only to his own daughter, but also to the youth of his community.

Set Goals for Himself

Lashley was born Franklin Roberto Lashley on July 16, 1976. His father was a drill sergeant in the U.S. Army, and the family moved frequently as his career required. In 1990, when young Franklin Lashley was only 14, his father divorced his mother and left the family. Clara Lashley settled her family in Junction City, Kansas, and raised her son and three daughters on her own, often on low-paying jobs. Franklin, the only male in the family, felt both alone and responsible. He grew determined to work toward a better life and became goal-oriented and driven at an early age. Seeking an outlet for both his energy and his ambition, he threw himself into athletics, becoming a wrestler like Hulk Hogan, the Road Warriors, and the other heroes he saw on television. His coaches also became male role models in his life, teaching him valuable lessons both on and off the mat.

Lashley honed his wrestling skills as a member of the Junction City High School Blue Jays, where his coach Robert Lester emphasized that athletic ability must be accompanied by excellence in other areas of life. In 1995, Lashley entered Missouri Valley College, where he continued his successful wrestling career as a MVC Viking under Coach Mike Macholz. Macholz taught his wrestlers the value of persistence and relentlessness in pursuit of a victory and the importance of achieving the right mental attitude in approaching a contest.

At MVC, Lashley began the series of championships that would characterize his career. During his freshman

At a Glance . . .

Born Franklin Roberto Lashley on July 16, 1976; one daughter: Kyra. *Education:* Missouri Valley College, BA, Human Service Agency Management, 1999; United States Army, 2000-02.

Career: Wrestler, 1990s–; National Association of Intercollegiate Athletics, National Wrestling Champion, 1997, 1998; Armed Forces Wrestling Champion, 2000, 2001; Conseil International du Sport Militaire (International Military Sports Council) World Games, silver medal, 2002; Ohio Valley Wrestling (as Blaster Lashley), 2003-2005; World Wrestling Entertainment, 2005–; WWE U.S. Champion, May 26, 2006–July 11, 2006; Extreme Championship Wrestling, 2006–; ECW World Heavyweight Champion, December 3, 2006–April 29, 2007 and June 3, 2007–June 11, 2007.

Selected awards: *Pro Wrestling Insider*, Rookie of the Year, 2005; Most Improved Wrestler, 2006.

season, he placed fourth in the National Amateur Championship, then won the championship three years in a row, in addition to achieving All-American status all four years of his college career. In 1997 and 1998, he won the National Athletic Intercollegiate Association's National Wrestling Championship.

In 1999, he graduated from college with a degree in human service agency management. He joined the Army, and qualified for its World Class Athletes Program. Stationed in Colorado Springs, Colorado, Lashley trained in the Olympic training camp there, where his workout included brisk walks up Pikes Peak, a famous high point of the Rocky Mountains. He became a two time Armed Forces Champion and won a silver medal at the 2002 Conseil International du Sport Militaire (International Military Sports Council) World Games.

Aimed to Wrestle Professionally

After leaving the Army, Lashley qualified an alternate spot on the 2004 Olympic team. But his hopes of making the team were scuttled by a freak accident; he damaged his knee while diving to avoid the gunfire of a bank robber. With Olympic gold out of reach, he renewed his focus on his goal to be a professional wrestling star. However, in order to make the change from amateur to professional, he had to make some changes in himself and his way of viewing his sport. Professional wrestling has a unique relationship to

amateur wrestling. Unlike other sports, in which the professional version closely resembles the amateur sport, professional wrestling has become a sort of spectacular theater, where good battles evil in the form of costumed wrestlers with colorful names.

The sport of wrestling has an ancient history that stretches back to the ancient cultures of Egypt, Greece, and Rome. Evidence of prehistoric wrestlers has even been found in early cave paintings. The nature of wrestling has always been highly dramatic, pitting two opponents against each other in intimate physical contact. During the 1940's in the United States, a type of professional wrestling emerged which exaggerated the dramatic aspects of the sport, adding elaborate costumes and rehearsed moves, creating an event that was more theater than athletic contest.

With the advent of television in the 1950s, the popularity of professional wrestling expanded to a wide audience. The introduction of cable television during the 1980s brought professional wrestling to even more fans, and high-powered production companies such as the World Wrestling Federation (WWF, later renamed World Wrestling Entertainment) added more drama. By the early 2000s, when Lashley entered the sport, professional wrestling was a carefully scripted, precisely choreographed, rehearsed spectacle, where the performers used props like tables, chairs, and ladders as weapons and were carefully trained to avoid injury.

In preparing to become a professional, Lashley's first step was to "beef up," to add pounds of bulging muscles. The majority of modern professional wrestlers have powerful physiques with huge sculpted muscles. Lashley was six feet three inches tall, and during his amateur career, had wrestled at 177 pounds. By the time he signed a contract with WWE in November 2003, he had added almost a hundred pounds of muscle, giving him the powerhouse look of a professional in the ring.

Became a "Villain"

Once his contract had been signed, Lashley was sent to the Ohio Valley Wrestling (OVW), a training ground for beginning professionals in Louisville, Kentucky. There, he learned the theatrical side of the sport and competed in his first professional matches. Lashley was given the role of a wrestling villain and the name "Blaster Lashley." Villains in the professional ring are called "heels," and Lashley worked in a group of heels called "Bolin Services," managed and promoted by Kenny Bolin.

Lashley finished his training and made his pro wrestling debut on December 4, 2004, in a "dark match," the untelevised warm-up for a televised match. He performed so well that his promoter Kenny Bolin offered other wrestlers $100 for each minute they could remain in the ring with him. Lashley spent two years in

OVW, wrestling in dark matches, before his television debut with WWE on September 23, 2005. Once again, he was victorious, delighting fans by doing pushups with his opponent on his back. As a WWE wrestler, Lashley dropped his heel persona along with the name Blaster. For the rest of his career Franklin Lashley would be Bobby Lashley and a "face," or wrestling hero.

In his first month with WWE, Lashley wrestled in ten matches, a fast pace that would continue in the coming years. On May 26, 2006, he appeared on the WWE program *Smackdown!*, where he defeated John Bradshaw Layfield to win the U.S. Championship. He continued to provide uproarious entertainment in WWE shows like *Smackdown!* and *Raw*, and in another WWE branch called Extreme Championship Wrestling (ECW). On December 3, 2006, he won the ECW World Heavyweight Championship, losing it again on April 29, 2007. He regained the title on June 3, 2007, then lost it again June 11, 2007. However, each gain and loss is part of the spectacle that keeps the fans tuning in to watch, and Lashley built a large following of loyal fans.

Throughout his rise to success in the flamboyant world of professional wrestling, Lashley remembered his youth of poverty and loss, and it remained important to him to give back to his community. In addition to the public charity work connected to his career, such as participating in a celebrity bowling match for the Make A Wish Foundation, he has become a regular visitor to Harrison High School near his Colorado Springs home. There he shares his success with his community, letting young fans try on his mammoth championship belt and acting as a mentor, speaking about the importance of setting and achieving goals. He has also become a committed father, giving his young daughter the time and attention he did not receive during his own childhood.

Sources

Periodicals

Detroit Free Press, March 23, 2007; April 1, 2007.
Flex, September 2007, p. 134-146.
Miami Herald, April 2, 2007.
New York Times, April 4, 2007, p. E1.
Seattle Times, February 20, 2007, p. D1.
Sports Illustrated for Kids, June 1, 2000, pp. 60-2.

On-line

"Biography for Bobby Lashley," *Internet Movie Database,* www.imdb.com/name/nm2048764/bio (September 7, 2007).
Bobby Lashley Online, www.bobbylashleyonline.com/ (September 7, 2007).
"Bobby Lashley," *The Accelerator's Wrestling Rollercoaster,* www.accelerator3359.com/Wrestling/bios/lashley.html (September 7, 2007).
"Bobby Lashley Interview," *New Zealand Pro Wrestling,* www.nzpwi.co.nz/home/index.php?option=com_content&task=view&id=2008&Itemid=88 (September 7, 2007).
"Lash-ing Out: Bobby Lashley Has Reached Prime Time," *Black Athlete Sports Network,* www.blackathlete.net/artman/publish/article_02037.shtml (September 7, 2007).
"Raw: Bobby Lashley," *World Wrestling Entertainment,* www.wwe.com/superstars/raw/lashley/ (September 7, 2007).

—Tina Gianoulis

Sister Gertrude Morgan

1900-1980

Artist, singer, preacher

Sister Gertrude Morgan was many things to many people. To residents and tourists who came to the French Quarter in New Orleans, Louisiana, she was a street preacher who dressed in a nurse's uniform, explained that she was the bride of Christ, and spoke and sang, through a megaphone, to anyone who would listen about the Kingdom of Heaven. To music fans she was a solo performer on a unique gospel music album, featuring just her voice and a tambourine, that demonstrated the close links between Southern African-American gospel music and its African roots. Among those music fans was Philadelphia DJ and producer King Britt, who released a remix of her music in 2005. To museum curators and art gallery owners she was the creator of religious folk art that gained a national reputation. And to the poor of New Orleans she was the operator of the Everlasting Gospel Mission, whose yard filled with four-leaf clover led to a door where they could find food and childcare when their backs were to the wall.

Morgan was born Gertrude Williams in LaFayette, Alabama, on April 7, 1900. She was the seventh of eight children of Edward and Frances Williams, and as a child she knew the desperately poor life of subsistence farming in the South. Her education lasted only until the third grade, when she left school to work in the fields. As a child she was drawn to art and scratched pictures in the dirt outside her family's home. The Williamses bounced around eastern Alabama, living in or near Girard (near Phenix City) and Opelika before settling in nearby Columbus, Georgia, where Gertrude became a member of the Rose Hill Memorial Baptist

Church. At age 28, she married a man named Will Morgan. She remembered that time in her life fondly, saying, according to Michael Kimmelman of the *New York Times,* she was "havin' a good time, goin' about my business, goin' to the picture show."

Ministered in "Headquarters of Sin"

It was during her 30s—the date is variously given as 1934 and 1937—that Morgan experienced the crucial religious revelation of her life. Sitting in her kitchen, she heard a voice that commanded her to "go and preach—tell it to the world!" according to the *Sister Gertrude Morgan* Web site. She heeded the call and began preaching in the streets. She worked as a nursemaid and cared for orphaned children as she could. After her husband left her, she was free to go where she wished. Reasoning that wide-open New Orleans had the greatest number of lost souls in need of her spiritual services; Kimmelman noted that she called the city "the headquarters of sin." She made her way there in 1939 and met two other missionary women, Margaret Parker and Cora Williams.

They started an orphanage and mission on Flake Avenue in the Gentilly neighborhood, and began dressing in sober black robes with white collars. Morgan dubbed herself Sister Gertrude Morgan, and in place of her earlier Baptist faith, she began attending the physically demonstrative services of the city's Holiness and Sanctified churches. The three women sang hymns on the streets of New Orleans to raise money for the mission.

At a Glance . . .

Born Gertrude Williams, April 7, 1900, in LaFay-ette, AL; married Will Morgan, ca. 1928 (marriage dissolved); died July 8, 1980, in New Orleans, LA. *Education:* Left school in third grade to do farm work with family. *Religion:* Raised Baptist; preached Holiness services in New Orleans.

Career: Heard call to preach, mid-1930s; moved to New Orleans, 1939; (with Margaret Parker and Cora Williams) started mission in Gentilly neighborhood; began drawing with crayons and soon to paint, mid-1950s; works exhibited by art dealer E. Lorenz Borenstein, beginning 1960; opened Everlasting Gospel Mission in Lower Ninth Ward neighborhood, early 1960s; recorded album, *Let's Make a Record,* 1970 (remixed by DJ Britt as *King Britt Presents Sister Gertrude Morgan,* 2005); stopped making art, 1974; many posthumous museum and gallery exhibits of artworks.

Morgan's spiritual life continued to develop in New Orleans. Around 1955 she experienced further revelations, one of which anointed her the bride of Christ. She began to dress in white instead of black and sometimes wore a nurse's uniform as she preached the gospel and sang in the city's much-visited French Quarter. A second revelation inspired her to begin illustrating her religious ideas in the form of visual art, and she began to draw and paint. At first she used crayons and thought that she could use her drawings in teaching religion to children. Christ, and her relationship to Christ, were among her favorite subjects for many years; she painted Christ on a throne that resembled the popular Barcalounger chair, depicted him in a tuxedo, and flying an airplane toward heaven. Although her signature varied, it consistently highlighted her devotion to Christ; she signed her works as "Your Boss's Wife," "Nurse to Doctor Jesus, " "Little Ethiopia Girl," "Everlasting Gospel Revelation Painter," or "Housekeeper for Dada God."

Discovered by Art Dealer

Morgan patterned her first works after prints in illustrated Bibles, but soon created more and more imaginative pieces. Any surface, from a scrap of cardboard to a lampshade to a guitar case an empty roll of toilet paper could serve her as a canvas, and she packed large numbers of angels and imaginary creatures into her depictions of the Book of Revelations, another of her favorite themes. In 1960, Morgan's artworks were discovered by New Orleans art dealer E. Lorenz

("Larry") Borenstein, who began to exhibit them at his Associated Artists Studio gallery on St. Peter Street in the French Quarter. The building that once held the art gallery is a 1750 building with a storied history that is now the Preservation Hall jazz venue.

Borenstein befriended Morgan, who had moved out of the Gentilly house after the death of Cora Williams in 1957 and lived at various places in the Lower Ninth Ward neighborhood, a section of the city that was later devastated by Hurricane Katrina in 2005. In the early 1960s she moved into a home at 5444 North Dorgenois Street owned by a widow named Jennie Johnson and opened her own Everlasting Gospel Mission there, holding services in which she employed only a Bible, her paintings, a pointer/drumstick, a tambourine, and a megaphone of rolled paper (itself painted with scenes from the Bible). In 1965 the house was damaged by Hurricane Betsy. Around that time Johnson died, and Borenstein and business partner Allan Jaffe purchased the home from her heirs, turning it over to Morgan for use in her missionary activities.

Sometimes Borenstein invited Morgan to perform in his gallery as well, and in 1970 he arranged with a visiting British sound engineer to record some of her music. Morgan entered into the spirit of the project with new music that reflected the occasion; one track on which she shouted "Hallelujah! Come on, let's make a record! I wanna make a record for my Lord" gave the album its title. Accompanying her guttural but clear voice with only a tambourine, Morgan created mosaics of sound and speech that drew on the deep past of Southern African-American music, reaching back to a time when it still directly reflected African practices. In "Power," she repeated the word "power," varying it as "more power" or "you got power," in short patterns over a rapidly pulsing beat on the tambourine, showing little or no influence of the harmonies of European-American music. Some of the songs had spoken passages mixed in, as Morgan would do when she gave a sermon. The album was issued on Borenstein's Preservation Hall Recordings label; more a cult favorite than a hit, it was nevertheless repeatedly reissued and remained widely available on CDs and on-line download services in the early 2000s.

Included Text in Artworks

Morgan's artworks continued to evolve in style in her later years, increasingly often taking on words themselves as an element. Sometimes she would illustrate words whose first letters spelled out the alphabet, and in what are thought to be her later paintings (her works had no dates, and an exact chronology for them is difficult to establish) she began to create abstract patterns composed of thousands of words that, Kimmelman wrote, "increasingly took up every spare millimeter of space in her pictures. They flowed, stream-of-consciousness, in rapt and incantatory style, which was also how she spoke."

In the 1970s Morgan's art gained national attention. Painter Andy Warhol was among her admirers, as was *Interview* magazine writer Rosemary Kent, who profiled Morgan for the magazine's first issue. In 1974, however, Morgan announced that God had instructed her to stop making art; the fame it had brought her, she said, was unacceptable in God's eyes. Her decision may have been influenced by her deteriorating eyesight. Some of the money used to buy the North Dorgenois house had come from the sales of Morgan's art in the first place; when she stopped painting, Borenstein observed (according to Kimmelman) that "I don't know how this is going to work out for her and the Lord, but it affects me about he same way as the gasoline shortage affects traveling salesmen." She continued to preach, write poetry, and operate her mission, and on July 8, 1980, she died in her sleep.

Morgan's reputation continued to expand after her death, and in the early 2000s both her artwork and her music were brought into the national spotlight. Morgan's paintings and drawings became the subject of a major exhibition organized in 2003 by the American Folk Art Museum in New York; the exhibition moved to the New Orleans Museum of Art and the Intuit gallery in Chicago. And Philadelphia DJ and remix producer King Britt issued the album *King Britt Presents Sister Gertrude Morgan,* surrounding the original vocals from *Let's Make a Record* with electronic beats. The album took on added significance and sales momentum as flooding in the aftermath of Hurricane Katrina devastated Morgan's Ninth Ward neighborhood in late August of 2005. King Britt was hooked on Morgan's music from the first time he heard "Power." "Man! First

it was her voice," he told Dan DeLuca of the *Philadelphia Inquirer.* "The honesty in her voice. And then, the message. In times like today, we really need a voice of hope. And this was it."

Selected works

Let's Make a Record, Preservation Hall, 1970.

Sources

Periodicals

Art in America, May 2005, p. 66.
New York Times, September 7, 2003, p. AR93; February 27, 2004, p. E27; August 2, 2004, p. E3.
News & Observer (Raleigh, NC), February 15, 2007.
Philadelphia Inquirer, September 23, 2005.

On-line

"Learn About Sister Gertrude," *Sister Gertrude: Let's Make a Record,* www.sistergertrude.com (July 15, 2007).
"The Minister's Art," *Artnet,* www.artnet.com/magazine/features/karlins/karlins4-9-04.asp (July 15, 2007).
"Sister Gertrude Morgan: A Biography," *Traditional Fine Arts Organization,* www.tfaoi.com/11/511/5aa94b.htm (July 15, 2007).

—James M. Manheim

Hamilton Naki

1926-2005

Laboratory assistant, trainer, researcher, gardener

A self-taught teacher and surgical researcher, Hamilton Naki showed a natural aptitude for medicine while working as a gardener at the University of Capetown, South Africa. Despite being barred from studying medicine and officially forbidden from entering whites-only operating theaters, Naki, working as a laboratory assistant, played an important role in developing the techniques Dr. Christiaan Barnard used to perform the first human heart transplant in 1967. After the end of apartheid in 1994 Naki's role in the pioneering transplant was exaggerated by the enthusiastic government and press of the new South Africa. In 2005 obituaries claimed that he was actually involved in the operation, which was not the case. He was, however, an important figure in the development of transplant surgery techniques, and since his death has become a symbol of the way the old regime in South Africa wasted its black citizens' talents.

Born in Ngcangane, South Africa, in 1926, Hamilton Naki grew up in poverty and received no formal medical education. For most of his life Naki lived under the system of apartheid, which operated in South Africa from 1948 to 1994. Under apartheid racial and ethnic groups were segregated; blacks were made citizens of "homelands" and forbidden to hold certain jobs and public positions. In 1940 at the age of 14 Naki left high school without graduating because his parents could not afford for him to continue and hitchhiked to Cape Town, where he was hired as a gardener at the University of Cape Town.

Naki's talent as a surgeon was first noticed by Professor Robert Goetz after he asked the gardener to help look after the laboratory animals. Naki began helping out as an assistant on Goetz's experimental work. He later explained that he learned his surgical skills by watching others, saying "I stole with my eyes," according to the *Economist*. Before long Naki was performing dissections and quickly acquired a reputation in the hospital for his skills, especially for the way he handled delicate membranes. When Goetz left the University of Cape Town, Naki served as laboratory assistant to Dr. Christiaan Barnard, according to the *New York Times*. Barnard was impressed by Naki's skills, in particular his ability to carry out very fine stitching in blood vessels.

Because of the apartheid laws Naki was forbidden from training as a surgeon and from working in the operating theater. But Barnard allowed him to teach his students and to assist in demonstrations. Naki's skills were so highly respected that students would go to him to be shown how to perform particular techniques. In all he helped in the education and training of over 3,000 surgeons, according to several news sources. His hand in training these medical students may have been exaggerated, according to a report by Michael Wines in the *New York Times*. Wines interviewed Dr. Rosemary Hickman, with whom Naki worked from 1967 to 1995. Hickman noted the exaggeration, but confirmed that "Naki was instrumental in a program in which second-year medical students were trained in anatomy by observing surgery on anesthetized pigs." She also noted that he "helped teach licensed doctors how to use laparoscopes, used for a form of minimally invasive surgery, after the technique was introduced to South Africa."

At a Glance . . .

Born Hamilton Naki on June 26, 1962, in Ngcangane, Eastern Cape, South Africa; died on May
29, 2005. Four children. *Education:* Received informal
training in surgery at the University of Cape Town.
Religion: Christian.

Career: University of Cape Town, South Africa, gar-
dener and groundsman, 1940-(?); University of Cape
Town, laboratory assistant to Robert Goertz, then
Christiaan Barnard, 1950s-70s; University of Cape
Town, J.S. Marais Surgical Laboratory, laboratory assis-
tant to Dr. Rosemary Hickman, 1970s-1991.

Awards: South Africa, Order of Mapungubwe, in recognition of public service, 2002; University of Cape
Town, honorary degree in medicine, 2003.

Most controversially Naki was reported to have been
involved in Barnard's 1967 operation to transplant the
heart of donor Denise Darvall at the Groote Shuur
Hospital. In the years following the 1994 democratic
election in South Africa, Naki's role in the operation
became a matter of pride to black South Africans. He
became an example of what might have been possible
for millions of people had their talents not been wasted
by the apartheid system. Naki was celebrated as the
black surgeon who had secretly been allowed to re-
move and prepare the donor's heart for Barnard.
When he died in 2005 obituaries in journals such as the
Economist, the *British Medical Journal* and the *Lancet* all made inflated claims to this effect on Naki's
behalf, claims the publications later retracted. Mr.
David Dent, who worked with Naki at the time of
Barnard's transplant, confirmed to Wines that "he had
a very good hand, but he never went to the hospital, or
into the hospital, or saw a human."

Naki was certainly an important figure in the development of the techniques Barnard used to perform his
groundbreaking transplant operation. Naki performed
many successful transplants on animals, developing
and refining the procedures that would later make
human transplants possible. His ability as a surgeon is
not in doubt, and he is certainly a key figure in the
history of transplant surgery. "He has skills I don't

have," Barnard told the Associated Press in 1993,
according to the *Washington Post*. "If Hamilton had
had the opportunity to perform, he would have probably become a brilliant surgeon." But Naki was never
given the opportunity. Although he was an important
part of the research team and appeared—identified as
a gardener—with Barnard in publicity shots, he was not
present in the operating theater when the first human
heart transplant took place. Perhaps because the apartheid system meant that his role had remained secret it
was later possible for an overenthusiastic media to
embellish his story. Feeling the pressure in old age, and
perhaps even beginning to believe it himself, Naki
eventually went along with the story of his participation
in the operation itself.

Naki's achievements in the context of strict segregation, limited education, and poverty remain impressive.
Naki had a strong Christian faith and spent his lunch
hours reading the Bible to alcoholics, drug addicts, and
the homeless in cemetery near to the hospital. He lived
his whole life in a one-room house without electricity or
running water. He was unable to afford an education
for his own four children. Some reports indicate that
Naki retired in 1991 on a gardener's salary and died
penniless. However, Hickman told Wines that Naki had
been promoted to laboratory assistant and retired from
that position. It is difficult to untangle the truth from
myth, especially now that both Barnard and Naki have
died. Yet Hickman assured Wines that "Naki was an
honest man" and confirmed his considerable talents. In
2002 he received South Africa's highest honor, the
Order of Mapungubwe; in 2003 he received an honorary degree in medicine from the University of Cape
Town. He died on May 29, 2005, aged 78.

Sources

Periodicals

Economist, June 9, 2005; July 14, 2005.
Jet, July 4, 2005 v108, p. 50.
Lancet (London), July 2, 2005, p. 22.
New York Times, June 11, 2005, p. B7; August 27,
2005, p. A2, A7.
Washington Post, June 13, 2005, p. B4.

On-line

"Gardener Behind Africa's Heart Pioneer," *BBC*,
http://news.bbc.co.uk/2/hi/africa/3011105.stm
(August 28, 2007).

—Chris Routledge

Apollo Milton Obote

1925-2005

Ugandan politician

A leader in the movement for Ugandan independence in the 1960s, Apollo Milton Obote presided over the withdrawal of the British colonial government in 1962 and became the country's first prime minister and later, its first president. Despite bold moves to improve Uganda's economy and modernize the country, Obote was not able to resolve tribal conflicts that threatened Ugandan unity, and in 1971 he was deposed in a coup led by Idi Amin, whose despotic eight-year-rule was marked by blatant human rights violations. In 1979, the Tanzanian military overthrew Amin, and in 1980 Obote was re-elected president.

Conditions in Uganda only grew worse under Obote's second administration. He continued Amin's brutal tactics against guerilla forces that opposed him. He also ordered the slaughter of civilians; an estimated 300,000 civilians were killed between 1981 and 1985, when Obote was ousted in another coup. Obote fled to Zambia, where he was granted political asylum and lived in comfort until his death in 2005.

Drawn to Revolutionary Politics

The third of nine children, Obote was born in the Apac district of northern Uganda. Because his father, a farmer, was a minor chieftain of the Lango tribe, Obote believed himself destined to become a leader and often proclaimed that "I was born of a ruling family." The young Obote attended missionary schools before entering Makerere University College in the capital city, Kampala, in 1948. After being expelled for leading a student strike, Obote finished his degree as a correspondence student.

Obote worked odd jobs as a laborer and a salesman in the southern Ugandan region of Buganda and then moved to Kenya, which was in the throes of a violent uprising against British rule that became known as the Mau Mau emergency. Obote joined the Kenya National Union, a political organization led by accused Mau Mau instigator (and later, first prime minister and president of independent Kenya) Jomo Kenyatta. Here Obote learned political skills that would help him go on to play a central role in the struggle for Ugandan independence.

Britain had ruled Uganda as a protectorate since 1894. Under this arrangement, Uganda—a sovereign but relatively small and vulnerable nation—signed a treaty accepting Britain as its protector. This meant that Britain provided diplomatic and military protection, organized government administrative functions, and imposed taxes. Many British policies benefited the Baganda, the largest ethnic group in Uganda, whose homeland of Buganda was a separate kingdom within Ugandan territory. But the British also favored Indian immigrants in Uganda, giving them a monopoly in the lucrative business of cotton ginning. By the early twentieth century, Ugandans were demanding an end to these and other policies that created division and injustice, and were growing increasingly impatient for full independence. After the end of World War II, Britain began planning the formal end of the protectorate.

At a Glance . . .

Born on December 28, 1925, in Akokoro, Uganda; died on October 10, 2005, in Johannesburg, South Africa; married Miria Obote; four children. *Education:* Attended Makerere University College, Kampala, Uganda, 1948-1950; completed his education through correspondence courses.

Career: Uganda National Congress, founder, 1955; Uganda legislative council, member, 1958-62; prime minister of Uganda, 1962-66; president of Uganda, 1966-71, 1980-85.

Created Alliances and Enemies

On returning to Uganda, Obote focused his energies on political organizing. Of central importance was the need to reach out to traditional tribal leaders to bridge the divides among them and gain their political support. In 1955 Obote formed the Uganda People's Congress (UPC), which attempted to draw Uganda's various tribal interests together so that separate factions would not threaten the country's unity on the eve of independence. In 1958 Obote joined the Uganda legislative council, continuing to forge tribal alliances that would ensure a UPC victory in the country's first independent election, scheduled for 1962. Eager not to alienate the powerful and influential Baganda, Obote made a deal: if they voted for the UPC, he would see to it that their king, Edward Mutesa II (known as King Freddy) would become president—a largely ceremonial post—while Obote himself would take the more powerful position as prime minister. Obote's bargain paid off, and in 1962 he was sworn in as Uganda's first prime minister, under President Mutesa.

Relations between Mutesa and Obote, however, did not go smoothly. Mutesa continued to push for recognition of Buganda as a separate kingdom—an aim that Obote thoroughly rejected. At the same time, Obote angered other tribal leaders by pushing an economic agenda that was strongly pro-communist and that weakened their own governing powers. In 1966, amid accusations of involvement in an illegal gold smuggling ring, Obote suspended Uganda's constitution and declared himself president, with almost absolute powers. When Mutesa strenuously objected, calling this move illegal, Obote exiled him to England, where he died in 1969. Many Buganda never forgave Obote for removing their beloved king and for abolishing the traditional powers of Uganda's tribal leaders.

Uganda experienced a short period of political stability and economic growth in the late 1960s. In 1969 Obote announced a Common Man's Charter, which

promoted classic socialist ideals such as workers' ownership of the means of production. This move immediately alienated western powers, who feared that Uganda, like some other newly-independent African nations, would form a strong alliance with the Soviet Union. In fact, Uganda followed a policy of nonalignment; its relations with the Soviet Union were friendly but not extensive or deep. Obote's policies, as described by Julian Marshall in the *Guardian*, were "a diluted form of socialism" that sought "substantial, but not majority, shareholding in foreign-owned businesses"—not the full-scale nationalization that was feared. Nor did Obote intend to decree such measures on his own—he expected to let Ugandans vote for his policies. Nevertheless, according to Marshall, Obote was seen by western countries as a kind of "socialist ogre of the emerging independent Africa."

Deposed by Amin

In 1971, while attending a conference of prime ministers in Singapore, Obote was overthrown by General Idi Amin and sought refuge in Tanzania. Many Ugandans supported this coup at first, but Amin's brutal tactics soon made him a hated tyrant. During Amin's eight-year rule, an estimated 500,000 Ugandans were tortured and killed. Obote repeatedly denounced Amin, gaining political support from the many thousands of Ugandans who fled Amin's regime for exile in Tanzania. In 1979 Tanzanian troops entered Uganda and deposed Amin, paving the way for Obote to resume power.

A general election in 1980 gave the presidency to Obote, but most observers believed the voting to have been rigged. Once in power again, Obote ordered Uganda's National Liberation Army to conduct a brutal campaign against the those who opposed him—chiefly the Buganda, the Acholi, and the especially the National Resistance Army, a guerilla movement in the western part of the country led by Yoweri Museveni. The National Liberation Army destroyed entire villages, killing thousands of civilians with impunity. Atrocities against civilians in the Luwero Triangle, a region north of Kampala, were especially notorious. Local officials reported that government forces killed between 100,000 and 200,000 civilians there, and detained and tortured several thousand others. At least 150,000 refugees from the region were forced to flee to International Red Cross refugee camps.

Obote was accused of imprisoning and torturing his political enemies and restricting basic freedoms throughout the country, making Uganda into a virtual police state. During his second administration, Uganda had one of the worst human rights records in the world. Makerere University law professor Sylvia Tamale, a teenager at the time, explained in a memoir published in *African Gender Institute Newsletter* that roadblocks, thievery, and rape were common throughout the country in the early 1980s. "Apart from the gang rapes that happened routinely in the war zone," she wrote, "there were many more horrendous stories: tales of mothers who were raped in full view of their children before being bludgeoned to death. Stories of machete-wielding soldiers who split open the bellies of pregnant women at roadblocks, 'to find hidden rebels!'" Tamale also described roadblocks where "the infamous 'panda gari' exercises usually happened. An impromptu roadblock would be mounted with a big truck by the roadside, onto which young men would be ordered to climb. The men would then be taken to various frontlines in the war zone and literally turned into cannon fodder. Very few ever rejoined their families." In all, an estimated 300,000 Ugandan civilians died during this conflict. According to some analysts, the brutality of Obote's regime was even worse than Amin's record.

Ousted in second coup

By 1985 factions within Obote's own army strongly opposed him, and they organized a coup that July. Obote fled to Kenya and then found permanent refuge in Zambia. Museveni took over as president of Uganda. Though many Ugandans believed Obote would eventually return, Museveni warned him that if he did so he would face criminal prosecution for the deaths of thousands who had perished during his regime in the 1980s.

Obote lived comfortably in Zambia for 20 years. He died at age 80 on October 10, 2005, in Johannesburg, South Africa, where he had been hospitalized for treatment of kidney disease. To the surprise of many Ugandans, President Museveni ordered a state funeral for the deposed leader. "We reviewed the turbulent history of Uganda and we saw the need for reconciliation," Museveni said in remarks reported by BBC News.

For some Ugandans, Obote was a champion of independence whose downfall was due mostly to external forces beyond his control, or to the policies of subordinates who acted without his authority. For others, however, he remains the architect of corruption and misrule that almost tore Uganda apart and left lasting scars on a country struggling to find its place in a rapidly modernizing world.

Sources

Books

Ingham, Kenneth, *Obote: A Political Biography*, Routledge, 1994.

Periodicals

Guardian, October 12, 2005.
New York Times, October 11, 2005, p. 9.
Washington Post, October 12, 2005, p. B6.

On-line

"'Duka-Duka!': Memories of the Ugandan Civil War," *African Gender Institute*, http://web.uct.ac.za/org/agi/pubs/newsletters/vol9/duka.htm (September 10, 2007).
"Government of Uganda—Past Leaders," *My Uganda,* www.myuganda.co.ug/govt/obote.php (September 10, 2007).
"Ugandans Mourn at Obote's Funeral," *BBC News,* http://news.bbc.co.uk/2/hi/africa/4363226.stm (September 10, 2007).

—E. M. Shostak

Helen L. Phillips

1919-2005

Opera singer, teacher

During the 1940s and 1950s Helen L. Phillips, a lyric-dramatic soprano, broke the color barrier at the Metropolitan Opera in New York City and at musical events elsewhere in the United States and abroad. She became the first black American to be hired by the Metropolitan Opera when she sang five performances of *Cavalleria Rusticana* during the Met's 1947-48 season. Phillips went on to a successful solo career that included tours of Austria and Germany for the U.S. State Department, as well as concert performances throughout the United States, Europe, Africa, and South America during the 1950s. Phillips drew international acclaim for her interpretations of black spirituals and German lieder.

Helen L. Phillips was born in 1919 and raised on Cottage Avenue in St. Louis, Missouri. Her father, the Reverend James Phillips, was a Baptist minister in neighboring Edwardsville, Illinois, and her mother, Julia Phillips, worked as a laundress. In 2005 Mary Tabor Engel, Phillips's last vocal student as well as a former reporter for the *New York Times*, *Boston Globe*, and *Christian Science Monitor*, told John M. McGuire of the *St. Louis Post-Dispatch* that John and Ruth Haskell and Ruth Haskell's brother, Robert Hanna, all of St. Louis, were primarily responsible for launching Phillips's career: "They knew Helen because her mother was Haskell's laundress, and Helen's sister, Lettie May Boys, was their cook."

Phillips's first public notice came at the age of 14 when she was chosen as a soloist for the dedication of Kiel Auditorium in St. Louis. At Sumner High School in St. Louis, Phillips was encouraged by the music director

Wirt Waltor. She graduated from Lincoln University, a historically black school in Jefferson City, Missouri. She later pursued graduate studies in sociology and music at Fisk University in Nashville, Tennessee. Although raised as a Baptist, as an adult Phillips became a Christian Scientist.

Seven years before Marian Anderson's historic debut with the Metropolitan Opera in the role of Ulrica in Verdi's *A Masked Ball* in January of 1955, Phillips broke the Met's unofficial color barrier for opera singers. She later recalled that her hiring was an apparent accident. The stage manager had called her agent and requested his best soprano because several members of the Met's chorus were absent. When Phillips arrived at the Met, the manager looked twice and then told her to hurry on backstage. Phillips was quoted in the *New York Times* as having told friends, "I just slipped in. Then after the performance, I slipped back out again." From December of 1947 through February of 1948 Phillips sang in the chorus for five performances of Pietro Mascagni's *Cavalleria Rusticana*. Although a troupe of black dancers had performed with the Met in 1933, Phillips was the first black chorister to perform with the opera. In 1962 Elinor Harper became the first black singer to sign a full-time contract with the Met chorus.

Phillips was fluent in German and, following World War II, she performed more than 500 concerts over a three-year period as part of a U.S. State Department tour of Austria and the former West Germany. During the 1940s and 1950s Phillips was the first black soloist to perform with Dr. Edwin Franko Goldman's Band,

At a Glance . . .

Born Helen L. Phillips in 1919 in St. Louis, MO; died on July 27, 2005, in New York City. *Education:* Lincoln University, BA; Fisk University, graduate studies in music and sociology. *Religion:* Christian Scientist. *Politics:* Republican.

Career: Singer, Metropolitan Opera chorus, 1947-48; U.S. State Department, concert tour of Austria and Germany, late 1940s; soloist with Dr. Edwin Franko Goldman's Band, New York City, 1940s-50s; Town Hall, New York City, debut, 1953; City Center, New York City, "Queenie" in *Show Boat,* 1954; St. Louis Symphony, soloist, 1955; symphony orchestra, Madrid, Spain, soloist; New York City, school teacher, voice teacher, vocal coach, 1960-2000(?).

singing in summer concerts in Central Park in New York City. An article about Phillips in the *St. Louis Post-Dispatch* in 1950 described her as a singer of the same stature as Marian Anderson and Todd Duncan.

Phillips embarked on a successful solo career during the 1950s. She debuted at Manhattan's Town Hall in 1953 and performed as a soloist with a symphony orchestra in Madrid, Spain. In 1954 she sang the part of Queenie in a production of *Show Boat* at New York's City Center. In 1955 she soloed with the St. Louis Symphony at Kiel Opera House. She also sang with the St. Louis Opera.

In a *St. Louis Post-Dispatch* article from 1955 she recounted traveling on the Orient Express railroad with her accompanist Richard Chamberlain. Two Russian soldiers passed by: "Noticing that we were Negroes, they entered [our compartment] and started deriding the United States and talking about the plight of Negroes in this country. During the course of the conversation, one took my glasses and refused to give them back. Then he tried to get fresh, and I slapped him good and hard."

Phillips never married. She later became a school teacher and, for the last 30 years of her life, worked as a voice teacher and vocal coach in New York City. Phillips died of heart failure on July 27, 2005, at the Isabella Geriatric Center in New York City. She left no immediate survivors. She was buried alongside her parents in Valhalla Cemetery in north St. Louis County. Engel told the *Post-Dispatch:* "Helen very quietly broke through racial barriers at a time when it was difficult for blacks to do so...When she went to a nursing home in Manhattan's Washington Heights, I would go see her, and she had pictures of her mother and father, an American flag and George W. Bush. She was an ardent Republican and a very genuine, spirited person. But she was feisty."

Sources

Periodicals

Los Angeles Times, August 9, 2005, B11.
New York Times, August 12, 2005, p. A17.
St. Louis Post-Dispatch, August 9, 2005, p. B1.
Washington Post, August 15, 2005, p. B5.

On-line

"*News & Notes*: Helen Phillips, First Black Soprano at the Met," *National Public Radio,* August 10, 2005, www.npr.org/templates/story/story.php?storyId= 4793728 (August 16, 2007).

—Margaret Alic

Preacher Moss

1967—

Comic, writer, lecturer

Preacher Moss, photograph. David S. Holloway/Getty Images.

Bryant Moss began practicing the art of satire at the age of seven, when he earned the nickname "Preacher" for his hilarious imitations of the pastor at his family's church. He maintained his interest in comedy and performing during his college years and his career as a special education teacher by developing a standup act and writing jokes for several respected comics. However, Moss wanted to do more than tell jokes; he wanted to create comedy that would educate and inspire his audiences, while making them laugh. A devout Muslim, Moss wanted to bring the Islamic principles of social justice, unity, and spiritual development into his work. He began to develop comedy shows that had a serious purpose—to increase understanding among people. First in his progressive comic lecture series, "End of Racism," then in the "Allah Made Me Funny" Muslim comedy tour, Moss has worked to build bridges of laughter across the fear and misunderstandings that divide people of different cultures.

Moss was born in 1967 in Washington, D.C., where his father worked as a training officer for the National Institutes of Health. His first lessons in social activism came from his parents who worked in the civil rights movement, his father as a member of the radical black power group, Black Panthers, and his mother, who had joined the movement after meeting Martin Luther King, Jr., when she was a teenager. They raised their son in the Christian faith in a Maryland suburb of the city and sent him to a local military academy for his schooling.

Began Performing Standup in College

Moss' gift for mimicry and humor became apparent at an early age, when friends at church encouraged him to do impressions of the minister. They dubbed him, first "Reverend Spitty Mouth," then "Preacher Moss," a nickname that Moss would adopt for his standup career.

Having been raised under the eye of strict parents, Moss decided to go away from home to college. He enrolled in Marquette University, a Milwaukee, Wisconsin, college that had been founded by the Jesuit order of Catholic priests. Milwaukee has a large majority of white citizens, and very few African Americans attended Marquette during the mid-1980s when Moss entered the college. Coming from the Washington,

At a Glance . . .

Born Bryant Reginald Moss in 1967 in Washington, DC; married Yasmin, 2003. *Education:* Marquette University, BA, journalism, 1988. *Religion:* Islam.

Career: Special education teacher, 1988-96; standup comic and comedy writer, 1988–.

Awards: Muslim Public Affairs Council, Media Award, 2005.

D.C., area, where a majority of the urban population was black, Moss experienced culture shock and isolation. True to his progressive upbringing, he worked with local groups to protest the policy of extreme racial segregation, called apartheid, in South Africa, while his own college had substantial investments in the racist white regime there.

Moss did not feel that he fit in at Marquette, or, indeed, in Milwaukee in general. As he had done as a child, he turned to comedy to express himself. Along with the journalism that he had come to Marquette to study, he began to take classes in comedy and to write and perform standup routines at a local comedy club. The comic stage allowed him to express his discomfort and soften his anger with humor.

Converted to Islam

While at Marquette, Moss also began to study Islam. He was first drawn to the subject by curiosity, but, as he learned more about the ancient religion, he began to feel a connection with Islam that he had not felt with Christianity. There had been Muslims in the United States for many centuries, some traveling with the very earliest Spanish explorers of the continent, others coming from Africa as slaves. During the 1920s and 1930s, some African Americans began to feel a special connection with Islam as a religion that did not devalue black identity, as Christianity so often seemed to do. In the early 1930s, a black Muslim mystic named Wallace Ford, who had taken the Muslim name Fard Muhammad, founded the Nation of Islam, an organization that sought to spread both principles of Islam and black nationalism among African Americans. Since then a number of African American Islamic groups have emerged. Because one of the basic beliefs of Islam is equality among races, many black Muslims practice their religion in multi-racial congregations.

In 1988, at the age of 20, Preacher Moss converted to Islam. He was concerned that his Christian parents would be upset by his conversion, so he broke the news gradually during his visits home, leaving his Qur'an, the holy book of Islam, or the rug he used for daily prayers where his parents would see them. They finally accepted his choice.

Moss graduated from Marquette University in 1988 with a degree in journalism. However, he did not work as a journalist, but instead took a job teaching emotionally disturbed children in Milwaukee, while continuing to do standup comedy. In 1994, Moss was the opening act for a comic named Darrell Hammond, who would later become a regular on the NBC classic comedy show *Saturday Night Live*. Hammond recognized Moss' talent and the two formed a lasting friendship. Hammond encouraged Moss in his comic career and hired him as a writer. Seeking to develop his comedy skills, Moss moved to Los Angeles. There, he continued to teach special education classes and worked as a writer for many well-known comics, including Damon Wayans and George Lopez. Although Moss achieved many successes as a writer, he was not satisfied. He wanted his work to mean more than laughs; he wanted his comedy to make changes in the world.

Created His Own Progressive Comedy Shows

While working for the innovative comedian Damon Wayans, Moss had learned that to create real comic art, it was important to communicate ideas, not merely tell jokes. He began to write his own show, a combination of comedy and instruction that he titled "End of Racism." Beginning in 2000, Preacher Moss toured hundreds of college campuses performing, teaching, and discussing poverty, racism, and civil rights. As Moss himself describes the show on his website, "'End of Racism' creates a rare atmosphere where people can address serious issues, release some anxieties, and have a dialogue of inclusion."

Moss had been performing "End of Racism" for four years when he got an idea for another kind of progressive comedy experience. That show had addressed one kind of prejudice, but as a Muslim, he was aware of another kind of prejudice that was spreading rapidly throughout the non-Islamic communities in the United States. Political events, such as the terrorist attacks that took place on September 11, 2001, coupled with ignorance about Islam, had resulted in widespread fear and intolerance. Many people in America did not know anyone personally who practiced the religion, and they had many misconceptions about who Muslims are and what they believe. Moss thought, what better medium than comedy to combat this fear and prejudice?

In May 2004, Moss and two other Muslim comics, Azeem and Azhar Usman, launched what they termed the "official Muslim comedy tour." Titled "Allah Made Me Funny," the show not only offered non-Muslims a chance to get to know a little about Islamic culture, but it provided a place where Muslims could gather to share humor about their own lives and experiences. Early in his comedy career, Moss had toured with Latino comic George Lopez and was impressed with the family feeling of connection that Lopez shared with his largely Latino audiences. Moss wanted to create that atmosphere of shared joy and struggle for Muslim audiences.

In planning the show, Moss consulted Islamic religious leaders who confirmed that laughter was permitted and even approved by the Prophet Mohammed, a major figure in the Islamic religion. According to Moss, the hadith—the collection of writings that teach about the Prophet's words and actions—includes chapters titled, "The Book of When the Prophet Laughed," and "The Time the Prophet Joked." Moss and the other comics on the tour made sure that their jokes were respectful and did not include sexual references or profanity. To ensure that Muslims would be comfortable attending the show, the comics requested that comedy clubs not serve alcohol or pork or allow smoking during performances. Though some non-Muslim patrons complained about this or condemned the idea of Islamic comedy altogether, many came and enjoyed the show.

In fact, "Allah Made Me Funny" was immediately popular, surprising even its creators. Muslim audiences enjoyed the chance to share "in-jokes" about their culture, and many non-Muslims were happy for the chance to see Muslim people telling the stories of their lives with warmth and humor. "Allah Made Me Funny" toured 30 U.S. cities during its first year, and went on to amuse audiences in Canada, Europe, Malaysia, Australia, New Zealand, and the Middle East. Wherever the show is performed local Muslim comics frequently join the show's originators onstage. London's newspaper, the *Independent on Sunday* quoted Moss' description of the show, "The idea is to provide a venue whereby Muslims and non-Muslims can feel safe, relevant, and inclusive...where humour [can] bridge gaps of bias, intolerance, and other social ills."

In 2003, Moss married Yasmin, an Indian Muslim living in Toronto, Canada. When not on tour, he lives in Long Beach, California, and visits his mother's home in Washington, D.C., frequently.

Sources

Periodicals

Independent on Sunday, Apr 1, 2007.
India-West (San Leandro, CA), January 27, 2006, p. C1.
Los Angeles Times, December 12, 2004, p. I10.
Recorder (Indianapolis, IN), May 6, 2005, p. C3.
Seattle Post-Intelligencer (Seattle, WA), October 1, 2005, p. C1.
Seattle Times (Seattle, WA) April 14, 2004, p. H29.
The Toronto Star, May 16, 2004, p. 15.
Weekend All Things Considered (Washington, D.C.) August 14, 2005, p. 1.

On-line

Allah Made Me Funny, www.allahmademefunny.com/comics.html (September 5, 2007).
"Comedy of the 'Allah Tour' Has Muslims Laughing," *Beliefnet,* www.beliefnet.com/story/169/story_16969.html (September 5, 2007).
"Poking Fun, In Good Faith: Muslim Comics Laugh In the Face of Intolerance," *Washington Post.com,* www.washingtonpost.com/ac2/wp-dyn?pagename=article&node=&contentId=A39975-2004Apr24&notFound=true (September 5, 2007).
"Poor Righteous Preacher," *Muslim Round Table Television,* www.p0wned.net/mrt/news/article-preacher.htm (September 5, 2007).
Preacher Moss, www.preachermoss.com/ (September 5, 2007).
"Clean Jokes and an Attempt to Foster Understanding," *The State.com: South Carolina's Homepage,* www.thestate.com/mld/thestate/entertainment/9502751.htm (September 5, 2007).

—Tina Gianoulis

E. Albert Reece

1950—

Physician, medical school dean

As an obstetrician/gynecologist (OB/GYN) and researcher, Dr. E. Albert Reece became one of the world's leading experts on diabetes-induced birth defects and prenatal diagnosis. He pioneered a technique called embryofetoscopy or embryoscopy to detect fetal birth defects. Reece and his collaborators discovered biochemical and molecular causes of diabetes-induced birth defects and pioneered methods for preventing such defects. In 2006 he became dean of the University of Maryland School of Medicine (SOM).

Attracted to Specialty in Obstetrics and Gynecology

E. Albert Reece was born in 1950 in Spanish Town, Jamaica, where his mother taught school and his father was a homebuilder. As a child Reece gave up music lessons to pursue his passions for soccer and cricket. After graduating from high school in Jamaica, Reece earned an honors degree from Cambridge University and a bachelor's degree *magna cum laude* from Long Island University in New York. He received his medical degree from New York University School of Medicine in 1978.

Reece told the University of Maryland Medical Alumni Association's *Bulletin* in 2006: "My interest in obstetrics and gynecology can be traced back to medical school. I liked surgery because of its rapid pace and contemporaneous answers, but I also enjoyed internal medicine because of its intellectual challenge and the long-term relationships an internist develops with pa-

tients. I chose my specialty because it combines these attractive elements."

Not only did obstetrics and gynecology combine two "attractive elements" for Reece, the specialty also offered him opportunities to explore new medical horizons. In the late 1970s Reece began studying why diabetic women were more likely to have children with birth defects. He told *Diabetes Forecast* in 1992: "I realized there were only a handful of people in the world who were actually looking at the mechanism that explains these defects, either in terms of animal models or basic research. So I concluded that there was a real need for basic studies."

Pioneered Embryoscopy

Reece's research focused on pregnant and lactating women with type 1 diabetes, as well as women with gestational diabetes mellitus (GDM), both of which can cause complications for the mother and fetus. During late pregnancy 3-5 percent of healthy women develop GDM, a resistance to the effects of insulin on sugar metabolism. Reece and his coworkers showed that this insulin resistance preserves sugar and fatty acids for the nutritional needs of the mother and fetus.

While at Yale University School of Medicine, Reece and Dr. Ruben Quintero researched viewing scopes that were small enough to examine a fetus for birth defects during its first trimester. Reece tested the safety of his procedure by examining the fetuses of women who were planning to have abortions. He then began using

At a Glance . . .

Born E. Albert Reece in 1950 in Spanish Town, Jamaica; married Sharon A. Reece; children: Kelly, Brynne, Sharon-Andrea. *Education:* Long Island University, BS; New York University School of Medicine, MD, 1978; Columbia University-Presbyterian Medical Center, OB/GYN internship, 1978-79, OB/GYN residency, 1979-82; Yale University School of Medicine, perinatology fellowship, 1982-84; University of the West Indies, PhD, biochemistry, 2000; Temple University, MBA, 2001.

Career: Yale University School of Medicine, Department of OB/GYN, New Haven, CT, assistant professor, 1984-86, associate professor, 1986-90; Temple University School of Medicine, Philadelphia, PA, Abraham Roth Professor, Department of Obstetrics, Gynecology and Reproductive Sciences, chair, 1991-2001; University of Arkansas for Medical Sciences, Little Rock, vice chancellor, College of Medicine, dean, professor in Departments of OB/GYN, Internal Medicine, and Biochemistry and Molecular Biology, 2001-06; University of Maryland, Baltimore, vice president for medical affairs, SOM, dean, John Z. and Akiko K. Bowers Distinguished Professor, 2006–.

Selected memberships: Arkansas Symphony, board; Association of American Medical Colleges, Administrative Board; Institute of Medicine, National Academy of Sciences, Board on Health Sciences Policy, vice-chair and chair of section on pediatrics, obstetrics and gynecology, committee on Guidelines for Human Embryonic Stem Cell Research; March of Dimes, Scientific Advisory Committee; National Council of Deans, Executive Committee.

Awards: Alpha Omega Alpha Medical Honor Society; Blacks Networking for Progress, Inc., honored for significant contributions in health care, 1994; Baltimore *Daily Record,* Influential Marylander, 2007.

Addresses: *Office*—Department of Obstetrics, Gynecology and Reproductive Sciences, University of Maryland School of Medicine, 655 W. Baltimore Street, Baltimore, MD 21201.

the technique on women at high risk of having a fetus with inherited defects. Reece performed his first 100 or so embryoscopies by inserting a needle-thin camera through the patient's vagina. Later he performed embryoscopies through the abdomen to reduce the risk of infection. Reece told Gina Kolata of the *New York Times* in 1993: "Embryoscopy opens a whole new world, a whole new frontier that we never had before. It's just unbelievable. You can make a diagnosis much more rapidly early in pregnancy and with a high degree of confidence." In 1997, when Reece was one of only three doctors in the country utilizing the procedure, he told *Good Housekeeping*: "People expect the worst, so they are absolutely joyous when things work out." Reece's techniques may eventually be utilized to cure or repair birth defects before birth.

In 1991 Temple University School of Medicine recruited Reece as chairman of its Department of Obstetrics, Gynecology and Reproductive Sciences and director of the Division of Maternal-Fetal Medicine. There Reece helped establish a Pre-Pregnancy Program to assist women in controlling their diabetes before becoming pregnant. His laboratory research focused on the first eight weeks of embryonic development when, in some diabetic women, the fetus may be nutritionally deprived, and on the role of the yolk sac in embryonic nutrition.

Appointed Dean at University of Arkansas

Reece did not limit his energy to medicine. In his spare time Reece earned a doctorate in biochemistry from the University of the West Indies, with a dissertation entitled *Cellular and Biochemical Mechanisms of Diabetic Embryopathy*, and an MBA from Temple's Fox School of Business and Management. His MBA, Reece told *SOMNews* in 2006, "influences my approach to management by making me much more analytic when evaluating new or existing ventures. I do more business and market analysis, return on investment and business plans to confirm my intuition and to give me greater confidence in initiating and/or staying with projects."

In 2001 Reece was named dean of the College of Medicine and vice chancellor for medical sciences at the University of Arkansas. There he doubled the school's research funding, recruited more than 30 well-funded scientists, initiated new multidisciplinary research centers, reformed the medical school curriculum, and launched three joint-degree programs and the state's first liver transplant program. He also helped create the Fay W. Boozman College of Public Health. In addition to his administrative responsibilities and research, Reece continued to see patients at the high-risk pregnancy clinic.

A series of tragedies at the university prompted Reece to form a panel charged with developing a system for identifying stress and mental disturbances in medical personnel and providing intervention. He described his initiative in the *Arkansas Times* as a "brotherly-sisterly approach. We are all our brothers' and sisters' keepers."

Moved to University of Maryland

Reece moved to Maryland as the nation's oldest public medical school was beginning a yearlong celebration of its bicentennial and as the SOM's research component and reputation were undergoing rapid growth. He immediately issued a series of open letters outlining his visions for medical research, for education, including an expansion of joint-degree programs and minors, and for the clinics of the University of Maryland Medical System. The latter included the development of cardiovascular disease and cancer magnet programs with the goal of becoming a National Institutes of Health-designated Comprehensive Cancer Center. Just as the SOM was planning a new research facility for regenerative medicine, including stem-cell research, Reece was appointed by the National Academy of Sciences to a new commission to monitor and revise standards for human embryonic stem-cell research.

University of Maryland Chancellor William E. Kirwan was quoted in the *Baltimore Sun* in 2006, describing Reece as a "visionary who can articulate a sense of what a medical school must be like in the decades to come. He sees the close connection between world-class research on one hand and clinical practice on the other...activities that many see as separate silos in medical schools."

As of 2007 Reece had published four monographs and some 450 peer-reviewed articles, book chapters, and abstracts, and was a sought-after lecturer. Some of his 11 books have appeared in multiple editions—unusual for specialized medical anthologies. Having brought some of his collaborators to Maryland, Reece continued to conduct research focusing on drugs for the prevention of type 2 diabetes.

Selected writings

Books

(With Donald R. Coustan, eds.) *Diabetes Mellitus in Pregnancy: Principles and Practice,* Churchill-Livingstone, 1988, 1995.

(With J. C. Hobbins) "Embryoscopy: An Evolving Technology for Early Prenatal Diagnosis," in *The Embryo: Normal and Abnormal Development and Growth*, M. Chapman, G. Grudzinskas, and T. Chard, eds., Springer-Verlag. 1991, pp 123-140.

(With John C. Hobbins, Maurice J. Mahoney, and Roy H. Petrie, eds.) *Medicine of the Fetus and Mother,* Lippincott, 1992, 1995, 1999.

(With I. Goldstein and J. C. Hobbins) *Fundamentals of Obstetric and Gynecologic Ultrasound*, Appleton & Lange, 1993.

(With D. R. Coustan and S. G. Gabbe, eds.) *Diabetes in Women: Adolescence, Pregnancy, and Menopause,* Lippincott, Williams & Wilkins, 2004.

(With J. C. Hobbins, eds.) *Clinical Obstetrics: The Fetus & Mother*, Blackwell, 2007.

Periodicals

(With others) "Clinical Research in the United States at a Crossroads: Proposal for a Novel Public-Private Partnership to Establish a National Clinical Research Enterprise," *Journal of the American Medical Association,* Vol. 291, No. 9, 2004, pp. 1120-1126.

(With others) "Effects of Pioglitazone and Metformin on [Beta]-Cell Function in Nondiabetic Subjects at High Risk for Type 2 Diabetes," *American Journal of Physiology: Endocrinology and Metabolism*, Vol. 292, No. 1, January 2007, p. E359.

(With Peixin Yang and Zhiyong Zhao) "Involvement of c-Jun N-Terminal Kinases Activation in Diabetic Embryopathy," *Biochemical and Biophysical Research Communications,* Vol. 357, No. 3, June 8, 2007, pp.749-754.

Sources

Periodicals

Arkansas Times, January 13, 2005, p. 9.

Baltimore Sun, June 8, 2006.

Daily Record (Baltimore, MD), June 8, 2006; November 30, 2006.

Diabetes Forecast, August 1992, p. 66.

Good Housekeeping, August 1997, p. 54.

New York Times, July 6, 1993, p. C3.

On-line

"E. Albert Reece, MD, PhD, MBA," *University of Maryland School of Medicine,* http://medschool.umaryland.edu/dean.asp (June 25, 2007).

"Off and Running: An Early Start for Maryland's New Dean," *MAA Bulletin*, www.medicalalumni.org/bulletin/fall_2006/president.html (June 27, 2007).

"Physician Spotlight: UAMS Dean E. Albert Reece," *Medical News of Arkansas,* http://arkansas.medicalnewsinc.com/news.php?viewStory=23 (June 27, 2007).

"A Q&A with Dean E. Albert Reece," *SOMNews,* http://medschool.umaryland.edu/dean_q_a.asp (June 18, 2007).

"Reece Appointed Dean of University of Maryland School of Medicine," *University of Maryland Medical Center,* www.umm.edu/news/releases/reece.htm (June 27, 2007).

"Reece, E. Albert M.D., Ph.D., M.B.A.," *University of Maryland School of Medicine,* http://medschool.umaryland.edu/facultyresearchprofile/viewprofile.aspx?id=9572 (June 18, 2007).

—Margaret Alic

Max Roach

1924-2007

Jazz drummer, composer, educator

Roach, Max, photograph. Tom Copi/Michael Ochs Archives/Getty Images.

Jazz drummer Max Roach expanded the boundaries of his art. He raised the profile of percussion within American music and served as a pioneer in using his craft as a method for socio-political advocacy for the African-American experience. Following in the musical footsteps of Big Sid Catlett and Kenny Clarke, Roach—as a member of bands led by such notable talents as Charlie Parker and Dizzy Gillespie—further developed the art of modern jazz drumming. Widely recognized as one of the founders of bebop or modern jazz, Roach refused to recognize such terms in reference to an African-American art form he believed was prejudicially named by those outside the musical community. Described by music writers as a "melodic drummer," Roach retained, within his solo work, logical constructions built creatively around the composition. As a drummer, educator, composer, and political activist, Roach looked to music as a liberating voice. Roach's use of drums and percussion instruments in orchestral ensemble, the integration of non-standard time signatures, and projects involving rap performers, kept him at the forefront of change within jazz and African-American music for more than six decades. His virtuosity as a percussionist set new standards and enriched American music.

Neighborhood Sounds Formed Musical Education Foundation

Maxwell Lemuell Roach was born in Newland, North Carolina, on January 10, 1924. At the age of four, Roach moved with his family to the Bedford-Stuyvesant district of Brooklyn. Roach's mother, a gospel singer, took him to church regularly and it was there that he received his first musical instruction on trumpet and piano. Roach studied keyboard harmony at age eight with his aunt and, within a year, played piano in the summer Bible school of the Concord Baptist Church. Roach's interest in music was heightened by the sounds of his Brooklyn neighborhood. "You could walk down the street; you heard people singing, you heard people playing," he recalled in Ira Gitler's book *Swing to Bop*. "The community was just fraught with music."

Introduced to the drums in high school, Roach joined the school marching band. By listening to radio shows and recordings, he heard the drumming of Jo Jones

At a Glance . . .

Born Maxwell Lemuel Roach, January 10, 1924, in Newland, North Carolina; married Mildred (divorced); Anne Marie "Abbey" Lincoln, married 1962 (divorced 1970); married Janus Adams (divorced); children: Ayodele, Dara, Daryl, Maxine, Raoul. *Education*: Manhattan School of Music, BA, music composition. *Religion*: Muslim.

Career: Harlem, various jam sessions, musician, 1942; recorded first session with Coleman Hawkins and Dizzy Gillespie, 1944; Benny Cater's Band, 1944; Parker-Gillespie quintet, member, 1944; recorded with Stan Getz, 1946; Charlie Parker's group, member, 1946-53; recorded with Miles Davis for *Birth of the Cool* sessions, 1949; co-founded Debut Record Company, 1952-57; formed a quintet with trumpeter Clifford Brown, 1954-56; worked and recorded with Sonny Rollins, 1956-58; worked with wife and vocalist Abbey Lincoln, 1960s; University of Massachusetts at Amherst, instructor, 1971; M'Boom percussion section, founder, 1972; recorded with Anthony Braxton and Abdullah Abrahim, 1980s; Bluemoon Records, record producer, 1980s; Jazz Institute, artistic director, 1980s; Max Roach's Double Quartet, founder, 1982; So What Brass Band, founder, 1990s.

Awards: Grand Prix International Du Disque 1977; NEA Jazz Master Award, 1984; John D. and Catherine T. MacArthur Fellowship Award, 1988; The Composer/Reader's Digest Commissioning Program Grant, 1988; Grammy Hall of Fame, inductee, 1995.

and swing drummer "Big" Sid Catlett, who recorded with trumpeter Dizzy Gillespie on such influential bebop numbers as "Salt Peanuts." Along with high school friends such as trumpeter Leonard Hawkins and saxophonist Cecil Payne, Roach listened to the latest jazz bands at the Apollo Theatre in Harlem. Playing in Brooklyn rehearsal bands, he read stock arrangements from the band books of Count Basie and Jimmie Lunceford. On weekends at Coney Island, he performed in the Darktown Follies and accompanied eighteen different acts in one day.

Local jam sessions became the main outlet for the development of Roach's rhythmic ideas. At these fiercely competitive exchanges, Roach's drum technique began to deviate from the standard swing pat-

terns of the period. While still a teenager, Roach often wore a penciled mustache in order to appear old enough to attend after-hours jam sessions at Harlem nightclubs like Monroe's Uptown House on 138th Street and Minton's Playhouse located in the dining room of the Hotel Cecil on 118th Street. At Minton's Roach encountered the house band's innovative drummer, Kenny Clarke, a Brooklyn neighbor who provided him with insight concerning technique and career opportunities. Years later, Clarke recounted in *Klook: The Story of Kenny Clarke*, how he "persuaded," Roach "to study at Julliard so that he could acquire the knowledge to become an all-around musician and do studio work and everything." At this time, Roach also received encouragement from Big Sid Catlett. As Roach told Burt Korall in *Drummin' Men*, "I didn't hear that much of Big Sid, except on records, apart from the little I heard on 52nd Street, but I was influenced by his kindness, his generosity."

Gained Reputation with Finest Bands of the Day

When most of the experienced jazz drummers left New York to serve in the armed forces during World War II, Roach's musical reputation and his ability to read music allowed him to find employment with some of the finest bands of the day. At age sixteen he played three nights at the Paramount Theatre with Duke Ellington's Orchestra, filling in for the ailing Sonny Greer. In Ira Gitler's *Jazz Masters of the Forties* Roach explained how "I had no rehearsal. The stage came up and I was sitting on Sonny's drums all about me. I followed Duke—his conducting was so hip while he played the piano."

After graduating from Boys High School with full honors in 1942, Roach played regular jobs with white groups, and in the evenings sought out more progressive sounds at Monroe's and Minton's. At these late-night club dates, he established a name for himself as one of the formidable "up-and-coming" modern jazzmen. In 1944, Gillespie and bassist Oscar Pettiford hired Roach for their group based at the Onyx on Fifty-Second Street. From the Onyx, Gillespie booked Roach and several members of a new group across the street at the Down Beat.

In February of 1944 Roach, through the intercession of Dizzy Gillespie, made his recording debut with veteran swing saxophonist Coleman Hawkins on the Keynote label. In the company of Hawkins, Gillespie and other talents such as Budd Johnson and Oscar Pettiford, Roach contributed to the numbers "Disorder at the Border," "Feeling Zero," and "Rainbow Mist." One of the first big-name musicians to hire Roach, Hawkins also nurtured the talents of a number of young modern jazzmen. In the liner notes to *Giants of Jazz: Coleman Hawkins*, Roach considered Hawkins as "the most adventurous of the established musicians of the period." A few months after the session with Hawkins, Roach went on the road with saxophonist Benny Carter's band.

Returning to New York in the spring of 1945, Roach joined the legendary Dizzy Gillespie-Charlie Parker quintet at the Three Deuces on Fifty-Second Street. Although he credited other drummers for his musical development Roach, as he explained in *The Legend of Charlie Parker*, attributed Parker as playing a major role in "...the way I play the drums. Bird was really responsible, not just because his style called for a particular kind of drumming, but because he set tempos so fast, it was impossible to play straight." To compensate for the polyrhythmic texture of bebop, Roach abandoned the steady four-four bass pedal and repetitive ride cymbal patterns of earlier jazz drummers. Through the variation of rhythm, he developed what has been called "melodic" drumming—an approach which freed the instrumentalist from his traditional role as strictly a time-keeping accompanist.

With Gillespie's departure from the group, Parker hired 19-year-old trumpeter Miles Davis, who formed a close friendship with Roach. In November of 1945 Roach, along with Gillespie, Davis, and bassist Curly Russell, recorded with Parker on the Savoy label. Released as "Charlie and His Re Boppers," the session yielded the classic numbers "Billie's Bounce," "Now's the Time," and "Thriving on a Riff." The session also included Parker's "Ko Ko"—a landmark bebop number which, as Gary Giddins noted in *Chasin' The Bird*, "braced by the cold winds of Max Roach's drums...struck with the violence and calm of a hurricane."

By December of 1945, Parker and Gillespie had replaced Roach in a newly assembled group. Roach then free-lanced in Fifty-Second Street clubs with groups led by Coleman Hawkins, Dexter Gordon, and J.J. Johnson. He recorded with Hawkins for the Sonora label, cutting the album *Coppin' the Bop*. His 1947 Dial recordings with Parker included "Scrapple From the Apple," and "Chasin' the Bird." In 1949, Roach attended a session that became part of Miles Davis's ground-breaking *Birth of the Cool* recordings. That same year, he played on pianist Bud Powell's legendary numbers "Tempus Fugit" and the Latin-influenced number "Uno Poco Loco." Around this time Roach also earned a bachelors degree in music theory from the Manhattan School of Music.

Pioneering Efforts Lauded

In his 1952 work, *A History of Jazz in America*, Barry Ulanov lauded Roach as "a rhythmic thinker; his solos are not like swing drummers', not dependent on sheer noise and intensity to make the point." Known for his crisp and precise rhythmic execution and melodic sense, Roach was in demand as both a performer and studio musician. That same year, he joined Charles Mingus and his wife Celia as co-founder of the Debut record label. This short-lived company recorded not only solo projects by Roach and Mingus, but also those of jazzmen such as Miles Davis, Thad Jones, Kenny Dorham, and J.J. Johnson. In May of 1953 Roach and Mingus, along with Gillespie, Parker, and Bud Powell, took part in an all-star concert at Toronto's Massey Hall. The concert, recorded on-stage by Mingus, was later released as the Debut recording *The Quintet: Jazz at Massey Hall*. In *To Be or Not to Bop*, Roach recalled the concert, "...everybody was in complete command, everybody had a wonderful time. It was a real happy, happy day."

In 1953, Roach arrived in Hermosa Beach, California to replace drummer Shelly Mann in the Lighthouse All-Stars. During the following year, Roach brought trumpeter Clifford Brown from New York to California and assembled a quintet that included Harold Land, pianist Richie Powell, and bassist George Morrow. In *West Coast Jazz*, Ted Gioia noted that Roach and Brown "were about to become the most prominent members in one of the finest—if not best—jazz combos of the early 1950s." From sessions recorded in Los Angeles during August of 1954, the quintet recorded its first LP *Brown and Roach Incorporated*. This release was followed in 1955 by the album *Clifford Brown and Max Roach*.

These recordings received acclaim from both musicians and music critics. Following the departure of Land from the quintet in 1955, Roach and Brown recruited the talents of saxophonist Theodore Walter "Sonny" Rollins. The horns of Brown and Rollins, along with Roach's inventively propulsive drumming, proved to be a brilliant combination. Rollins' recording debut with the group occurred on the 1956 album, *Clifford Brown and Max Roach at Basin Street*. Like the group's earlier recordings, *At Basin Street* showcased Roach's masterful extended solos. The quintet's success, however, was cut short in June of 1956 when Brown and Powell were killed in an automobile accident. "Max used to tell me all the time how he loved playing with Brownie," related Miles Davis in his memoir *Miles*. "His death really got to Max and he didn't pull out of it for a long time."

After the deaths of Brown and Powell, Roach performed in a trio with Rollins and bassist George Morrow. In April of 1956, he appeared on saxophonist Johnny Griffin's album, *Introducing Johnny Griffin*. Two months later, he provided accompaniment for Rollins' groundbreaking solo album, *Saxophone Colossus*. A brilliant showcase of material, this album included "St. Thomas," a Caribbean-inspired number in which, as Ira Gitler observed in the album's liner notes, "Max shines in his featured spot, once again demonstrating his musical approach to the drums." Roach's performance on the album *Blue 7* "shows," as Gunther Sculler commented in *Jazz Panorama*, "that exciting drum solos need not be just an un-thinking burst of energy—they can be interesting and meaningful compositions." In December of 1956 Roach, along with bassist Oscar Pettiford, formed the rhythm section for Thelonious Monk's Riverside album *Brilliant Corners*. Roach's contributions to *Brilliant Corners* included playing the tympani on Monk's classic "Bemsha Swing." As Thomas Fetterling remarked in *Thelonious Monk: His Life and Music*, "[Roach] supplanted his kit with tympani, giving the rather simple theme a powerful allure. During [Sonny] Rollins' solo he makes the tympani thunder." In February of 1958, Roach and Pettiford formed a trio with Rollins for the saxophonist's celebrated Riverside album, *Freedom Suite*.

Advocated for Civil Rights

Roach entered the 1960s committed to the struggle against racism. His outspoken views on race were reflected in the 1960 Atlantic album *We Insist! Freedom Now*. In July of the same year, he joined Mingus in a protest against the cancellation of the Newport Jazz Festival by staging a "rebel festival" at the nearby Cliff Walk Manor Hotel. The alternative event attracted such talents as Coleman Hawkins, Jo Jones, Ornette Coleman, and vocalist Anne Marie "Abbey" Lincoln. Soon after the event, in a 1961 issue of *Down Beat*, Roach boldly stated that he would "never again play anything" that did not "have social significance." That same year, Roach infused the voice of racial protest into his recording of *Percussion Bitter, Sweet*. This album showcased a number of original compositions in the company of such musicians as Eric Dolphy, Booker Little, Julian Priester, Clifford Jordan, and Mal Waldron. Vocalist Abbey Lincoln appeared on the tracks, "Garvey's Ghost," which was dedicated to the Jamaican-born black nationalist leader Marcus Garvey, and the ballad "Mendacity," which sardonically mocked American democracy and its promise of racial equality.

Roach married Abbey Lincoln in 1962 and, over the next decade, the two collaborated extensively, even after the marriage eventually ended in divorce. Trained as a rhythm and blues singer, Lincoln expanded her musical horizons by recording with jazz accompanists. In *Down Beat*, Lincoln described the "handsome, sophisticated," Roach as an inspiring companion who "gave me sanctuary." Devoted to expanding the horizons of African-American music, Roach fused jazz with elements of Negro spirituals to create a voice of artistic expression and social protest. As drummer-bandleader, Roach wrote and arranged choral and orchestral works, the first of which appeared on the album *It's Time* in 1962. In September of the same year, Roach and Mingus provided the accompaniment for Duke Ellington's Blue Note recording, *Money Jungle*. The album, which placed Ellington with "two musicians of the next generation, both of whom idolized him, produced some splendidly forthright, if none too well recorded, playing by all three." remarked Brian Priestly in *Mingus*.

In 1971 Roach began teaching at the University of Massachusetts at Amherst, where he became a key figure in establishing a jazz major. That same year, he recorded *Lift Every Voice and Sing*, (dedicated to Paul Robeson) with a twenty-two member gospel choir. In 1972, he founded the M'Boom, a ten-man percussion ensemble featuring over one hundred different Third World instruments, including vibes, steel pans, marimbas and chimes. In 1979 and 1980, he joined pianist Cecil Taylor for a series of concerts and spent the rest of the decade recording with jazzmen such as Abdullah Abrahim, Cecil Bridgewater, and Odoen Pope. Peter Keepnews of the *New York Times,* remembered the Max Roach Double Quartet of the mid-1980s as perhaps Roach's "most ambitious experiment," for in it Roach gave string musicians equal footing with others in the ensemble, allowing them to improvise and swing as never before. In 1987, Roach further pursued his diverse musical vision by contributing to the score of "Swingin' The Dream" an adaptation of William Shakespeare's "Midsummer's Night Dream." During the following year, he appeared with the Japanese drum troupe Kodo, and became the first jazz musician to win a MacArthur Foundation grant for creative genius.

Throughout the 1990s, Roach was involved in numerous collaborations and creative settings. He recorded the two-CD set, *To the Max!*, in 1992 and performed with the Atlanta Symphony Orchestra. Always attentive to new musical ideas, Roach viewed rap as a creative improvisational form and collaborated with MTV's rap-music host Fab Five Freddie in recording the program *From Bebop to Hip-hop*. Roach's sextet performed with the Abyssinian Baptist choir in 1997. In 1998, Roach performed with his So What Brass Quintet, which was comprised of five brass instruments and drums, and with dancers in choreographer Donald Byrd's production "Jazz Train." He performed live until at least 2001, when he appeared with his Quartet at the 2001 JazzFest in New Orleans. Roach's last recording followed in 2002 with trumpeter Clark Terry. Jazz critic Kevin Whitehead found Roach's style on *Friendship* spare when compared with his dynamic recordings from the 1970s, according to his review of the recording for National Public Radio; yet Whitehead concluded that Roach still "phrases with the clarity and grace of a tap dancer."

Roach's musical career offers a timeline of the creative legacy of modern African-American music. His ability to embrace new musical ideas throughout his career exemplified his vast creative vision and boundless desire to interpret the world around him. While alive, Roach took it as his "mission," commented Ben Sidran in *Talking Jazz: An Oral History*, "to keep the long revolution marching forward to a new beat." He died on August 16, 2007, in New York City. Roach's "superior quality of sound," as Wynton Marsalis observed in a 1988 *New York Times* article about jazz, "is one of the marvels of contemporary music." For his percussive talents, Marsalis described Roach as "a peerless master." For setting standards in American music and for using his music to advocate for his culture, Roach remains a man to be admired.

Selected works

Recordings

Coleman Hawkins, 1944, Classic Records, (France), 1995.
(With Charlie Parker)
The Very Best of Bird, Warner Brothers.
Bird: The Complete Charlie Parker on Verve, Verve, 1989.
The Legendary Dial Masters, Vol. I, Stash, 1989.
Charlie Parker, Swedish Schnapps, (sessions including Roach recorded 1949 and 1951), Verve, 1991.
Charlie Parker, Jazz Masters 15, Verve, 1994.
Yardbird Suite, The Ultimate Charlie Parker Collection, Rhino, 1997.
(With others)
Dexter Gordon, Dexter Rides Again, (1946), Savoy, 1992.
Miles Davis, Birth of the Cool, (1949) Capitol, 1989.
Compact Jazz, Bud Powell, (1949-1950), Verve, 1993.
The Amazing Bud Powell, Vol. 2, (1951), Blue Note, 1989.
The Quintet, Jazz at Massey Hall, (Debut 1953), Original Jazz Classics, 1989.
Clifford Brown, Brownie, (1954-1956), Emarcy, (ten CD box set).
Charles Mingus, Jump Monk, Debut (Debut 1955), Original Jazz Classics, 1990.
Thad Jones, (Debut 1955), Original Jazz Classics, 1991.
Sonny Rollins, Saxophone Colossus, (1956), Prestige, 1987.
Introducing Johnny Griffin, (1956), Blue Note, 1987.
Thelonious Monk, Brilliant Corners, (1956), Original Jazz Classics, 1987.
Sonny Rollins, Freedom Suite, (Riverside 1958), Original Jazz Classics, 1983.
Abbey Lincoln, Straight Ahead, Candid, 1961.
Duke Ellington, Money Jungle, Blue Note, (1962), 1987.
Max and Dizzy: Paris 1989, A & M, 1989.
Friendship, Columbia, 2003.
(As bandleader)
Brown and Roach Incorporated, Emarcy, 1954.
Clifford Brown and Max Roach, Emarcy, 1955.
Clifford Brown and Max Roach At Basin Street, EmArcy, (1956), 1990.
Max Roach Plus Four, Emarcy, (1956-1957), 1990.
Deeds Not Words, Riverside, 1958.
We Insist! Freedom Now, Candid, 1960.
Percussion, Bitter, Sweet, ABC Paramount Impulse! (1962), 1993.
Max Roach with the New Orchestra of Boston and the So What Brass Quintet, Blue Note, 1996.

Films

Blue Note: A Story of Modern Jazz (interviewee), 1997.
How to Draw a Bunny (composer), 2002.

Sources

Books

Bird, The Legend of Charlie Parker, edited by Robert Reisner, Da Capo, 1962, p. 194.
Davis, Miles, with Quincy Troupe, *Miles: The Autobiography*, Simon & Schuster, 1989, p. 204.
Fetterling, Thomas, *Thelonious Monk: His Life and Music*, foreword by Steve Lacey, Berkley Hill Books, 1997, p. 157.
Giddins, Gary, *Chasin' The Bird: The Triumph of Charlie Parker*, Beech Tree, 1987, p. 88.
Gillespie, Dizzy, *To Be, or Not to Bop*, Doubleday & Company, Inc., 1979, pp. 374-75.
Gioia, Ted, *West Coast Jazz: Modern Jazz in California 1945-1960*, University of California Press, 1992.
Gitler, Ira, *Jazz Masters of the Forties*, Collier Books, 1966.
Gitler, Ira, *The Masters of Bebop*, Da Capo, 2001.
Gitler, Ira, *Swing to Bop: An Oral History of the Transition of Jazz in the 1940's*, Oxford University Press, 1985.
Hennesey, Mike, *Klook, The Story of Kenny Clarke*, University of Pittsburgh Press, 1994, pp. 63-64.
Jazz Panorama: From the Birth of Dixieland, From the Pages of Jazz Review, Collier Books, 1958, p. 248.
Korall, Burt, *Drummin' Men: The Heartbeat of Jazz, The Swing Years*, Schirmer Books, 1990, p. 193.
Mathieson, Kenny, *Giant Steps: Bebop and the Creators of Modern Jazz, 1945 65*, Canongate, 1999, p. 125.
Owens, Thomas, *Bebop: The Music and Its Players*, Oxford University Press, 1995.
Priestly, Brian, *Mingus: A Critical Biography*, Da Capo, 1982.
Sidran, Ben, *Talking Jazz: An Oral History*, Da Capo, expanded edition, 1995, p. 77.
Taylor, Arthur, *Notes and Tones: Musician-to-Musician Interviews*, Da Capo Press, 1993.
Ulanov, Barry, *A History of Jazz in America*, Viking, 1952, p. 288.

Periodicals

The Black Perspective in Music, 1990.
Down Beat, March 21, 1968; July 24, 1969; March 16, 1972; September 1989; November 1978; November 1990; February 1992; May 1993; November 1993; November 1998.
Los Angeles Times, August 17, 2007, p. B8.
Musician, January 1994.

New York Times, July 31, 1988, p. A21; August 25, 2007, p. C10.

Philadelphia Tribune, June 12, 1998, p. E2.

Pulse!, November 1992.

Washington Post, August 17, 2007, p. B6.

On-line

"Marian McPartland's Piano Jazz: Max Roach," *National Public Radio,* www.npr.org/programs/piano-jazz/previousguests/summer2007/roach.html (August 27, 2007).

"Max Roach," *DrummerWorld,* www.drummerworld.com/drummers/Max_Roach.html (August 27, 2007).

"Music Review: *Friendship* from Clark Terry and Max Roach," *National Public Radio,* www.npr.org/templates/story/story.php?storyId=1277286 (August 27, 2007).

"Pioneering Jazz Drummer Max Roach Dies at 83," *National Public Radio,* www.npr.org/templates/story/story.php?storyId=12847242 (August 27, 2007).

Other

Liner notes: *Saxophone Colossus*, Prestige, 1956, written by Ira Gitler; *Giants of Jazz: Coleman Hawkins*, Time Life Records, 1979, written by John McDonough.

—John Cohassey and Sara Pendergast

Renee Stout

1958—

Sculptor, mixed-media artist

Renee Stout is an acclaimed artist whose sculptures and mixed-media installations explore human relationships and the roots of her African heritage. Many of her works evoke dreams, memories, spirits, and the need for healing. The power of female sexuality and the search for identity are also central themes, as are critiques of social injustice. Her work has been described as "strange and scary, as well as beautiful and awe-inspiring" by critics, according to Penelope Blair of *Savoy*.

Deeply influenced by African art, Stout uses a wide array of materials, including found objects, in her work. Many of her pieces evoke mystery, or suggest elusive stories. As Stout states on her Web site, "I see each one of my pieces as a fragment or installment in an ongoing narrative that's my contribution to telling the story of who we are as a society at this point in time."

Inspired by Fetish Objects

Born in Kansas in 1958, Stout grew up in Pittsburgh, Pennsylvania, where her first exposure to African art occurred during visits to the city's Carnegie Museum. Interested in drawing since earliest childhood, she received considerable encouragement from her family and, in fourth grade, was invited to attend special classes at the museum for elementary school students. The teacher required students to visit the natural history exhibits and to draw objects on display. One such object, an African figure studded with nails, fascinated Stout. Though she did not understand its cultural significance, she returned to this exhibit whenever she

visited the museum; she was to draw much of her future inspiration as an artist from this introduction to African art.

Stout studied art and trained to be a painter at Pittsburgh's Carnegie-Mellon University. Her first works were in the realist tradition of artists such as Edward Hopper, but Stout soon realized that such an approach would prove too limiting for her creative vision. She wanted to explore spiritual and psychic themes that could not be adequately expressed through realistic renderings of landscapes, buildings, or still lifes on canvas.

After a year's artist-in-residency at Northeastern University in Boston, Stout moved to Washington, D.C. Stout related to Eric D. Bookhardt of *Gambit Weekly* that "Washington made her more aware of her African-American identity, as well as the societal chaos that was all around her in the nation's capital. A painted canvas was no longer enough." In Washington, she discovered the work of found-object artist Joseph Cornell and assemblage artist Betye Saar, and began experimenting with three-dimensional creations, including sculptures inspired by Kongo *minkisi*—African fetish figures believed to possess powers to affect human lives. Her 1988 piece, *Fetish #2*, is a life-size figure made from a plaster cast of the artist's own nude body. As described by Michelle A. Owen-Workman in *Readers, Advisors, and Storefront Churches: Renee Stout: A Mid-Career Retrospective*, the piece is a "veritable study of [Stout's] own existence." The figure stands straight, arms at its sides; it is adorned with various power objects such as small pouches of medicines,

At a Glance . . .

Born in 1958, in Junction City, KS. *Education:* Carnegie-Mellon University, BFA, 1980.

Career: Artist, 1980s–; University of Georgia, Athens, GA, visiting professor, 1995.

Awards: Northeastern University, Afro-American Master Artists in Residency Program, 1984-1985.

Addresses: *Web*—www.reneestout.com.

cowrie shells, dried flowers, a photograph of a baby, and a postage stamp from Niger. The figure, according to Owen-Workman, symbolizes "Stout's ultimate power over her own life and the path to knowledge she was seeking." Part of the Dallas Museum of Art's permanent collection, the piece brought Stout national attention.

In 1993 Stout had her first major solo exhibition, "Astonishment and Power: Kongo Minkisi and the Art of Renee Stout," at the Smithsonian's National Museum of African Art. Holland Cotter observed in the *New York Times* that the show was often "soul-stirring and beautiful." While appreciating the questions that the show raised about the relationship between African and Western art, however, the critic felt that the show did not succeed fully in answering them. Cotter described the potency and "tantalizing presence of hidden substances" apparent in the minkisi, but felt that Stout's pieces were, by contrast, disappointing. "Set beside Kongo examples," Cotter wrote, "her minkisi throw the gulf between the traditional non-Western religious image and the Western art object—however referential, even reverential, that object may be—into clear relief. They are, simply put, spiritual and esthetic worlds apart." The show attracted significant attention and confirmed Stout's stature as an important young artist.

Intrigued by Vodou

Since the late 1980s Stout has continued to explore themes of self-empowerment and healing. In the early 1990s she became increasingly interested in spiritual traditions from Africa, including vodou—a religion that developed in Haiti among West African slaves who combined their native spiritual traditions with influences from Roman Catholicism, the religion of their French colonial masters. A strong expression of the dual traditions of vodou is found in Stout's "Hoodoo Holy" (2000). In the center of this piece is a bottle, ostensibly filled with holy water—part of Catholic ritual. The assemblage also includes written instructions for

making a vodou potion. Inside the bottle, however, is not water but a collection of special aromatic oils. As Owen-Workman observed, "Within one simple image, Stout has created an icon that simultaneously denotes healing, the washing away of sins, and renewal."

Many of Stout's works are associated with two personas that have intrigued her: "Madame Ching" and "Fatima Mayfield." Madame Ching was an old "conjure woman" in Pittsburgh when Stout was a child; though Stout never knew her, the artist often passed Madame Ching's house and was intrigued by the atmosphere of secrecy and spells that surrounded it. As a working artist, Stout developed a character based on Madame Ching but also incorporating the vodou goddess of love and sexuality. Several of Stout's pieces, including "Traveling Root Store" (1995) and "Madame Ching's Love Products" (1995), depict the potions that this character dispenses to her customers, who need help with their love lives. Fatima, whom Stout describes on her Web site as her "alter ego," is a fictional fortune-teller in New Orleans, who inherits her aunt's root store and preserves the healing traditions associated with it. "Fatima's Sign" (2001) is a representation of an advertising sign for this root store. It lists store hours as well as descriptions and prices of the various products on offer: Florida Water, Money Drawing Kits, Wishing Stones, Holy Spirits Bath Set, Abundance Charms, Jinx Removing Bath, Against Envy Powder, She's All Mine Oil, and many more.

A similar work is "Amor II," painted to resemble an old-fashioned poster or magazine advertisement for a product called "Lover's Incense." Words at the bottom state that "Fatima Recommends!" several additional products, including Mt. St. Helens Ash (For Men) and Wine of Erzulie. In an interview with Stout in *Black Artists of D.C. Newsletter,* Toni Nelson admired the humor in these works, and admitted that they are so realistic that "I was personally getting ready to go to Fatima's on Florida Avenue." What particularly attracted her to African religions, Stout told Nelson, is that "women are essential to the whole worldview of balance. I am affected by the fact that there's no femininity in the world today."

Made Political Statements

Stout has also made work with more overt political content. "Point of View" (1994) critiques the media for presenting inaccurate images of African Americans and other ethnic groups. The three-dimension piece includes a black-and-white photograph of a black man aiming a gun directly at the viewer; at the bottom are pieces of street trash such as bullet casings, a crack bag, and cigarette butts. Text on the back of the piece reads: "The man who posed for this picture is actually a Maryland mailman and art collector. When he is off duty he likes to wear baggy clothes because they are comfortable. Women often clutch their purses when they pass him on the sidewalk."

Another three-dimensional piece, "The Chairman Watching the Game" (1997), expresses outrage at the role of powerful multinational corporations in instigating violence in such places as Rwanda. The piece is structured as a sort of board game, with the figure of the chairman watching from above as black and white soldier figures enact a game. The two black figures, who point guns at each other, are identified as Hutus and Tutsis; the white figures are the "Gang of 8"—a reference to the Group of 8 nations with the largest economies. Included in the piece are such game instructions as "Finance Civil War 40 pts; Encourage Hanging of Dissenters 60 pts; Destroy Culture 100 pts."

A series of Stout's works address the need for gun control legislation. She began by making an actual gun for herself—an act she hoped would reveal how to work anger into her art. As Stephen Bennett-Phillips explained in *Readers, Advisors, and Storefront Churches*, "It was Stout's way of holding-up the viewer, jolting him or her into asking why it was there." Stout went on to create guns for other figures she esteemed as revolutionaries, such as South African political leader Winnie Mandela as well as historical figures, including ex-slave and Underground Railroad leader Harriet Tubman and Latin American guerilla fighter Che Guevara. Other pieces in the series include "Baby's First Gun" (1998), a satirical response to school shootings, with cute images of a baby and a gun as a toy. None of the guns in the series contain actual working parts.

Stout has enjoyed several solo exhibitions across the United States, and her work is included in the collections of major museums, including the Metropolitan Museum of Art, New York City; the Corcoran Gallery of Art, the National Museum of American Art, and the National Gallery of Art, Washington, DC; Rhode Island School of Design; and the Detroit Institute of Arts. As Sarah Valdez observed in an *Art in America* review of a 2002 exhibit, "Stout immerses herself in the notion that there's more going on in the world than meets the eye. She is tuned in to a powerful domain of secrets and souls that just might trump the logic of the material world."

Selected works

Solo exhibitions

Astonishment and Power: Kongo Minkisi and the Art of Renee Stout, 1993.

Dear Robert, I'll See You at the Crossroads, 1995.
Madam's Secrets, 1996.
Dueling Dualities, 1997.
Rantings in the Night Studio, 1999.
Readers, Advisors, and Storefront Churches, 2002 and 2005.
Fatima's Dreams, 2003-2004.
Fragments of a Secret Life, 2005.
Church of the Crossroads, 2006.

Sources

Books

Contemporary Women Artists, St. James Press, 1999.
Farrington, Lisa E., *The Herstory of Black Art Creating Their Own Image The History of African-American Women Artists*, Oxford University Press, 2005.
Owen-Workman, Michelle A., and Phillips, Stephen Bennet, *Readers, Advisors, and Storefront Churches: Renee Stout: A Mid-Career Retrospective*, University of Missouri-Kansas City, 2002.

Periodicals

Art in America, January, 2002, p. 111.
Gambit Weekly (New Orleans, LA), August 16, 2005, p. 41.
New York Times, July 18, 1993, p. A27.
Savoy, Spring 2005, p. 84.
Washington Post, October 20, 2005, p. C5; January 26, 2006, p. H1.

On-line

"Ms. Herb Doctor Is In," *Best of New Orleans*, www.bestofneworleans.com/dispatch/2004-06-08/art_review.html (August 8, 2007).
Renee Stout, www.reneestout.com/ (August 8, 2007).
"Renee Stout," *Smithsonian American Art Museum*, http://americanart.si.edu/search/artist_bio.cfm?ID=6586 (August 8, 2007).
"Unapologetic and Infinite BLACK Found! Exhibit Charts New Ground for DC Artists," *Black Artists of D.C. Newsletter*, http://blackartistsofdc.org/EL01Summer06.pdf (August 8, 2007).

—E. M. Shostak

Tamar-kali

1973(?)—

Vocalist, songwriter

Brooklyn singer/songwriter Tamar-kali plays primarily hard rock and hardcore punk rock—which makes her unusual in a white-dominated field. But she refuses to be categorized or restricted by racial boundaries. "I've never heard something I dug, and then after I saw who the messenger was said, 'Oh, I don't like it anymore.' You know what I mean? Either you feel it or you don't," Tamar-kali told Cheryl Corley of National Public Radio. One of New York City's most consistent club draws, Tamar-kali has been involved in a variety of projects that attest to her creativity and her faith in her own musical instincts.

Born around 1973, Tamar-kali is a native of Brooklyn. Her stage name refers to the Hindu goddess Kali, who is associated with both violence and sexuality. As a child, Tamar-kali spent summers in the Sea Islands region of South Carolina, home to the Gullah or Geechee culture, a form of African-American culture that preserves West African traditions to an unusually strong degree. Her debut extended-play album was called *The Geechee Goddess: Hardcore Warrior Soul.* Tamar-kali's attraction to the arts grew partly from loneliness. She immersed herself in music, and she later wished she had bought even more music than she did. "I was so isolated as an only child with both parents," she recalled to Mike Believe of the *Exit the Apple* Web site. "I wish I had taken advantage of all that time alone; it was a perfect time to collect."

By 1992, Tamar-kali had begun performing around New York. Among her first ongoing gigs was as a member of the durable band Funkface, a multicultural and multiracial group whose music fuses James Brown-style funk, hard rock guitars, and Jamaican reggae. Tamar-kali found herself especially drawn to the rock aspect of the group's sound. "This is about a music that spoke to me…very clearly around the time [I was] about 19, where I think a lot of young African-American people in America start questioning their identity, looking towards their history," she told Corley. "And hardcore definitely was a music that I could express my frustrations and the anger that you originally come to when you learn from your history and you're dealing with society's ills and things like that."

Seeking out chances in New York's hardcore scene (hardcore is a generally more intense variant of punk rock), Tamar-kali signed on with an all-male band called Song of Seven. She became the lead singer after the band's former vocalist joined the top-rank punk group the Bad Brains, whom Tamar-kali had grown up listening to. At times, the experience of being a black woman in the world of hard rock was isolating, and Tamar-kali gravitated toward other African Americans who liked the music. "It's like you meet someone and you're like, 'Omigod, you're one, too,'" she told Teresa Wiltz of the *Washington Post.* "Oh my God, I'm not a freak. Thank God."

Along the way, she made ends meet by doing day jobs she didn't particularly enjoy. Once, she told Believe, she was hired to hand paint "some ugly…statues, you know the, tchotchke kind that your tacky Aunt Gracie got all over the house, clowns, geisha girls. I didn't last a full day and the fumes were crucial." Later she found work that was more to her liking: teaching belly dancing. "Folks have been getting a purely sexual

At a Glance . . .

Born c. 1973 in Brooklyn, NY; married to Greg Tate, a journalist and organization executive.

Career: Musician, 1992–; joined band Funkface, 1993; worked as belly dance instructor; formed production company, Flaming Yoni Productions.

Addresses: *Office*—Flaming Yoni Productions, 1151 Dean St., Suite 4B, Brooklyn, NY 11216. *Web*—www. flamingyoni.com/home.html.

interpretation" of that ancient art form, she pointed out to Believe, but for Tamar-kali belly dancing was more a celebration of the life force as manifested in women's bodies than just an erotic dance.

Tamar-kali's own personal style also had spiritual overtones. "My body is a work of art," she explained to Joy Duckett Cain of *Essence*. The artwork encompassed 16 separate body piercings, including those in navel, tongue, and breasts, and at least seven tattoos representing meaningful symbols in the artist's life. As she recalled to Cain, "My piercings and tattoos are never contrived."

Some people suggested, Tamar-kali told Cain, that she was emulating the culture of whites, in which body modification was more common than among African Americans. "No. I'm on that Masai stuff," she retorted. "I'm on that Cherokee stuff. I'm on that Mohawk stuff. I'm doing what some brothers and sisters set the path for me to do; I'm just following the path. I think of myself as a contemporary tribalist. It's still all about the tribe, no matter how we try to get away from it."

Tamar-kali's distinctive style served her well when she began to launch a solo career in the early 2000s. In the words of her Web site biography, "her strength as a woman in a male-dominated genre led to creative conflict and compelled her toward her own expression as a writer and vocalist." Known in the New York music industry for her soaring voice, which combined rock and gospel qualities, she sang backup for such acts as the alternative rock band Fishbone and the innovative Atlanta hip-hop duo Outkast. By 2005 she had formed a production company of her own, Flaming Yoni Productions, and released *The Geechee Goddess: Hardcore Warrior Soul*.

A major push forward to Tamar-kali's career came when she was one of four artists featured in the nationally distributed documentary *Afro-Punk: The Rock' n' Roll Nigger Experience* (2003). That project, combined with her debut album and her uninhibited live shows, often placed her in the featured listings of New York's entertainment publications in 2005 and 2006. In the summer of 2005 she opened for jazz giant Cassandra Wilson at a SummerStage concert held in New York's Central Park. Her fame spread beyond New York with an appearance at the National Black Arts Festival in Atlanta in 2004 and later in other cities.

Tamar-kali returned in 2006 with a trio of new projects: *5ive Piece* is a rock-oriented recording, while the singer described *Pseudoacoustic* as "inspired by such genius lamentors as [jazz singer] Nina Simone, [melancholy French pop vocalist] Edith Piaf, [Belgian singer-songwriter] Jacques Brel, and [and alternative rocker] Kate Bush." On *Psychochamber Ensemble est. 1998* Tamar-kali headed an all-female string group composed of electric and acoustic bass, viola, violin, and cello; the band performed versions of songs from *5ive Piece* as well as original string compositions. This varied group of projects seemed likely to further Tamar-kali's reputation as one of the New York music scene's most original figures. Tamar-kali is married to Greg Tate, a columnist for *Vibe* magazine and the co-founder of the Black Rock Coalition.

Selected discography

The Geechee Goddess: Hardcore Warrior Soul, Flaming Yoni, 2005.
5ive Piece, Flaming Yoni, 2006.
Pseudoacoustic, Flaming Yoni, 2006.
Psychochamber Ensemble est. 1998, Flaming Yoni, 2006.

Sources

Films

Afro-Punk: The Rock 'n' Roll Nigger Experience (documentary), 2003.

Periodicals

Essence, May 2001, p. 164.
Newsday, May 18, 2005, p. A14.
Washington Post, July 15, 2000, p. C1.

On-line

Tamar-kali, www.flamingyoni.com/home.html (August 12, 2007).
"Tamar-Kali: geechee goddess," *Exit the Apple,* http://exittheapple.com/fresh/index.php/2004/ Tamar-kali (June 14, 2007).

Other

"Tamar-kali: A Punk Artist with Soul," *News & Notes,* National Public Radio, www.npr.org/templates/ story/story.php?storyId=9238260&ft=1&f=1039, March 30, 2007.

—James M. Manheim

Tampa Red

1904(?)-1981

Blues vocalist, musician

Although his name is rarely mentioned today among the pantheon of blues greats, Tampa Red was one of the most influential musicians in the history of the blues. He was one of the first bluesmen to migrate to Chicago, and he played a key role in the city's blues music scene for many years. "It's Tight Like That" and his other entertaining "hokum"-style hits recorded with pianist "Georgia Tom" Dorsey were important milestones in the transformation of the blues from a rural folk music to a form of modern urban entertainment. And he was the first African-American musician to record using a resonator-type Hawaiian steel guitar, introducing a new musical vocabulary to blues instrumental work. Tampa Red's importance was recognized by African-American audiences in his own time—he recorded some 335 78 rpm records, more than any other blues artist. Reissues have helped illuminate his recorded legacy, but he remains a blues artist ripe for rediscovery.

Tampa Red was born Hudson Woodbridge in Smithville, Georgia, probably on January 8, 1904; he himself gave various birthdates to investigators. His parents, John and Elizabeth Woodbridge, died when he was young, and he and his brother Eddie were sent to live with a grandmother with a surname of Whittaker in Tampa, Florida. He took her family name for official purposes. The nickname that stuck once he went on the road came from the city of his upbringing combined with his light skin or the red hair some recalled (surviving black-and-white photographs seem to show him with dark hair). Tampa Red had his first lessons on the guitar from his brother, a local performer, and he picked up some pointers from a street musician named Piccolo Pete.

When blues recordings by Mamie Smith and Gertrude "Ma" Rainey began to hit the market in the early 1920s, Tampa Red, who could play guitar, piano, and kazoo, added more licks to his style and began to play in honky-tonks around Florida, going as far afield as St. Augustine. By the mid-1920s he had moved north to Chicago, anticipating a massive migration of blues musicians to the city's South Side. Soon he was performing on the streets and in the new bars that were springing up to serve blacks who had found work in Chicago's rail yards, slaughterhouses, and steel mills. He met another musician from the Southeast, pianist Tom Dorsey (unconnected with bandleader Tommy Dorsey), who called himself Georgia Tom. Dorsey had begun accompanying Rainey and other female blues artists on recordings, and he steered similar work toward Tampa Red.

In 1928 the pair was signed to the Paramount label by its canny talent scout, J. Mayo Williams, and the two immediately hit paydirt with the 78 rpm single "It's Tight Like That." The sound of the recording was something new in the world of the blues, distinct from either the raw emotion of the rural Southern guitar blues or the regal power of Bessie Smith and the other queens of the urban stage. Tampa Red's vocals were smooth, sly, and almost half-spoken as he rendered the song's mildly raunchy lyrics, put together from a slang expression of the day and bits of various earlier blues songs.

At a Glance . . .

Born Hudson Woodbridge on January 8, 1904 (an approximate date, as Woodbridge offered various dates) in Smithville, GA; married Frances; died on March, 19, 1981, in Chicago, IL.

Career: Street and club musician, Chicago, mid-1920s; teamed with Tom Dorsey as Tampa Red and Georgia Tom, 1928; Paramount label, recording artist, 1928; Vocalion label, recording artist, 1928-32; Bluebird label, recording artist, 1934; RCA Victor label, recording artist, 1945; odds jobs mostly outside of music industry, 1953-60; Bluesville label, recording artist, 1960.

Awards: Blues Foundation Hall of Fame, inducted 1981.

The record reputedly sold five million copies, and between 1928 and 1932 Tampa Red and Georgia Tom frequently toured and reentered the studio to record similar material such as "Sellin' That Stuff" and "No Matter How She Done It." The upbeat new style soon had its own name, hokum, and the pair sometimes recorded under the name of the Hokum Boys. Tampa Red himself enjoyed a varied performing and recording career, sometimes using other names such as Jimmy Eager or Honey Boy Smith. Some called him, "the guitar wizard," and blues historian Gérard Herzhaft opined in the *Encyclopedia of the Blues* that "when one listens again to his best recordings of 1928, their modernism is striking." His National-brand steel guitar was as influential as his vocals, and a host of other bluesmen, including Son House, Bukka (Booker) White, Bo Carter, Blind Boy Fuller (Fulton Allen), Peetie Wheatstraw, and Scrapper (Francis Hillman) Blackwell, took up the instrument in the wake of his success.

Recording companies slashed their release schedules during the economic depression of the early 1930s, putting an end to the high-flying career of Tampa Red and Georgia Tom. Dorsey, in the wake of personal tragedy, renounced secular music and went on to a gospel career as Thomas A. Dorsey, composing "Peace in the Valley," "Take My Hand, Precious Lord," and other classic religious numbers. But Tampa Red bounced back in the blues field, signing with the budget-priced Bluebird label in 1934. With black record buyers suffering the effects of the depression, Tampa Red's 35-cent Bluebird discs (as opposed to 75 cents for a mainline RCA-label release) caught on fast. He branched out from straight blues, such as his standard "Anna Lou Blues," into swing, boogie, and other related styles.

Settling into a durable gig at Chicago's C&T Club in the late 1930s, Tampa Red played in various combinations with guitarist Big Bill Broonzy and pianist Big Maceo (Maceo Merriweather), among other up-and-coming blues musicians. The home of Tampa Red and his wife, Frances (for many years located near the corner of State and 35th streets in the heart of the South Side), was a frequent stop for aspiring blues musicians, especially because of his friendship with key blues producer Lester Melrose; the house also served as temporary lodging and rehearsal space for the up-and-comers who made Chicago blues a household phrase.

Tampa Red's popularity flowered anew after World War II as he worked with a new generation of young players, including pianist Sunnyland Slim (Albert Luandrew), at such clubs as the Purple Cat. In 1945 he signed with the RCA Victor label, an association that lasted through 1953. A new wave of influence from Tampa Red spread through the blues repertory as his 1949 hit "When Things Go Wrong for You (It Hurts Me Too)," a harbinger of a new emotional complexity in the blues, was famously covered by guitarist Elmore James. Other rising stars, including B.B. King and Robert Nighthawk, also covered Tampa Red's songs.

In 1953 Tampa Red's wife, Frances, died. He was hit hard emotionally, and his career suffered—she had also served as his business manager. His struggles with alcohol worsened, and several times in the late 1950s he was hospitalized several times. In the early 1960s he reemerged with a trio of albums on Chicago's Bluesville label, but the polish that had propelled his career for so long worked against him in the authenticity-prizing musical atmosphere of the 1960s. Living on the South Side, he eventually drifted out of music completely, and in 1974 he was placed in Chicago's Sacred Heart Nursing Home. He died penniless on March 19, 1981, in Chicago, and was buried in nearby Glenwood. Posthumous honors included induction into the Blues Foundation Hall of Fame and reissue of his complete recordings on Austria's Document label, but his contributions to the blues tradition remain imperfectly understood.

Selected discography

Don't Tampa with the Blues, Bluesville, 1961.
Don't Jive with Me, Bluesville, 1961.
How Long, Bluesville, 1963.
Complete Recorded Works, 15 vols., Document, 1991-93.
Bluebird Recordings, 1934-1936, Bluebird, 1997.
Essential, Classic Blues, 2001.
Blues: Slide Guitar Wizard, Chicago 1931-1946, Fremeaux & Associés, 2004.

Sources

Books

Contemporary Musicians, volume 25, Gale, 1999.

Harris, Sheldon, *Blues Who's Who,* Arlington House, 1979.

Herzhaft, Gérard, *Encyclopedia of the Blues,* 2nd ed., trans. Brigitte Debord, University of Arkansas Press, 1997.

Russell, Tony, *The Blues—From Robert Johnson to Robert Cray,* Schirmer, 1997.

On-line

"The History of the Blues Slide Guitar," *South Australian Roots and Blues,* www.sablues.org/features8.htm (July 15, 2007).

"Tampa Red," *All Music Guide,* www.allmusic.com (July 15, 2007).

"'Tampa Red' Whittaker," *Georgia Encyclopedia,* www.georgiaencyclopedia.org/nge/Article.jsp?id=h-1662 (July 15, 2007).

—James M. Manheim

Tamara Tunie

1959—

Actress

Tamara Tunie established a successful acting career with major roles on stage, in television, and in films. Since 1987 she has appeared in the daytime serial, *As the World Turns*. In addition, she has been a member of the cast of the prime-time series, *Law & Order: Special Victims Unit*, since 2000. Balancing her television work with film and stage roles, Tunie has become known as one of the busiest and most versatile African-American actresses of the early 2000s. In addition to her acting work, Tunie has also blossomed into a successful producer of Broadway productions.

Tunie, Tamara, photograph. Brad Barket/Getty Images.

to pursue a career in the arts. She won a scholarship to Carnegie Mellon University, where she studied drama and earned a B.F.A. in 1981. She then moved to New York City and began seeking acting work, with the help and support of her acting coach, Billie Allen. In 1982 Tunie landed a role in the musical *Lena Horne: The Lady and Her Music*, in which Horne starred. It was a thrilling experience for the young actress to work onstage with Horne, an icon of African-American musical theater and one of Tunie's personal idols.

Tunie enjoyed what she has described as a happy, normal childhood—though some of her friends were initially afraid to play at her house. She grew up with her four siblings above the family's funeral home in McKeesport, Pennsylvania; both of her parents were morticians. She considered it quite normal, she confided to *Ebony* interviewer Kevin Chappell, to live above dead people and learn not to play noisily during wakes. But "sometimes it was tough getting my friends to come over."

Though Tunie thought of becoming a doctor, she fell in love with performing while in high school and decided

By the mid-1980s Tunie had found steady work in television. In 1987 she was cast as Jessica Griffin Harris, a district attorney on the daytime serial *As the World Turns*. Her portrayal of Harris as a strong, successful professional woman gained the actress a strong fan base as well as critical acclaim, and Harris became one of the most popular characters on the series. Having established her importance to the series, Tunie worked hard to persuade its writers to create a role for Allen. The writing team was persuaded and wrote Allen into the show as Harris's mother, Louise. In an interview on Pittsburgh's WPXI, Tunie observed that she enjoyed playing a character who got to

At a Glance . . .

Born on March 14, 1959, in McKeesport, PA; married Greg Generet (second marriage). *Education:* Carnegie Mellon University, BFA, 1981.

Career: Actress.

Memberships: Figure Skating in Harlem, vice-chair.

Awards: Antoinette Perry Award, co-producer, 2007, for *Spring Awakening*.

Addresses: *Office*—c/o *As the World Turns*, CBS-TV, Inc., 524 West 57th Street, Suite 5330, New York, NY 10019.

investigate interesting things, adding that "What I love about it is that the cops always have to come to me for the answers, and I tend to have them."

Tunie landed a role on the prime-time hit series *NYPD Blue* in 1994, playing Lillian Fancy, wife of police lieutenant Arthur Fancy. She appeared in this recurring role through 1997, but the part never became more than a supporting one and it was eventually phased out. Meanwhile, Tunie had left *As the World Turns* in 1995 to pursue a wider range of acting opportunities. She landed parts in several feature films, working with such noted actors as Al Pacino, Keanu Reeves, and Charlize Theron in *The Devil's Advocate* and with Samuel L. Jackson in *Eve's Bayou,* in which she was cast as the narrator. Tunie also appeared in a small role in *Snake Eyes*, working with director Brian de Palma and a cast that included Nicolas Cage, Gary Sinese, John Heard, and Luis Guzman.

Within a year after returning to *As the World Turns* in 1999, Tunie found herself juggling roles in both daytime and prime-time series. In 2000 she joined the cast of *Law & Order: Special Victims Unit*, playing medical examiner Melinda Warner. She was prosecuting criminals by day as a passionate district attorney, and conducting forensic examinations on victims of sex crimes by night. In addition, Tunie was cast in a third series, *24*, in which she played Counterterrorism Unit (CTU) division director Alberta Green during the cult hit's first season in 2001. Working on this show, Tunie told the WPXI interviewer, was particularly exciting for her because the program broke so much new ground in the television medium.

Tunie worked with Samuel L. Jackson again in the film *The Caveman's Valentine*, playing the wife of Jackson's character, a paranoid schizophrenic who lives in a cave in New York City who becomes involved in a murder investigation. In 2007 she was in negotiations to play U.S. Ambassador Rebecca Lacie in *The Koi Keeper*, a film about the abduction of the young daughter of U.S. diplomats in Bangkok.

Though television and film roles have kept Tunie busy, she has also found time to do theater work. In 1995 she played Helen of Troy in the New York Shakespeare Festival production of *Troilus and Cressida*. That same year she appeared with Denzel Washington in an acclaimed production of *Julius Caesar* on Broadway. Tunie added another Shakespeare production to her resume in 2000 when she starred as Cleopatra in the New Jersey Shakespeare Festival production of *Antony and Cleopatra*. Reviewing this play for the *New York Times*, Alvin Klein noted Tunie's "thoroughly modern, trendy allure" in this role.

In 2006 the rock musical *Spring Awakening*, which Tunie co-produced, opened on Broadway. It heralded a promising new direction for Tunie's theater career. The show, directed by Michael Mayer and choreographed by Bill T. Jones, was a sensation, winning eight Tony Awards, including best musical. It also won four Drama Desk Awards, including Outstanding Musical, as well as the New York Drama Critics Circle Award for best musical.

Following this spectacular success in her first project as a producer, Tunie signed on as a co-producer of the Broadway production of *Radio Golf*, the last work by Pittsburgh playwright August Wilson. Tunie told *Pittsburgh Post-Gazette* writer Christopher Rawson that she would love to act in a Wilson play, but that "I think this [producer] was the role I was [meant] to play" in bringing Wilson's work to Broadway. "I'm passionate about Pittsburgh and theater, and August Wilson comprises both," she added. "My agenda is to bring as much African-American support to the table as possible." As co-producer, Tunie said, she hoped to be able to market the play successfully and attract substantial African-American audiences—including those who do not regularly attend plays. Critics hailed *Radio Golf* as a humane work that celebrated the dignity in ordinary lives. "*Radio Golf* is the coda to a magnificent and heroic life work that illuminated the historic destiny of former slaves and free men still enslaved," wrote John Heilpern in the *New York Observer*. "It gave shattering voice to the voiceless; it created leading roles for underemployed black actors of unsurpassed talent and brought an African-American audience into a predominantly white Broadway.... Theater will never forget August Wilson."

Aside from her career in entertainment, Tunie lives a full life. She lives in New York City with her second husband, Greg Generet, and serves as vice-chair of Figure Skating in Harlem, a not-for-profit organization that provides skating instruction and other opportunities for girls in Harlem.

Selected works

Films

The Devil's Advocate, 1997.
Eve's Bayou, 1997.
Snake Eyes, 1998.
The Caveman's Valentine, 2001.
The Koi Keeper, 2007.

Television

As the World Turns, 1987-1995, 1999—.
Law & Order: Special Victims Unit, 2000—.
24, 2001.

Theater

Lena Horne: The Lady and Her Music, Broadway, 1982.
Troilus and Cressida, New York Shakespeare Festival, 1995.
Julius Caesar, Broadway, 1995.
Antony and Cleopatra, New Jersey Shakespeare Festival, 2000.

Producer, *Spring Awakening*, Broadway, 2006.
Producer, *Radio Golf*, Broadway, 2007.

Sources

Periodicals

Ebony, August 1, 2005.
New York Observer, May 22, 2007.
New York Times, September 23, 2000; May 20, 2007.
Pittsburgh Post-Gazette, March 28, 2007.

On-line

"*As the World Turns*: Tamara Tunie," *CBS*, www.cbs.com/daytime (July 31, 2007).
"Interview with Tamara Tunie," *WPXI*, www.wpxi.com/video/11424606/index.html (July 31, 2007).
"Tamara Tunie," *Hollywood.com*, www.hollywood.com/celebrity/Tamara_Tunie/1121411#fullBio (July 31, 2007).

—E. M. Shostak

Gene Washington

1947—

Football player, business executive

Gene Washington made his name on the field as a wide receiver for the San Francisco 49ers in the 1970s, but he made his mark after leaving the gridiron, becoming one of professional football's most high-profile executives. His success reflected a philosophy that he expounded upon in a speech he gave at Stanford University in 2004 entitled "How to Make Black America Better." "If you want to compete in the real world, you're going to face a lot of 'isms'—sexism, racism, nepotism, and you've got to be as educated as you can be," as quoted by the *Daily Stanford*. He pointed to the examples of business leaders such as Kenneth Chenault of American Express and Stanley O'Neal of Merrill Lynch who relied on education to become successful and wealthy. "If you want political equality, you better have some money," he continued according to the *Daily Stanford*. "Money is the mother's milk of politics." He concluded by encouraging young African Americans to look to these business leaders, not professional athletes, for truly inspiring role models.

Played a Decade of Professional Football

Gene Washington was born on January 14, 1947, in Tuscaloosa, Alabama. After graduating from high school, he headed to California's Stanford University in part to take advantage of the school's commitment to integrate minorities into their student body. Though he was just one of 25 African-American students on a campus of 10,000, Washington blazed trails, becoming the first black member of the Delta Tau Delta fraternity

as well as an All-American on the football field. As a wide receiver for the Stanford Cardinals, Washington was one of the school's most valuable players. For three games in the 1968 season, he was the game leader in receiving yards. That year, he also set the school's all-time receiving record with a total of 1,117 yards. Two decades later, when the Stanford Athletic Hall of Fame was established, Washington was inducted as a member.

After graduating in 1969, Washington entered the National Football League (NFL) professional football draft and was selected 16th overall in the first round by the San Francisco 49ers. As a wide receiver, he again proved his merit with 1,100 receiving yards in 1970 and an average of 745 yards per season over his 49'ers career. His skill earned him repeated spots on the league's All-Star team and he played in four consecutive Pro Bowls from 1969 to 1972. In 1979, after nine years with the 49'ers, Washington was traded to Detroit. After a less than spectacular season with the Lions, he retired from professional football and moved back to California.

As a football star in California, Washington was often tapped to appear in films and televisions series. In 1972, he had a recurring role as a football player on the detective drama *Banacek*. The same year, he appeared on *The Mod Squad*. In 1974, he had another recurring role on *McMillan & Wife*. On the big screen, Washington played bit parts in several blaxploitation films of the 1970s including *The Black Six, Black Gunn,* and *Lady Cocoa.* In the 1980s, Washington returned to Stanford in an administrative posi-

At a Glance . . .

Born on January 14, 1947, in Tuscaloosa, AL; children: Kelly and Daniel. *Education:* Stanford University, 1969.

Career: San Francisco 49ers, wide receiver, San Francisco, CA, 1969-78; Detroit Lions, wide receiver, Detroit, MI, 1979; Stanford University, assistant athletic director, mid-1980s-1993; National Football League (NFL), director of football development, 1993; director of football operations, 1994–.

Memberships: Goodrich Petroleum Corporation, director, 2003–; Delia's Inc., director, 2006–; National Park Foundation, board member; New York Bancorp Inc., director; Home Federal Savings Bank, director.

Awards: *Sports Illustrated,* Most Influential Minorities in Sports, ranked 29th, 2003, 25th, 2004; Stanford Athletic Hall of Fame, inductee.

Addresses: *Office*—National Football League Inc., 280 Park Ave., New York, NY 10017.

tion with the athletics department. By the early 1990s, he had risen to the position of Assistant Athletic Director. In that role, he also co-founded the school's Athletic Hall of Fame. It was also during this time that Washington befriended Stanford's then-provost, Condoleezza Rice, who went on to become the Secretary of State under George W. Bush.

Enforced Discipline and Fair Play on the Field

In 1993, Washington was hired as the Director of Football Development for NFL. That role was expanded to Director of Football Operations the following year. The position required that he move to New York City, headquarters of the NFL. By that time, he had married and divorced and his two children, Daniel and Kelly, stayed behind with their mother in California. In addition to overseeing all aspects of the game of football within the NFL, Washington's job entailed one duty that earned him a lot of derision in the sports press. He was responsible for the on-field conduct of the players. Sports writer Dan Patrick noted on ESPN.com, "It's Washington's job to monitor what's appropriate and professional versus outlandish and immature." In effect, Washington became the NFL's disciplinarian.

Working with a team of NFL officials, Washington established codes of conduct that covered everything from the height of a player's socks to his behavior in the end zone. Dancing, taunting, and slow-motion foolery were banned. Washington explained to *South Coast Today*, "You'd have that kind of celebration every game, every time someone scored." It not only took away from the dignity of the sport but, more importantly, wreaked havoc with live coverage where minutes of air-time costs tens of thousands of advertising dollars. Though these measures caused both fans and players to snicker that the NFL had become the "No Fun League," a move against unwarranted violence on the field brought success. "We feel there's no place in the game for extracurricular hits," Washington told *The Sporting News*. In response to pot shots and fighting, Washington hit back where it hurt: the players' pockets. He issued dozens of five-figure fines to players in response to unfair hits. It seemed to have worked. By 2001, the NFL reported a reduction in the number of helmet-to-helmet hits on quarterbacks.

When not monitoring players, Washington built a high profile away from the field. He joined the boards of directors of several organizations including New York Bancorp, Goodrich Petroleum Corporation, the Home Federal Savings Bank, and the National Park Foundation. In 2003, he returned to Stanford to help their business school create the NFL-Stanford Executive Education Program executives in the football league. He also began giving motivational speeches on African-American success. However, Washington received some of his most persistent celebrity due to his friendship with Rice. He accompanied her to several White House events including a 2007 dinner with Queen Elizabeth II. "Talking to the Secretary of State and the Queen of England, that's not like talking to first-round draft picks in the green room," he quipped to *NFL.com*. "That's nice, of course. But as we say in Alabama, this was really high cotton." Whether rubbing shoulders with world leaders or overseeing the nation's football players, Washington too fulfills this old Southern saying which translates as doing very well indeed.

Sources

Periodicals

Sporting News, November 21, 1994.

On-line

"NFL Well Represented at State Dinner," *NFL.com,* www.nfl.com/nflnetwork/story/10172460 (July 20, 2007).
"NFL Head Stresses Individual Responsibility in 'Black America,'" *Daily Stanford,* http://daily.stanford.edu/article/2004/2/27/

nflHeadStressesIndividualResponsibilityInBlackAmerica (July 20, 2007).

"Washington Hits Hard, Plays Fair," *ESPN.com*, http://espn.go.com/talent/danpatrick/s/2002/1022/1449438.html (July 20, 2007).

"Where to Draw the Line in the NFL," *South Coast Today*, http://archive.southcoasttoday.com/daily/12-01/12-10-01/c12sp113.htm (July 20, 2007).

—Candace LaBalle

Carrie Mae Weems

1953—

Photographer, artist

In a career spanning two decades, photographer Carrie Mae Weems has garnered impressive art world success. Her works—more than a dozen major series and hundreds of individual pieces—explore issues of racism, sexism, and oppression, and blend the boundaries of history, anthropology, and beauty. Using both fine photography and vernacular text, Weems shocks, seduces, and shames. "My responsibility as an artist is to work, to sing for my supper, to make art, beautiful and powerful, that adds and reveals; to beautify the mess of a messy world, to heal the sick and feed the helpless; to shout bravely from the rooftops and storm barricaded doors and voice the specificity of our historical moment," Weems said of her work, according to the *Women in Photography International* Web site. Her body of work is an eloquent testament to the belief that activism and beauty are not opposing forces. Her work has been shown and collected by prestigious institutions including The Whitney Museum of American Art, The Museum of Modern Art (MOMA), The Getty Museum, and the National Museum for Women in the Arts. She has received numerous awards including a National Endowment for the Arts and has been the subject of a documentary series on creativity.

Found Artistic Voice Through Photography, Folklore

Descended from Mississippi sharecroppers, Carrie Mae Weems was born in 1953 in Portland, Oregon, where her parents had migrated before she was born. Her father worked in tanning factory to support the family which included Weems's mother, brother, and sister. After graduating from high school, Weems moved to San Francisco where she hoped to study modern dance. Fate intervened in the form of a camera, a gift she received on her 21st birthday. Then working in a clothing factory, Weems first turned her lens on the activities of union organizers, documenting the labor unrest brewing in the late 1970s. Ardently political, she viewed the camera as a tool of activism. Weems was inspired to expand into art, however, after coming across a book of photographs by black photographers. She enrolled at the California Institute of the Arts and earned a bachelor's in fine arts in 1981.

Weems continued directly into graduate school at the University of California in San Diego, earning a master's degree in photography in 1984. Her thesis exhibition gave the first hint that Weems possessed a unique, powerful vision. Entitled "Family Pictures and Stories," the series of works merged black-and-white photography with text in order to explore the history of her sharecropping family and their migration Northward. In greater context, the series gave visual context to the legacy of thousands of black American families who migrated away from their Southern pasts to pursue dreams in the North. The unintended result, and a major factor motivating Weems, was the loss of their historical roots. The sharecropper was a direct descendent of the slave, another factor influencing the work. A reviewer writing for *Artforum International* noted, "For Weems, this slave past, with all its intimations of Africa, is central to black experience, and it forms a leitmotif running through her oeuvre."

Weems's incorporation of text with photography was inspired by *The Sweet Flypaper of Life*, a 1955 collaboration of two influential Harlem Renaissance artists, writer Langston Hughes and photographer Ray DeCarava. The book offered intimate portraits of life in Harlem accompanied by equally tender text. Weems was also influenced by the writer and anthropologist Zora Neale Hurston who published black folklore and wrote fiction using black American dialect. Weems pursued this influence further, enrolling in the University of California at Berkeley where she earned a master's in folklore in 1987. That same year, she debuted "Ain't Jokin'," a series of portraits of proudly posed black subjects juxtaposed against the harsh text of racist jokes. Her next series, 1998's "American Icons," featured elegant still lives of ugly artifacts—household items and advertisements featuring racist stereotypes. Photos of Aunt Jemima salt-and-pepper shakers and Uncle Tom dolls illustrated, "how casually hate-based culture seeps into our homes and consciousnesses," noted a review in *Art Papers*.

Used Beautiful Imagery to Explore Ugly Realities

By the 1990s, Weems had begun to make a name for herself in the art world, working as a visiting professor or an artist-in-residence at art centers and schools throughout the country, as well as participating in dozens of group and solo exhibitions. However, her first major artistic acclaim came with her 1990 series, "Untitled (Kitchen Table Series)," a set of large-scale black-and-white photographs featuring a black woman (portrayed by Weems) and a kitchen table. Accompanied by text panels, the series evoked themes of love, desire, longing, and domesticity, revealing the complexities inherent in the everyday life of a black woman. "I was trying to respond to a number of issues," Weems told the on-line journal *ChickenBones*, "Woman's subjectivity, woman's capacity to revel in her body, and woman's construction of herself, and her own image." Received with almost unanimous acclaim, the series cemented Weems's status as an emerging artistic force.

Weems's 1991 series "Colored People" challenged color classifications with a collection of oversized Polaroid photos of black-skinned people of various shades further tinted by Weems's own pen. She assigned them names such as "Honey Colored Boy," "Golden Yella Girl," and "Blue Black Boy." Her 1992 "Sea Islands Series" explored the Gullah culture still evident on the islands located just off the Georgia and South Carolina coasts. A stopping point for slave ships, the Sea Islands became home to African-American communities that maintained close ties with their African ancestry. The series evoked their rich cultural past through beautiful, moody photography and sparse, dialect-driven text printed on ceramic plates, each beginning with the phrase, "Went looking for Africa."

Enthusiastic response to Weems's work led to her first retrospective, an overview of her art from 1978 to

1992. Inaugurated at the National Museum of Women in the Arts in 1993, the show marked the first time the museum featured a solo show by an African-American artist. Of the retrospective, the *Washington Post* wrote, "Over the course of this show we see Weems make photographic images of ever greater formal beauty and narrative intensity." The exhibition later traveled to eight contemporary musuems around the country including Museum of Modern Art in San Francisco, the Contemporary Arts Center in Cincinnati, and the Portland Art Museum in Oregon. Positive reviews in each place, further established Weems's national reputation. Topping off this success, Weems was awarded a prestigious National Endowment of the Arts grant in 1994. She was also named the 1994 Photographer of the Year by the San Francisco Ansel Adams Center.

Earned Artistic Acclaim and International Fame

Weems's subsequent work refined what *Art in America* called Weems's "come-hither look followed by a sucker punch." Through evocative photography, provocative text, and a variety of medium including etched glass, richly patterned wallpaper, flowing fabric banners, and seductive audio recordings, Weems continued to seduce the viewer with imagery before challenging them with cultural, racial, sexual, and historical inconsistencies and shame. The 1995 series "From Here I Saw What Happened and I Cried" was created in response to a Getty Museum exhibit of photos of black Americans from the late 19th century. The 32 photographs, some posed by Weems, others adapted from the Getty collection, were tinted blood red and encased behind thick glass etched with harshness. One photo of a proud-faced black woman in a fine gown says, "They said you were the spitting image of evil."

In 1998, Weems's exhibition "Ritual and Revolution" traveled overseas to the Dak'art Biennale of Contemporary Art in Dakar, Senegal and to a private gallery in Berlin, Germany. The series, which also toured the United States, featured sheer banners suspended from the ceiling printed with photos of monuments and memorials, prisoners and protesters. Throughout the gallery, an audio loop of Weems's voice said "I was with you." The implication, according to the *Boston Herald,* was that "every monument to colonial victory shrouds an untold human story, of individual lives led in history's daunting shadow." In 1999, along with pop art star David Hockney and music legend Max Roach, Weems was featured in the PBS series *Behind the Scenes,* which explored the creative process. That same year, she was also the subject of a retrospective at the Everson Museum in Syracuse, New York. Featuring her works since 1992, the exhibition took the viewer on an evocative journey through what *Art in America* called "meditations on the politics of culture."

In 2000, Weems completed "The Hampton Project" in reaction to a series of photos from 1900 that documented the education of African Americans at Hampton University. Weems's work featured original photographs, printed banners, and audio loops juxtaposed against some of the photos from 1900, as well as images from modern history, including black students being hosed by white police officers in Alabama. She followed this with the 2002 series "Dreaming in Cuba" which offered photographic commentary on the attempt to live orderly domestic lives under the shadow of political and economic disorder. 2003's "The Louisiana Project," commemorating the Louisiana Purchase, featured the artist as muse leading the viewer through the complex history of Louisiana and its swamp-tangled roots of racism. By 2004, Weems had begun to incorporate video into her repertoire, debuting the films *Coming Up for Air* and *May Days Long Forgotten.* She told *Art Papers* that video represented, "an amazing shift that allows us to finally negotiate the space between museum culture and popular culture." For an artist who has successfully highlighted the nation's complex, often ugly socio-political history through the creation of seductive, achingly beautiful art, the move to video may well find Weems making the leap from art house activism to broad cultural impact.

Selected works

Solo exhibitions

Biennale of Contemporary Art, Galerie Nationale d'Art, Dakar, Senegal.
Contemporary Arts Museum, Houston, TX.
International Center of Photography, New York, NY.
J. Paul Getty Museum, Malibu, CA.
Museum of Modern Art, New York, NY.
Museum of Modern Art, San Francisco, CA.
National Museum of Women in the Arts, Washington, DC.
2nd Johannesburg Biennale, Africus Institute for Contemporary Art, Johannesburg, South Africa.
Whitney Museum of American Art, New York, NY.

Sources

Periodicals

Art in America, June 1996, p. 103; May 1999, p. 122.
Art Papers, September/October 2004.
Artforum International, February 1993, p. 79.
Boston Herald, December 3, 1999, p. 11.
New York Times, December 22, 1995; May 22, 1998; August 11, 2000, p. E34.
Washington Post, January 7, 1993.

On-line

"Carrie Mae Weems," *Charles Guice Contemporary,* http://charlesguice.com/artists_cmw.html (July 16, 2007).

"Carrie Mae Weems," *ChickenBones: A Journal for Literary & Artistic African-American Themes,* www.nathanielturner.com/carriemaeweems.htm (July 16, 2007).

"Carrie Mae Weems," *PPOW Gallery,* www.ppowgallery.com/artists/CarrieMaeWeems/bio.html (July 16, 2007).

"Distinguished Photographers 2005 Award," *Women in Photography International,* www.womeninphotography.org/Events-Exhibits/DistinguishedPhotog/CarrieMaeWeems_2005/Weems.html (July 16, 2007).

—Candace LaBalle

Alek Wek

1977—

Model, author, humanitarian

Wek, Alek, photograph. AP Images.

Sudanese model Alek Wek represents a fresh, 21st-century attitude from within the fashion industry and the images it sends out into the world about who or what is beautiful. Wek, possessing far darker skin than her African-heritage supermodel predecessors, was called "the hottest face in fashion" by *Newsweek*, and her late 1997 appearance on the cover of one of the world's leading fashion magazines was a virtual media event in itself. Like other top models, the Sudanese Wek is statuesque, but as a writer for *People* magazine enthused, "few have her smile, and none have Wek's dramatically cropped hair, cherubic cheeks and flawless coal-black skin that has set the modeling world abuzz." A keen businesswoman, Wek used her singular fame on the catwalk and magazine covers to launch her own accessories and handbag company, and to call for humanitarian aid for her homeland.

Fled War-Town Hometown

A writer for the *New York Times*, Constance C. R. White, interviewed Wek shortly after her appearance on the November 1997 cover of *Elle* and found that "the only thing more startling than her 5-foot-11- inch ebony beauty is her erudite humor and self-assuredness." A less-than-storybook life may account for some of that poise. Wek was born in Wau, Sudan, on April 16, 1977, one of nine children born to a southern Sudan family of Dinka heritage. A civil war that erupted in the mid-1980s interrupted their relatively placid lives in their home-town, and as a result of the conflict, Wek's father, a teacher, was injured and went to the Sudanese capital of Khartoum for medical treat-ment. When the fighting near their home worsened, Wek talked her way onto a military plane that was taking refugees out of the area and to Khartoum. She was just ten, had nothing on her except the clothes she was wearing—and left her mother and brothers and sisters behind. "We couldn't all go together," Wek recalled in an interview with *People*, "so I decided I had to go on my own."

Fortunately, the rest of the family were able to join her in Khartoum soon afterward, and they grieved together when their father died. At that point, an older sister of Wek's living in London launched a complicated process to get her siblings out of the country. Only Alek, her

At a Glance . . .

Born on April 16, 1977, in Wau, Sudan; daughter of Athian (a teacher) and Akoul (a social worker) Parak. *Education*: Attended college in London, England, mid-1990s.

Career: Ford Models, New York City, model, 1996; IMG Models, New York City, model, 1997–; Alek Wek 1933 Ltd., founder, 2001; W.E.K., Working to Educate Kids, non-profit organization, founder 2006.

Awards: MTV, Model of the Year, 1997; *i-D Magazine*, Model of the Decade, 1997.

Addresses: *Agent*—IMG Models, 304 Park Ave S, New York, NY 10010. *Web*—www.alekwek1933.com.

mother, and one other sister made it to England as refugees; the other siblings landed elsewhere in Europe. Since leaving Khartoum, Wek and her family have never been reunited all at once because all possess various travel restrictions on their visas.

From Street Fair to Catwalk

Wek's transition from the Sudan to parochial school in London as an immigrant was not an easy one in the early 1990s. Classmates teased her because of her looks. "It was painful to be called names," she remembered in the interview with *People*, but pointed out that she refused to become discouraged, and that after just being herself for a while, "they got used to me." By 1995, Wek was a college student enjoying a street fair in London one day when someone approached her and asked if she was interested in modeling; Wek refused to take the stranger seriously at first, but the woman was with Models One, a top London agency. Intrigued, Wek then had some professional photos taken, and suddenly saw herself in an entirely new light: as she told *People*, her first reaction to the images was, "Oh, my God, this is me!" Her only obstacle to launching a modeling career was convincing her mother to let her abandon her college studies.

Wek was quickly offered plum assignments, assuaging any worries her mother might have had. She appeared in some British and Spanish fashion magazines, and arrived in New York City in June of 1996. Her long legs, dark skin, and clipped hair adorning a near-sculptural head excited interest there as well, but she has been adamant about not being barricaded into the "tribal" category. Initially signed with Ford Models, Wek grew unhappy with the way management "sold"

her to clients. When her agent decamped to IMG Models, Wek followed. "Some people at said I would never sell, I was too dark," Wek told the *New York Times*'s White. Some also predicted she would never win any cosmetics advertising jobs, but then Wek landed an assignment to represent makeup artist Francois Nars's new product line.

Soon international cosmetics giant Clinique was courting Wek as well, as were designers Isaac Mizrahi and Moschino. She appeared on runways in New York, Paris, and Milan throughout the rest of the year and into 1997, and also had cameos in videos from Janet Jackson and Busta Rhymes. But it was her appearance on the November 1997 cover of *Elle* magazine that made Wek one of the hottest models in the industry: despite gains made by all women of color against lingering beauty stereotypes, black models still landed on the covers of top magazines only infrequently. Furthermore, the ones that did were more likely lighter-skinned women such as Naomi Campbell or Tyra Banks.

Started Media Stir

Elle's editor, Gilles Bensimon, shot the cover himself, putting Wek in white on a white background. With the starkly contrasting colors, Bensimon was trying to project the idea "'Nobody is out, everybody is in,'" as he told the *New York Times*'s White. "I thought, if I was African-American, I never would see myself in magazines," Bensimon reflected. Yet the fact that Wek is not actually African-American has caused somewhat of a stir, and though the *Elle* cover incited an onslaught of extremely positive reader mail at the magazine, her agent at IMG does receive some negative letters. Some find fault with Wek's look, seeing her rise as evidence of a new form of stereotype from the other end of the spectrum, the "primitive" or "exotic" tag. Wek, who refuses to appear at model calls that ask for black models, is perplexed that her rise to the upper echelons of the fashion industry has generated controversy. "I can't understand the fuss," Wek told *Newsweek*'s Allison Samuels. "In my village there is no problem because we all look the same. Here there is so much difference in skin—so much is thought about it, and that's sad." Yet the controversy paled in comparison to her growing fame. Wek "really opened up the way for anyone to come after," explained Candace Matthews, president of ethnic hair care company SoftSheen-Carson, to Megan Scott of the *Seattle Times*. Indeed, Wek landed such mainstream recognition as an MTV honor as Model of the Year in 1997 and a listing among *People* magazine's 50 Most Beautiful People in 1999.

After a decade of "turning the fashion industry's idea of marketable beauty on its head," as Denise Campbell of *Black Enterprise* put it, Wek broadened her own horizons. She started AlekWek1933 Ltd in 2001 to offer her own line of fashion accessories and handbags.

The 1933 in her company's name honors the year her father, Athian, was born. "My father passed away when I was 12," Wek explained to Marc Karimzadeh of *WWD.* "I didn't want to remember him how he died—[1933] is more a celebration of life. It would have been amazing for him to see me and the opportunities I have had." A great honor to her father, Wek also formed her company to express her own deep interest in design, which she'd nurtured for years. "I wanted to have a medium that would allow the artist in my heart to evolve," Wek told Campbell. She involved herself in all aspects of design and production, creating bags—made of find Italian leathers, alligator, lamb, and even canvas—that ran the gamut in style from chic and formal to casual and sporty. Wek also appeared in her first film, *Four Feathers,* in 2002.

Wek did not take her growing celebrity lightly. She understood the great distance she had come from her time as a refugee. After her first return trip to Sudan in 1998, Wek offered a steady stream of support to her homeland. Witnessing tremendous devastation in Sudan on a trip in 2004, Wek set herself on a mission. "[S]eeing what the war destruction has done to the country and to the people triggered a call in my head that I've got to come back and do something," Wek recalled to Lauren Johnston of *Newsday.com.* She launched a non-profit organization called W.E.K. (Working to Educate Kids) in 2006 to provide educational opportunities to children in New York City and Sudan. She also determined to share her own story to inspire others. Her autobiography *Alek: From Sudanese Refugee to International Supermodel* was published in 2007. "Let fashion not fool you," Wek said to *People* contributor Charlotte Triggs. "There's a bigger world out there than our small bubble where we feel so fabulous. The best thing that this industry has given me is a voice. So in a way, it's my responsibility

to give back and shed light on a place where the people are voiceless."

Selected works

Books

Alek: From Sudanese Refugee to International Supermodel, Amistad/HarperCollins, 2007.

Films

Four Feathers, 2002.

Sources

Periodicals

Black Enterprise, September 2006, p. 170.
Ebony, September 2007, p. 32.
Newsweek, November 24, 1997, p. 68.
New York Times, November 16, 1997, sec. 9, p. 2.
People, February 2, 1998; September 3, 2007, p. 101.
Seattle Times, May 3, 2006, p. F5.
WWD, July 23, 2001, p. 7.

On-line

"Alek Wek: From Refugee to Supermodel," *Newsday.com,* www.newsday.com/entertainment/ny-alek0912,0,5585408.story (September 12, 2007).
"Fashion: Alek Wek: Model Profile," *New York Magazine,* http://nymag.com/fashion/models/awek/alekwek/ (September 12, 2007).

—Carol Brennan and Sara Pendergast

Emil Wilbekin

1968—

Journalist

Wilbekin, Emil, photograph. Lawrence Lucier/Getty Images.

Emil Wilbekin served as editor in chief of the immensely successful *Vibe* magazine for four years between 1999 and 2003, and helped bring the publication to a wider audience who were seeking more in-depth coverage of African-American music and culture than was available in other magazines. Wilbekin had been with *Vibe* since its launch in the early 1990s, and later moved on to a position with Ecko, the urban apparel brand. One of a few openly gay black men who are also trendsetters in the realm where rap and hip-hop music intersect with fashion, Wilbekin notes that his sexual orientation was seldom an issue. "There's this philosophy in hip-hop about keeping it real, whatever you are," he explained to *New York Times* journalist Lynda Richardson, "that you represent that, and that you are honest about that. Being honest about being openly gay is not a problem."

Wilbekin was born in 1968 in Cincinnati, Ohio. His father, Harvey, had just left his first career as a structural engineer with the city to attend law school and enter private practice, and his mother, Cleota, was also an attorney. Wilbekin and his brother Erik were often teased by classmates when they were teens for their household's resemblance to the fictional family por-

trayed on the hit NBC sitcom of the era, *The Cosby Show*. In high school, Wilbekin served as president of the local Jack and Jill chapter, a nationwide social organization for African-American teens. His relatively prosperous and safe upbringing did not place him that far out of the orbit of most rap and hip-hop music movers and shakers, he told Richardson in the *New York Times*. "The thing that is interesting about hip-hop is that a lot of hard-core rappers are from very middle-class households," he noted.

Wilbekin graduated from Hampton University, his father's alma mater, in 1989, and went on to Columbia University's Graduate School of Journalism in New York City. Following his second degree, he remained in Manhattan and worked for a number of publications in a short span of years either as an in-house editorial associate or freelancer, including *Metropolitan Home* and the Associated Press. He began at *Vibe* magazine in 1992, just a few months before its debut issue arrived on newsstands the following year. The respected music-oriented magazine was founded with the help of legendary record producer Quincy Jones, and quickly became a must-read for its solid coverage of entertainment-industry figures such as Michael Jackson, Jennifer Lopez, Snoop Dogg, and

At a Glance . . .

Born in 1968, in Cincinnati, OH; son of Harvey E. (a lawyer government official) and Cleota (a lawyer; maiden name, Proctor) Wilbekin. *Education:* Earned degrees from Hampton University, 1989, and the Columbia University Graduate School of Journalism.

Career: Freelance writer, editorial associate, or stringer for *Metropolitan Home,* Associated Press, the *Chicago Tribune,* and *People* magazine, early 1990s; *Vibe* magazine, writer, 1992-95, fashion editorial director, 1995-97, and editor in chief, 1999-2003; Vibe Ventures, editorial director and vice president for brand development, 2003-2004; Marc Ecko Collection, vice president for development, and member of editorial board for *Complex* magazine, July 2004–. Contributor to the *New York Times, Rolling Stone,* and *Emerge.*

Memberships: American Society of Magazine Editors (ASME), board member; Design Industries Fighting AIDS (DIFFA), board member; 24 Hours for Life, board member; Brotherhood SisterSol, board member.

Addresses: *Office*—Ecko, 40 W. 23rd St., New York, NY 10010.

Run DMC. Though it focused on African-American urban music and culture, *Vibe* lured readers from all ethnic groups.

Wilbekin held various editorial positions at *Vibe* as its circulation numbers climbed, and was named fashion editorial director in 1995. Over the next four years, under his direction, *Vibe* increased its fashion coverage with a focus on African-American trendsetters and black-owned companies, such as Sean Jean, the label founded by musician and label-owner Sean "Diddy" Combs, and Baby Phat, a similar venture launched by Kimora Lee Simmons and her music-mogul husband Russell Simmons. *Vibe*'s new emphasis on fashion lured additional readers and boosted the number of advertisers on its pages.

Wilbekin was named editor in chief of *Vibe* in 1999, and the publication continued to be a revenue source for its parent company, Miller Publishing, with him at the helm. In 2002 *Vibe* won a National Magazine Award from the American Society of Magazine Editors in the General Excellence category for magazines with circulation between 500,000 and 1 million readers. It beat out stiff competition for the industry honor, including *Wired* and the *New Yorker,* and the win also

marked the first time that a publication aimed at an African-American readership had won in the General Excellence category. It remained, however, a magazine focused on music, with Wilbekin explaining in the May 2002 interview with the *New York Times* that "*Vibe* is like what *Rolling Stone* was to rock 'n' roll in the 70's. In *Vibe,* most of our coverage is urban or black, but we also look at the world broadly from a global perspective. We really consider the magazine multicultural."

There were a few critics of *Vibe,* however, who found the magazine's editorial voice just not as politically aware as some thought it could be for an African-American publication with such wide influence in the community. A *Village Voice* article titled "Fronting for the Enemy: Gay Men Who Make Homophobic Rappers Look Good," examined the dichotomy presented by the fact that rap lyrics from some artists were blatantly homophobic, though music-industry executives and the stylists who made them look good for the album covers and magazine features in *Vibe* and other publications were often gay. The writer, Chris Nutter, even singled out Wilbekin for being an openly gay man running a magazine that regularly placed some of the most homophobic recording artists on its cover. "I have the power to raise questions about it, but it's not my job to police every album and tell every rapper they're doing something wrong," Wilbekin said in his defense.

In 2003, Wilbekin left his position as *Vibe*'s editor in chief to become editorial director and vice president for brand development with Vibe Ventures, the magazine's branding division. He left a year later to work for the Marc Ecko Collection as a vice president for development, but continued to be invited onto media outlets as an expert commenter on the subjects of African-American culture, music, and fashion. He remains best remembered in the industry, however, for his long tenure at *Vibe* at a time when African-American pop music was playing an increasingly prominent role in mainstream American life. Asked if he objected to being hailed as a "urban visionary," he replied, "I actually think it's very appropriate," he told Kerrie Frisinger in an interview for the *Daily Press* of Newport News, Virginia. "I saw something greater for urban life and culture than the artists and producers saw for themselves."

Sources

Daily Press (Newport News, VA), November 13, 2004.
Mediaweek, May 20, 2002, p. 41; July 14, 2003, p. 32.
New York Observer, August 16, 1999, p. 6.
New York Times, May 17, 2002; May 20, 2003; June 17, 2004.
Village Voice, June 20, 2001.
WWD, August 10, 2000, p. 4B; September 30, 2003, p. 12.

—Carol Brennan

Frederick B. Williams

1939-2006

Minister

Frederick B. Williams was an influential Harlem minister and canon in the Episcopal Church. For three decades before his death he presided over an historic congregation in New York City whose base, the Church of the Intercession, was a national landmark. During those years he worked tirelessly to bring federal and state funds to the ailing neighborhoods that surrounded his parish, and became an unofficial spokesperson against racism in all forms. The *New York Times* paid tribute to Williams in an obituary written by journalist Douglas Martin, who called him a minister "whose preaching ranged from proper Episcopalian to old-fashioned Gospel, but whose wisecracks were pure New York."

Williams was born in Chattanooga, Tennessee, on April 23, 1939, to parents Walter and Matlyn, and came into his teen years as an intellectual prodigy who entered Morehouse College in Atlanta at the age of 15. After graduating in 1959, he spent a year at Howard University before enrolling at General Theological Seminary in New York City to earn a second undergraduate degree, this one a Bachelor of Sacred Theology. The Seminary was the oldest institution in the United States for the training of ministers in the Episcopalian faith, the church that is the American branch of the worldwide Anglican Communion, whose mother church is the Church of England.

After graduating in 1963, Williams was ordained and assigned to St. Luke's Episcopal Church in Washington, D.C., and in 1966 became the rector of St. Clement's Episcopal Church in Inkster, Michigan, a predominantly African-American suburb of Detroit.

During his six years there, Williams became active in a nationwide group of black Episcopalian ministers, an organization that took formal shape in 1968 with their co-founding of the Union of Black Clergy and Laity (UBCL) of the Episcopal Church, which sought to eradicate institutional bias in the church. At its inaugural meeting, Williams was elected a UBCL vice president, a post from which he continued his reform efforts.

In late 1972, Williams was named the newest rector of the Church of the Intercession in New York City. This Episcopal congregation dated back to the 1840s and met in a famous neo-Gothic building at the border of Harlem and Washington Heights in Manhattan, where Broadway and West 155th Street intersect. At the time, the Church of the Intercession was a chapel of Trinity Church, located much further south in Manhattan on Wall Street, an arrangement that stretched back several generations, and its congregation had just 500 members. The surrounding neighborhoods were falling into serious decay, and many of the longtime elite New York families who were once its members had fled to the suburbs. Williams set to work revitalizing the landmark church, which included attracting new members and finding funds to repair the disintegrating building. In 1976, the Church of the Intercession once again became a separate parish. Its members now included future New York City mayor David N. Dinkins and his family.

Williams was one of first African-American religious figures to publicly discuss the threat of Acquired Immune Deficiency Syndrome (AIDS), speaking out as

At a Glance . . .

Born Frederick Boyd Williams on April 23, 1939, in Chattanooga, TN; died on April 6, 2006, in New York, NY; son of Walter Howard and Matlyn (Goodman) Williams. *Education:* Morehouse College, BA, 1959; attended Howard University, 1959-60; General Theological Seminary, Bachelor of Sacred Theology, 1963; Colgate-Rochester Divinity School, DMin, 1975. *Religion:* Episcopal.

Career: St. Luke's Episcopal Church, curate, Washington, DC, 1963-65; St. Clements Episcopal Church, Inkster, MI, rector, 1966-72; Union of Black Clergy and Laity of the Episcopal Church, co-founder, 1968, and second vice president; Harlem Congregations for Community, co-founder, 1986, and chair during the 1990s; Episcopal Divinity School, Jones lecturer, 1999; Diocese of Botswana, Africa, honorary canon; Church of the Intercession, rector; Episcopal Divinity School, visiting professor, 2000-2003; General Theological Seminary, adjunct professor.

Awards: Most Venerable Order of St. John of Jerusalem, 1999; recipient of several honorary degrees.

early as 1985 and once even organizing a conference of 50 prominent religious authorities, of whom just 15 attended. By the mid-1980s his church pastorship was blossoming into a more community-inclusive activism around Harlem; a time when New York City's historic black neighborhood had become a watchword for urban blight. The church also stood near Harlem's border with the equally challenged area of Washington Heights, with a predominantly Hispanic population. In 1990, a major New York City hospital, St. Luke's-Roosevelt, announced it would shutter its maternity ward at Amsterdam Avenue and 114th Street, located in the Harlem-adjacent neighborhood of Morningside Heights, and transfer the 42 beds to a more centrally located Midtown campus of the hospital. Williams led the successful campaign to keep the maternity ward in the area, arguing that urban neighborhoods like his had the highest infant mortality rates in the United States. "If they move these services, it means that there will be no more babies cared for in a reasonable and responsible manner in Harlem," the *New York Times* quoted him as saying.

Williams was also a vocal supporter of an African-American teenager named Lemrick Nelson Jr., who was tried and acquitted for the 1991 slaying of Yankel Rosenbaum. Rosenbaum was a Jewish rabbinical student from Australia who was slain during the infamous Crown Heights riots in Brooklyn in 1991, when tensions between African-Americans and conservative Lubavitcher Jews reached a crisis point. Nelson, who was 16 at the time of the stabbing, was acquitted on criminal charges, but prosecutors filed a wrongful-death suit against him following that for violating Rosenbaum's civil rights. Williams raised money for Nelson's legal defense fund, and he publicly excoriated authorities for what many in the black community perceived as blatant bias fueled by the protests and political clout of the Jewish community in the city. "There is almost a blood lust in the air," *New York Times* reporter Joe Sexton quoted Williams as saying as the 1994 federal court trial was underway. "This is a legal lynching." The U.S. Attorney General's office even opened an investigation into charges of misconduct on the part of prosecutors for pursuing a second indictment against Nelson.

Williams was a co-founder of the Harlem Congregations for Community Improvement (HCCI), a coalition of some 90 other churches who pooled the resources of their congregations to improve the area with the help of state and federal dollars. He chaired the HCCI for a number of years, and oversaw one of its first major triumphs: the completion of nearly 2,000 new housing units in 1994 in the Bradhurst area of north Harlem, many of them earmarked for low-income residents. In addition to his church duties and community work, Williams also taught at his alma mater, the General Theological Seminary, and was a visiting professor at the Episcopal Divinity School in Cambridge, Massachusetts, from to 2000 to 2003.

Williams's parish prospered under his leadership. Its membership numbers had doubled in the two decades since he took over. The noted South African cleric Bishop Desmond Tutu, a friend of his, sometimes presided over services at the Church of the Intercession on visits to the United States. Williams died of a heart attack on April 6, 2006, at the age of 66.

Sources

Periodicals

New York Times, February 9, 1968, p. 57; October 15, 1970, p. 29; March 5, 1990, p. B1; June 13, 1990, p. B2; January 6, 1994, p. B1; August 18, 1994; April 8, 2006, p. C10.

—Carol Brennan

Mattiebelle Woods

1902-2005

Journalist

For more than half a century, newspaper columnist Mattiebelle Woods documented the vibrant black social scene in Milwaukee, Wisconsin. Her columns not only kept Milwaukee's African Americans up-to-date on black groups, clubs, and social events, but helped to promote community unity and pride. Warm, sincere, and spirited, Woods became a beloved figure in her home city and beyond as she devoted her seemingly endless energy to supporting charities, working for voting rights, and building self esteem in African-American youth. Her lifelong love of fun and festivity prompted friend and fellow journalist Eugene Kane to write in the Milwaukee *Journal Sentinel* upon her death, "For her, there was nothing better than a crowded room filled with talk and music, old friends or new friends and names to put in the newspaper. Remembering the late, great Mattiebelle Woods, I can imagine her first words in heaven: 'What time does the party start?'"

Mattiebelle Woods was born on October 31, 1902, in Louisville, Kentucky, the only child of Ira and Annabelle Woods. When Woods was around three, the family moved to the city of Milwaukee, on the shore of Lake Michigan. Though she was not born there, Woods would always consider herself a native of Milwaukee.

Annabelle Woods worked as a cleaner, both at the historic Astor Hotel and in the homes of wealthy German immigrants. She often brought her daughter with her to work, and Woods grew up in the company of these white families. She attended West Division high school in Milwaukee, and, at the age of 19, married George Beard. Soon after the marriage, Beard

was killed in an automobile accident, leaving Woods alone with their baby daughter Kathryn. She worked at a variety of jobs to support her small family and married again in 1925. That marriage ended in divorce, and Woods determined to remain on her own, saying with characteristic playful directness: "The second husband cured me of marriage," as quoted in *Jet*. After her divorce, she returned to using her maiden name, though she would not change it back legally until 2004.

By the 1940s, Woods had raised her daughter to adulthood, and she began to look for other places to devote her considerable energy. Already very concerned about the welfare of her people, she became involved in the earliest phases of the civil rights movement. She also began to write for local black newspapers. Though she had never attended college or studied journalism, Woods was a natural writer who had a lively style and a genuine interest in people. In 1952, she introduced the column that she would write continuously for the next five decades. "Partyline," an account of club meetings, social events, and parties in Milwaukee's black community, was first published by the Milwaukee edition of the African-American weekly the *Chicago Defender*.

In addition to her column in the *Defender*, Woods wrote for the *Milwaukee Star*, another local African American publication, and worked as a freelance Milwaukee correspondent for the prominent national magazines *Jet* and *Ebony*. Though much of her writing was devoted to covering the activities of her own community, Woods met and interviewed many famous

At a Glance . . .

Born Mattiebelle Woods on October 31, 1902, in Louisville, KY; died on February 17, 2005; married George Beard, 1921 (widowed); married 1925 (divorced); children: Kathryn Bedford. *Religion:* African Methodist Episcopal Church.

Career: *Milwaukee Globe, Milwaukee Star,* society reporter and columnist, 1940s; *Chicago Defender,* Milwaukee edition, society reporter and columnist, 1952-?; *Jet Magazine,* freelance contributor, 1956-?; *Ebony Magazine,* freelance contributor, 1956-?; *Milwaukee Courier,* society columnist and editor, 1964-2005.

Selected memberships: National Association for the Advancement of Colored People; United Negro College Fund, chair, 1954; Urban League.

Selected awards: NAACP, President Award, 2002; Wisconsin Black Media Association, Lifetime Achievement Award; Wisconsin Legislature, 2005 Senate Joint Resolution 6 Honoring Mattiebelle Woods, 2005; Black Women's Network, Woman of Color Honoree, 2005; Milwaukee Press Club, Legend of Milwaukee, 2007.

people, including W.E.B. DuBois, Eleanor Roosevelt, Ray Charles, and Martin Luther King, Jr., who stayed at her house when he visited Milwaukee.

Some readers who did not know Woods and her fierce devotion to supporting her community approached her column with a scornful attitude, assuming that the social events she wrote about were of little importance. Woods responded to these critics by pointing out that most black people could not hope to see their name printed in the white press unless they had been arrested. By printing the names and celebrating the activities of ordinary black citizens, Woods hoped to increase pride and self-confidence within her community and to foster lasting connections by publicizing African-American culture.

Woods expressed her hopes and vision for her community in her other activities as well. Beginning with her early civil rights work during the 1940s, she became deeply involved in voter registration programs, insisting that voting was a civic duty of all concerned citizens. A staunch member of the Democratic Party, she campaigned for progressive black candidates and worked at the polls during elections. She also worked in a wide variety of charitable organizations, becoming co-chair of the United Negro College Fund in 1954.

Of her many civic activities, Woods was perhaps most devoted to nurturing and supporting the young people in her community. A mentor and adviser to many generations of Milwaukee's black youth, she used her words and her example to promote confidence and self-esteem among young people who often had little other encouragement to believe that they could succeed. Hoping to encourage self-respect and poise among African American girls, she founded and directed the Ms. Bronze Milwaukee pageant in 1955 and the Miss Black Teen Wisconsin contest in 1970. Woods became such an important figure in the city she loved that, on her 98th birthday, Milwaukee mayor John Norquist proclaimed "Mattiebelle Woods Day."

Though she devoted herself to many serious causes, Woods also loved to have a good time. Five feet tall and petite, she attended many of the social events she wrote about, usually wearing an elegant evening gown and high heels. Even into her old age, she was renowned as an agile dancer. At the age of 101, she wowed the audience when she appeared on television's *Showtime at the Apollo* and performed the "electric slide" on stage, dropping to the floor and rising again effortlessly.

Mattiebelle Woods died in Milwaukee on February 15, 2005. She was 102 years old, and, during the last week of her life had typed out her final "Partyline" column on her typewriter as she had every week for over fifty years. The Tuesday before her death was an election day, and she had assisted at the polls as usual. She had been a dynamic public figure in her adopted city for decades, and her death made an impact on the entire Milwaukee community. Mayor Tom Barrett mourned her loss with the rest of the city, saying, "She went a hundred miles per hour for a hundred and two years," according to *JS Online*. Woods's unique contribution to documenting the life of Milwaukee's black community was honored in 2006 when the J. William and Mary Diederich College of Communication at Milwaukee's Marquette University established the Mattiebelle Woods Scholarship.

Sources

Periodicals

Jet, November 15, 2004, pp. 60-4; March 14, 2005, p. 57.
New York Amsterdam News, March 3-9, 2005, pp. 10-11; October 12-18, 2006, p. 10.

On-line

"Journalist and Activist Mattiebelle Woods," *U.S. Senator Herb Kohl,* www.senate.gov/~kohl/press/statements/2005303507.html (June 5, 2007).

"Milwaukee Legends Announced at City Birthday Party," *Milwaukee Press Club,* http://72.14.253.104/search?q=cache:UnXLEFFf5fwJ:www.milwaukeepressclub.org/news/view/24+mattiebelle+woods&hl=en&ct=clnk&cd=27&gl=us&client=firefox-a (June 5, 2007).

"100 Miles Per Hour For 102 Years: Courier Columnist May Have Been Oldest Working U.S. Journalist," *JS Online,* www.jsonline.com/story/index.aspx?id=303103 (June 5, 2007).

"Richard Prince's Journal-isms: Mattiebelle Woods, Working Journalist, Dies at 102,"*The Maynard Institute,* www.maynardije.org/columns/dickprince/050218_prince/ (June 5, 2007).

"Woods Was the Life of the City's Parties," *JS Online,* www.jsonline.com/story/index.aspx?id=302970 (June 5, 2007).

—Tina Gianoulis

Samuel F. Yette

1929—

Journalist, photographer

In the summer of 1956 Samuel F. Yette teamed with photographer and author Gordon Parks to create a four-part series on racial segregation for *Life* magazine. As a reporter for the Washington and Baltimore *Afro-American*, Yette covered the major events of the civil rights movement, including the Montgomery bus boycott, the organizational meetings of the Southern Christian Leadership Conference (SCLC), and the 1957 march on Washington. He was fired as *Newsweek* magazine's Washington correspondent after the publication of his 1971 book, *The Choice,* in which he claimed that there were "genocidal schemes" high up in the U.S. government to commit "guerilla warfare" against black Americans. As a freelance journalist and columnist Yette continued to spark dialogue and incite controversy with his outspoken and sometimes radical analyses.

Founded Student Newspaper

Samuel Frederick Yette, pronounced "Yet," was born on July 2, 1929, in Harriman, Tennessee, the 13th child of Frank Mack and Cora Lee (Rector) Yette. Although his mother had only an eighth-grade education, she saw to it that all of her children went to college. Yette told the National Visionary Leadership Project: "We had extraordinary parents...they raised families dedicated to education...no matter what we had to do to get an education." Indeed, some of Yette's siblings were forced to leave Tennessee for secondary school. Yette was able to attend Campbell High School

in nearby Rockwood, where he was mentored by the principal John Brown Olinger.

Yette's interest in journalism was kindled in childhood as he read the newspaper to his father every evening. After one year at Morristown College in Tennessee, Yette transferred to Tennessee State University where he founded and edited the student newspaper *The Meter* and served on the student council. When the Korean War draft threatened to interrupt his education, the university's president called the governor of Tennessee and arranged for Yette to finish school first.

In his first integrated educational experience, Yette graduated at the top his class from the U.S. Air Force's Fixed-Wire Communications School. However racial discrimination and harassment almost kept him from completing Officer Candidate School.

Launched Journalism Career

Yette became a high school English teacher and coach, a sportswriter for the *Chattanooga Times,* and a sportscaster at WMFS radio. In 1955 he enrolled in journalism school at Indiana University in Bloomington, as one of only two black students. Despite a racist environment, he reported on politics and medicine for the *Indiana Daily Student.* When he was inducted into Sigma Delta Chi, the national journalism fraternity, in 1956 Yette persuaded the university to allow noted black journalist Carl T. Rowan to speak at his induction ceremony. Yette's master's thesis was entitled *A Comparative Study of* Life *and* Ebony *Magazines.*

At a Glance . . .

Born Samuel Frederick Yette on July 2, 1929, in Harriman, TN; married Sadie Lee Walton, 1958 (died 1983); children: Frederick Walton, Michael Lewis. *Education:* Tennessee State University, BS, English, 1951; Indiana University, MA, journalism, 1959. *Military Service:* U.S. Air Force, communications and information officer, second lieutenant, 1951-53, reserve captain, 1953-63. *Religion:* Baptist. *Politics:* Independent.

Career: Campbell High School, Rockwood, TN, teacher and coach, 1953-54; Howard High School, Chattanooga, TN, teacher, 1954-55; *Chattanooga Times,* sportswriter, 1954-56; freelance journalist and photographer, 1956–; *Afro-American Newspapers,* Washington, DC, Baltimore, MD, reporter, 1956-57, columnist 1976-79; *Ebony* magazine, associate editor, 1957-59; Tuskegee Institute, Tuskegee, AL, Information Office Director, 1959-62; *Journal Herald,* Dayton, OH, city hall reporter, 1962-63; OEO, Washington, DC, special assistant for civil rights, 1965-68; *Newsweek,* Washington, DC, correspondent, 1968-72; Howard University, Washington, DC, journalism professor, 1972-80s, University Scholar, 1977-80s; Cottage Books & Posters, Silver Spring, MD, proprietor, 1982–; BET, Washington, DC, political commentator, 1987-88; WHMM-TV, *Talk TV Politics,* host, 1991-92; syndicated columnist, 1995–; Knoxville College, Knoxville, TN, writer-in-residence, 2006.

Memberships: Anthony J. Cebrun Journalism Center, board member; Capitol Press Club, vice president; Morristown College, trustee; Sigma Delta Chi; Society of Professional Journalists, president of Washington Chapter.

Awards: Prentiss Institute, doctor of humanities, 1971; Black Academy of Arts and Letters, Non-Fiction Work of Distinction, for *The Choice,* 1972; Capitol Press Club, Special Book, Award for *The Choice,* 1972; Society of Professional Journalists, Hall of Fame, 2000.

Addresses: *Office*—Cottage Books & Posters, PO Box 2071, Silver Spring, MD 20915.

Gordon Parks, *Life*'s first black staff photographer, would become famous for his photo essays of segregated, poverty-stricken America contrasted with the glamour of elite white society. Yette's travels through Alabama with Parks made them lifelong friends and sparked Yette's interest in photography. He described the experience in a *Tennessee Tribune* profile in August of 1996: "As reporter, researcher, pack-horse, camera-loader, Kian scout, front-man and chauffeur for Gordon, I began to appreciate the importance of photography as a powerful—and sometimes indispensable—tool in modern storytelling. On train rides, he would suck up magazines or newspapers and have me select the best and worst pictures, and tell why. I learned also of the responsibility the journalist assumes for the welfare of those he exposes in his process."

When the *Life* series appeared in 1957, Yette's career as a journalist took off. He was almost shot while covering a 1957 trial in Florida for the *Afro-American*. As the first black reporter at the *Dayton Journal Herald*, Yette made enemies when he took the City Hall beat away from racist reporters in 1962. He covered Dr. Martin Luther King, Jr., and came to know him well. In 1963 Yette served as the Peace Corps's press liaison for Sargent Shriver's trip to Africa and the following year he was appointed executive secretary of the Corps.

Fired by Newsweek

After two years as special assistant for civil rights at the U.S. Office of Economic Opportunity (OEO), Yette became *Newsweek*'s first black Washington correspondent. Suddenly he was a public figure, appearing on *Meet the Press* and other television programs. No one at *Newsweek* knew about the book he was writing.

The basic premise of *The Choice*—"Blacks are given a choice in this country: 'to accept their miserable lot or die'"—was bound to cause controversy. In his second chapter, "The Great Society Pacification Programs," Yette analyzed Lyndon Johnson's politics of black containment: "President Johnson's 'unconditional war on poverty' never became a general war.... The rhetoric and occasional good intentions aside, the effect of it all was mainly to further the establishment war against those in the society already defeated. OEO, in fact, would become a new vehicle for black oppression–at white profit. President Kennedy had taken official notice of black discontent; President Johnson would move to pacify it." Yette was quoted in the *Tennessee Tribune* in April of 1996: "The book dealt with things they did not want people to know about at the time. There were those well-placed in our government who were determined to have a final solution for the race issue in this country—not unlike Hitler's 'Final Solution' for Jews 50 years earlier in Germany. I wrote this and documented it. It caused the Nixon White House to say to *Newsweek* in effect, 'Don't come back until you are rid of him.'" Yette sued *Newsweek* over his firing. The ensuing court battle went on for six years. Although the initial verdict was in Yette's favor, the decision was eventually reversed and the U.S. Supreme Court declined to hear his appeal.

In *The Choice* Yette reported that the Nixon administration was planning to revoke the *Washington Post*'s Miami television license and give it to President Richard Nixon's friend Bebe Rebozo. According to Yette this revelation initiated the *Post*'s break with the administration, enabling to paper to pursue its Watergate reporting, which led eventually to Nixon's resignation. Yette also claimed that an award-winning *Post* story—concerning the role of U.S.-produced Asian rice sales in the Vietnam War—had been lifted from *The Choice*.

Joined Howard University Faculty

Yette joined Howard University as its first tenured journalism professor and continued writing and lecturing. In September of 1977 he was one of five journalists invited to tour the People's Republic of China. During a 1979 sabbatical he was the only journalist invited to accompany SCLC delegates on their historic peace mission to Lebanon to meet with Yasser Arafat, leader of the Palestinian Liberation Organization. Over the course of that year Yette pursued his growing interest in photojournalism and began marketing his photographs.

Yette's photograph of the Great Wall was sold as a poster in the Chinese pavilion at the World's Fair in Knoxville, Tennessee. Sales from the poster financed the republication of *The Choice* by his own company, Cottage Books, founded in 1982. In 1984 Yette and his son published a pictorial history of the civil rights movement.

Following his retirement from Howard in the mid-1980s, Yette continued to work as a freelance journalist and photographer, contributing to numerous publications including *People, Time,* and *National Geographic,* and mounting several photographic exhibitions. He documented the 1984 and 1988 presidential campaigns of the Rev. Jesse L. Jackson. In 1987 and 1988 Yette was a political commentator on Black Entertainment Television (BET) and in 1991 and 1992 he hosted *Talk TV Politics* on WHMM-TV.

In 1995 Yette launched a weekly syndicated black newspaper column. In a 1996 column he called Israeli Prime Minister Benjamin Netanyahu "Hitler's unacknowledged disciple" and charged that "Jewish political power...hold[s] American politicians hostage, often while betraying this nation's best interests." In response to pressure from the Jewish community the *Philadelphia Tribune,* which had printed the column twice, disavowed it.

Yette's political views were clearly stated in the *Philadelphia Tribune* in 1995: "I am for affirmative action, desegregation in general, self-reliance, gun registration, nationally organized boycotts, Congress' declaration before war, campaign finance reform, strict separation of church and state, sex education, the nationalization of the United States postal service, progressive income tax and parental notification for abortions."

Selected writings

Books

The Choice: The Issue of Black Survival in America, Putnam, 1971, Cottage, 1982, 1996.
(With Frederick Walton Yette) *Washington and Two Marches, 1963 and 1983: The Third American Revolution,* Cottage, 1984.

Periodicals

"Samuel F. Yette Charges 'Imitation and Thievery,'" *Afro-American Red Star,* July 6, 1996, p. B1.
"Learned Behavior Characterizes Some Jews Actions," *Philadelphia Tribune,* October 18, 1996, p. A2.
"Samuel F. Yette: Columnist," *Tennessee Tribune,* Vol. 8, No. 30, November 13, 1996, p. 6.

Sources

Periodicals

Jewish Exponent, November 7, 1996, p. 1.
Philadelphia Tribune, July 18, 1995, p. 8.
Tennessee Tribune, April 9, 1996, p. 5; August 27, 1996, p. 20.

On-line

Cottage Books & Posters, www.merchantamerica. com/blackbooks-posters/index.php?ba=home (August 16, 2007).
"Distinguished Journalist and Author Samuel F. Yette Takes Post at Knoxville College," *Knoxville College,* http://knoxvillecollege.edu/press/YetteKCPress-Conf.pdf (August 16, 2007).
"Samuel F(rederick) Yette," *Contemporary Authors Online,* http://galenet.galegroup.com/servlet/Bio-RC (August 16, 2007).
"Samuel Yette," *National Visionary Leadership Project,* http://209.213.221.46/nvlpmembertier/ visionariest1/visionarypages/2004visionaries/yette-samuel/index.asp (August 16, 2007).
"Samuel Yette Biography," *HistoryMakers,* www.the-historymakers.com/biography/biography.asp?bioindex=800&category=mediaMakers (August 16, 2007).

—Margaret Alic

Young Jeezy

1977—

Rap and hip-hop artist, producer

Young Jeezy, photograph. Scott Gries/Getty Images.

Raised in poverty by a single mother, young Jay Jenkins learned to make money and earn respect in the few, mostly unlawful, arenas open to him on the streets of his Atlanta neighborhood. Starting out in such enterprises as selling illegal cell phones in alleys, Jenkins had a driving ambition to escape the dead-end life that seemed inevitable for some inner-city youth. He was drawn to rap music because hip-hop artists and their songs appeared to be the only cultural medium telling the truth about the lives of young people of color in the inner city.

Jenkins eventually entered the music industry as a producer, but he did not stay behind the scenes for long. In 2001 he released his first album under the rap name "Lil' J," and by 2003 he had become Young Jeezy, one of the most popular rappers; first in Atlanta, then throughout the South, and finally across the United States. Young Jeezy's authentic experience on the streets endears him to his fans, but not to critics of rap and hip-hop culture, who condemn the references to drugs and guns in many of his lyrics. However, Jeezy sees himself as a teacher as well as an entertainer. As someone who knows the hopeless life of the streets, he

hopes to motivate young men like himself with a message of hope and honesty. As he says on the Web site of his record label, Def Jam, "I don't just do music for the clubs, I do music for the struggle. I do music for...the kids who ain't got no sense of direction. I'm trying to restore some of the morals back into the game, as far as the street."

Grew Up in Southern Ghetto

Jay Jenkins was born on October 12, 1977, in Columbia, South Carolina. His parents were not married, and his mother soon took her baby son back to her home in Macon, Georgia. Jenkins was raised by his mother and grandmother in Macon and moved to Atlanta as a teenager. There he lived in the rough Fourth Ward area of town, where he quickly learned how hard life could be for a poor African-American youth. Young Jeezy described the roots of his ambition in an interview with Nooreen Kara on the British Web site *The Situation,* "I don't want to be a statistic. I don't wanna be dead or in jail without nothing. It happens a lot where I'm from; people get killed, people go to jail, and people forget about them. I won't let that happen to me."

At a Glance . . .

Born Jay Jenkins on October 12, 1977, in Columbia, SC; children: one son.

Career: Corporate Thugz Entertainment, co-founder and chief executive officer, 1998–; Boyz N Da Hood, rap artist, 2004; solo artist, 2005–.

Addresses: *Office*—c/o Corporate Thugz Entertainment, 2221 Peachtree Rd., Suite D-602, Atlanta, GA 30309. *Web*—www.corporatethugzent.com.

Determined to survive and succeed, Jay Jenkins took whatever opportunities came his way, legitimate or not. He understood early that on the streets his image was all-important and, after earning $200 working for his uncle's construction company, he asked for the money to be paid with one twenty dollar bill and the rest in ones, so that he would have a bigger roll of cash to show his friends. Along with working for his uncle, Jenkins became what he would later call a "hustler," selling whatever he could to make money. Beginning with stolen goods, such as cell phones, he soon progressed to stealing cars and selling drugs.

Jenkins was still focused on a way out of the street life, however, and hip-hop music seemed to offer an opportunity. Hip-hop culture rose out of poor urban black culture, and though Jay Jenkins had little education, his early years had given him authentic credentials to enter the rap music business. With a friend named Demetrius Ellerbee (stage name "Kinky B"), he started a music company called Corporate Thugz Entertainment in 1998, intending to work behind the scenes as a music producer. He soon began to feel that he had the talent and experience to become a positive voice within U.S. hip-hop culture and the young, black, urban community.

Began Career as Rapper

Jenkins began releasing mixtapes of his work, first as Lil' J, then as Young Jeezy. Mixtapes, or homemade compilations of a rapper's work, are a staple of the hip-hop music scene and are eagerly bought by fans who value their underground nature. In 2001, Lil' J's first CD, *Thuggin' Under the Influence,* was released, followed in 2003 by *Come Shop Wit' Me.* Produced by Corporate Thugz Entertainment, *Come Shop Wit' Me* was Jenkins first appearance as Young Jeezy, and the album sold tens of thousands of copies.

In 2004, rap legend P Diddy approached Young Jeezy about making an album for his Bad Boy Records label. Jeezy agreed to make one album as part of a studio

group called Boyz in Da Hood, which included fellow rappers Big Gee and Big Duke. The three released the album *Boyz in Da Hood*, which reached number five on the *Billboard Magazine* chart of 200 most popular albums.

Young Jeezy was determined to make it as a solo performer, and in 2005 he signed with the respected rap record label Def Jam. His first major label album, *Let's Get It: Thug Motivation 101,* sold 172,000 copies during the first week of its release, rocketing to number two on *Billboard's* chart. In 2006, Def Jam released *Inspiration: Thug Motivation 102,* which was also popular with Jeezy's fans. In 2007, Young Jeezy joined two rapper friends, Slick Pulla and Blood Raw, to form a new group they called USDA, or United Streets and Dopeboyz of America. Together they made an album called *Cold Summer, The Authorized Mixtape.*

Wrote Controversial Lyrics

Young Jeezy's gangster past, gravelly voice, and street-smart style gave him credibility among fans of rap, but the explicit references to drugs, guns, and sex have been controversial. During the early part of his career, Atlanta radio stations were reluctant to play his songs. Critics of Young Jeezy's lifestyle also point to two arrests, one in March 2006 in Miami for carrying a concealed weapon, and one in Macon, Georgia, in May 2007 for disorderly conduct. Jeezy has for the most part remained unconcerned about mainstream response to either his music or his life. Though he has worked to become successful, he has consistently refused to become commercial and has little interest in crossing over to other genres. He has always considered the poor people of the street to be his true audience, and they, he feels, will understand his message.

Jeezy's sharp lyrics and tight rhymes deliver vivid images, and he considers himself to be like a motivational speaker, using his words to inspire change in his listeners. His message is down-to-earth and gritty, like the hard life of the hustler. In songs like "Talk to 'Em", he speaks to the younger generation about the hard, cold side of the gangster life. "Soul Survivor" is an uplifting anthem of endurance and triumph over hard times, and "Don't Get Caught" offers advice about the incomparable black male experience of being stopped by the police.

One of Young Jeezy's biggest controversies arose out of one of his street nicknames, "Snowman." Some commentators on the rap scene claim that Jeezy got the name because of his habit of adorning himself with "ice," or glittery jewelry, but many others point out that "snow" is a street name for cocaine, which Jeezy admits to selling during his youth. When Young Jeezy's music company began selling t-shirts with a picture of a glowering snowman, the news network CNN issued a story about the drug connection. In response, many high schools banned the shirts, prompting Jeezy to explain to Nooreen Kara, "You can't just look at the snowman and say that it glorifies one thing. It doesn't glorify drug use, it glorifies the ultimate hustler, the struggle, the movement, the people who ain't got it and are trying to get it."

When Hurricane Katrina hit the U.S. Gulf Coast in August 2005, Jeezy demonstrated that his support for the poor and the disenfranchised went further than the words of his songs. He not only collected enough food, water, clothing, and other supplies to fill twelve trailer trucks that he sent to help survivors, but he opened his own large house in Georgia to over a dozen refugees left homeless by the storm.

In 2006, Jeezy launched his own line of clothing. He had intended to call it USDA, like his music group, but the U.S. Department of Agriculture objected, and Jeezy changed the name to 8732, the letters USDA when entered into a phone for a text message. Such in-jokes are an important part of the culture of rap music, allowing fans to feel a part of an outlaw society.

In spite of disapproval from the critics of gangsta rap, Young Jeezy has continued to develop his career, doing guest appearances on the albums of such rap stars as Fabolous and Lil' Wayne and live performances like the March-April 2007 Street Dreams Tour. On November 12, 2006, he performed several songs on Black Entertainment Television's first annual Hip-Hop Awards.

Selected discography

Thuggin' Under the Influence (as Lil' J), 404 Music Group, 2001.
Come Shop Wit' Me, Corporate Thugz Entertainment, 2003.
Let's Get It: Thug Motivation 101, Def Jam, 2005.
The Inspiration: Thug Motivation 102, Def Jam, 2006.
Trap or Die (with DJ Drama), Aphilliates, 2006.

Tha Streets iz Watchin' (with DJ Drama), Aphilliates, 2006.
$nowman, Bcd Music Group, 2006.
You Can't Ban the Snowman, Bcd Music Group, 2006.
Young Jeezy Presents USDA: Cold Summer, The Authorized Mixtape, Def Jam, 2007.

Sources

Periodicals

Billboard, December 16, 2006, p. 38; June 2, 2007, p. 43; June 9, 2007, p. 71.
Entertainment Weekly, October 7, 2005, p. 74.
Esquire, February 2006, p. 66-8.
The Fader, September 2006, p. 106-14.
New York, December 11, 2006, p. 88-90.
Rolling Stone, November 16, 2006, p. 86-8; December 28, 2006, p. 114.

On-line

Corporate Thugz Entertainment, www.corporatethugzent.com (August 6, 2007).
Kara, Nooreen, "Young Jeezy: Interview," *The Situation,* www.thesituation.co.uk/us_interviews/06/young_jeezy/young_jeezy.html (July 23, 2007).
Reid, Shaheem, "Young Jeezy Opens His Home To Gulf Coast Disaster Victims," *MTV,* www.mtv.com/news/articles/1509747/20050916/jeezy_young.jhtml (July 23, 2007).
"Weapons Charges Against Young Jeezy Dropped," *Dirty South Rap Dot Com,* http://dirtysouthrap.com/news/2006/05/17/weapons-charges-against-young-jeezy-dropped/ (July 23, 2007).
"Young Jeezy," *Def Jam Recordings,* www.defjam.com/site/artist_home.php?artist_id=567 (July 23, 2007).

—Tina Gianoulis

Cumulative Nationality Index

Volume numbers appear in **bold**

American

Aaron, Hank **5**
Abbott, Robert Sengstacke **27**
Abdul-Jabbar, Kareem **8**
Abdur-Rahim, Shareef **28**
Abele, Julian **55**
Abernathy, Ralph David **1**
Abu-Jamal, Mumia **15**
Ace, Johnny **36**
Adams Earley, Charity **13, 34**
Adams, Eula L. **39**
Adams, Floyd, Jr. **12**
Adams, Jenoyne **60**
Adams, Johnny **39**
Adams, Leslie **39**
Adams, Oleta **18**
Adams, Osceola Macarthy **31**
Adams, Sheila J. **25**
Adams, Yolanda **17**
Adams-Campbell, Lucille L. **60**
Adams-Ender, Clara **40**
Adderley, Julian "Cannonball" **30**
Adderley, Nat **29**
Adkins, Rod **41**
Adkins, Rutherford H. **21**
Ailey, Alvin **8**
Akil, Mara Brock **60**
Al-Amin, Jamil Abdullah **6**
Albright, Gerald **23**
Alcorn, George Edward, Jr. **59**
Alert, Kool DJ Red **33**
Alexander, Archie Alphonso **14**
Alexander, Clifford **26**
Alexander, Joyce London **18**
Alexander, Khandi **43**
Alexander, Margaret Walker **22**
Alexander, Sadie Tanner Mossell **22**
Alexander, Shaun **58**
Ali, Hana Yasmeen **52**
Ali, Laila **27, 63**
Ali, Muhammad **2, 16, 52**
Allain, Stephanie **49**
Allen, Byron **3, 24**
Allen, Debbie **13, 42**
Allen, Ethel D. **13**
Allen, Marcus **20**
Allen, Robert L. **38**
Allen, Samuel W. **38**
Allen, Tina **22**
Allen-Buillard, Melba **55**
Alston, Charles **33**
Amaker, Norman Carey **63**
Amaker, Tommy **62**

Amerie **52**
Ames, Wilmer **27**
Amos, Emma **63**
Amos, John b8, **62**
Amos, Wally **9**
Anderson, Anthony **51**
Anderson, Carl **48**
Anderson, Charles Edward **37**
Anderson, Eddie "Rochester" **30**
Anderson, Elmer **25**
Anderson, Jamal **22**
Anderson, Marian **2, 33**
Anderson, Michael P. **40**
Anderson, Mike **63**
Anderson, Norman B. **45**
Anderson, William G(ilchrist), D.O. **57**
Andrews, Benny **22, 59**
Andrews, Bert **13**
Andrews, Raymond **4**
Angelou, Maya **1, 15**
Ansa, Tina McElroy **14**
Anthony, Carmelo **46**
Anthony, Wendell **25**
Archer, Dennis **7, 36**
Archie-Hudson, Marguerite **44**
Arkadie, Kevin **17**
Armstrong, Louis **2**
Armstrong, Robb **15**
Armstrong, Vanessa Bell **24**
Arnez J, **53**
Arnold, Tichina **63**
Arnwine, Barbara **28**
Arrington, Richard **24**
Arroyo, Martina **30**
Artest, Ron **52**
Asante, Molefi Kete **3**
Ashanti **37**
Ashe, Arthur **1, 18**
Ashford, Emmett **22**
Ashford, Evelyn **63**
Ashford, Nickolas **21**
Ashley-Ward, Amelia **23**
Atkins, Cholly **40**
Atkins, Erica **34**
Atkins, Juan **50**
Atkins, Russell **45**
Atkins, Tina **34**
Aubert, Alvin **41**
Auguste, Donna **29**
Austin, Gloria **63**
Austin, Jim **63**
Austin, Junius C. **44**
Austin, Lovie **40**

Austin, Patti **24**
Avant, Clarence **19**
Ayers, Roy **16**
Babatunde, Obba **35**
Bacon-Bercey, June **38**
Badu, Erykah **22**
Bahati, Wambui **60**
Bailey, Buster **38**
Bailey, Clyde **45**
Bailey, DeFord **33**
Bailey, Philip **63**
Bailey, Radcliffe **19**
Bailey, Xenobia **11**
Baines, Harold **32**
Baiocchi, Regina Harris **41**
Baisden, Michael **25**
Baker, Anita **21, 48**
Baker, Augusta **38**
Baker, Dusty **8, 43**
Baker, Ella **5**
Baker, Gwendolyn Calvert **9**
Baker, Houston A., Jr. **6**
Baker, Josephine **3**
Baker, LaVern **26**
Baker, Maxine B. **28**
Baker, Thurbert **22**
Baldwin, James **1**
Ballance, Frank W. **41**
Ballard, Allen Butler, Jr. **40**
Ballard, Hank **41**
Bambaataa, Afrika **34**
Bambara, Toni Cade **10**
Bandele, Asha **36**
Banks, Ernie **33**
Banks, Jeffrey **17**
Banks, Michelle **59**
Banks, Tyra **11, 50**
Banks, William **11**
Banner, David **55**
Baquet, Dean **63**
Baraka, Amiri **1, 38**
Barber, Ronde **41**
Barber, Tiki **57**
Barboza, Anthony **10**
Barclay, Paris **37**
Barden, Don H. **9, 20**
Barker, Danny **32**
Barkley, Charles **5**
Barlow, Roosevelt **49**
Barnes, Roosevelt "Booba" **33**
Barnes, Steven **54**
Barnett, Amy Du Bois **46**
Barnett, Etta Moten **56**
Barnett, Marguerite **46**

Barney, Lem **26**
Barnhill, David **30**
Barrax, Gerald William **45**
Barrett, Andrew C. **12**
Barrett, Jacquelyn **28**
Barrino, Fantasia **53**
Barry, Marion S(hepilov, Jr.) **7, 44**
Barthe, Richmond **15**
Basie, Count **23**
Basquiat, Jean-Michel **5**
Bass, Charlotta Spears **40**
Bassett, Angela **6, 23, 62**
Bates, Daisy **13**
Bates, Karen Grigsby **40**
Bates, Peg Leg **14**
Bath, Patricia E. **37**
Baugh, David **23**
Baylor, Don **6**
Baylor, Helen **36**
Beach, Michael **26**
Beal, Bernard B. **46**
Beals, Jennifer **12**
Beals, Melba Patillo **15**
Bearden, Romare **2, 50**
Beasley, Jamar **29**
Beasley, Phoebe **34**
Beatty, Talley **35**
Bechet, Sidney **18**
Beckford, Tyson **11**
Beckham, Barry **41**
Belafonte, Harry **4**
Bell, Derrick **6**
Bell, James "Cool Papa" **36**
Bell, James A. **50**
Bell, James Madison **40**
Bell, Michael **40**
Bell, Robert Mack **22**
Bellamy, Bill **12**
Bellamy, Terry **58**
Belle, Albert **10**
Belle, Regina **1, 51**
Belton, Sharon Sayles **9, 16**
Benét, Eric **28**
Ben-Israel, Ben Ami **11**
Benjamin, Andre **45**
Benjamin, Regina **20**
Benjamin, Tritobia Hayes **53**
Bennett, George Harold "Hal" **45**
Bennett, Gwendolyn B. **59**
Bennett, Lerone, Jr. **5**
Benson, Angela **34**
Bentley, Lamont **53**
Berry , Halle **4, 19, 57**
Berry, Bertice **8, 55**

Cumulative Occupation Index

Volume numbers appear in **bold**

Government and politics--international

Cumulative Subject Index

Volume numbers appear in **bold**

Active Ministers Engaged in Nurturance (AMEN)
King, Bernice **4**

Actors Equity Association
Lewis, Emmanuel **36**

Actuarial science
Hill, Jessie, Jr. **13**

ACT UP
See AIDS Coalition to Unleash Power

Acustar, Inc.
Farmer, Forest **1**

ADC
See Agricultural Development Council

Addiction Research and Treatment Corporation
Cooper, Andrew W. **36**

Adoption and foster care
Baker, Josephine **3**
Blacque, Taurean **58**
Clements, George **2**
Gossett, Louis, Jr. **7**
Hale, Clara **16**
Hale, Lorraine **8**
Oglesby, Zena **12**

Adventures in Movement (AIM)
Morgan, Joe Leonard **9**

Advertising
Barboza, Anthony **10**
Burrell, Tom **21, 51**
Campbell, E. Simms **13**
Chisholm, Samuel J. **32**
Coleman, Donald **24, 62**
Cullers, Vincent T. **49**
Johnson, Beverly **2**
Jones, Caroline R. **29**
Jordan, Montell **23**
Lewis, Byron E. **13**
McKinney Hammond, Michelle **51**
Mingo, Frank **32**
Olden, Georg(e) **44**
Pinderhughes, John **47**
Roche, Joyce M. **17**

Advocates Scene
Seale, Bobby **3**

Aetna
Williams, Ronald A. **57**

AFCEA
See Armed Forces Communications and Electronics Associations

Affirmative action
Arnwine, Barbara **28**
Berry, Mary Frances **7**
Carter, Stephen L. **4**

Cumulative Name Index

Volume numbers appear in **bold**

Aaliyah 1979-2001 **30**
Aaron, Hank 1934— **5**
Aaron, Henry Louis *See Aaron, Hank*
Abacha, Sani 1943— **11**
Abbott, Diane (Julie) 1953— **9**
Abbott, Robert Sengstacke 1868-1940 **27**
Abdul-Jabbar, Kareem 1947— **8**
Abdulmajid, Iman Mohamed *See Iman*
Abdur-Rahim, Shareef 1976— **28**
Abele, Julian 1881-1950 **55**
Abernathy, Ralph David 1926-1990 **1**
Abrahams, Peter 1919— **39**
Abu-Jamal, Mumia 1954— **15**
Ace, Johnny 1929-1954 **36**
Achebe, (Albert) Chinua(lumogu) 1930— **6**
Acogny, Germaine 1944— **55**
Adams Earley, Charity (Edna) 1918— **13, 34**
Adams, Eula L. 1950— **39**
Adams, Floyd, Jr. 1945— **12**
Adams, H. Leslie *See Adams, Leslie*
Adams, Jenoyne (?)— **60**
Adams, Johnny 1932-1998 **39**
Adams, Leslie 1932— **39**
Adams, Oleta 19(?)(?)— **18**
Adams, Osceola Macarthy 1890-1983 **31**
Adams, Paul 1977— **50**
Adams, Sheila J. 1943— **25**
Adams, Yolanda 1961— **17**
Adams-Campbell, Lucille L. 1953— **60**
Adams-Ender, Clara 1939— **40**
Adderley, Julian "Cannonball" 1928-1975 **30**
Adderley, Nat 1931-2000 **29**
Adderley, Nathaniel *See Adderley, Nat*
Ade, Sunny King 1946— **41**
Adeniyi, Sunday *See Ade, Sunny King*
Adjaye, David 1966— **38**
Adkins, Rod 1958— **41**
Adkins, Rutherford H. 1924-1998 **21**
Adu, Helen Folasade *See Sade*
Agyeman Rawlings, Nana Konadu 1948— **13**

Agyeman, Jaramogi Abebe *See Cleage, Albert B., Jr.*
Aidoo, Ama Ata 1942— **38**
Aiken, Loretta Mary *See Mabley, Jackie "Moms"*
Ailey, Alvin 1931-1989 **8**
Ake, Claude 1939-1996 **30**
Akil, Mara Brock 1970— **60**
Akinnuoye-Agbaje, Adewale 1967— **56**
Akomfrah, John 1957— **37**
Akunyili, Dora Nkem 1954— **58**
Al-Amin, Jamil Abdullah 1943— **6**
Albright, Gerald 1947— **23**
Alcindor, Ferdinand Lewis *See Abdul-Jabbar, Kareem*
Alcorn, George Edward, Jr. 1940— **59**
Alert, Kool DJ Red 19(?)(?)— **33**
Alexander, Archie Alphonso 1888-1958 **14**
Alexander, Clifford 1933— **26**
Alexander, John Marshall *See Ace, Johnny*
Alexander, Joyce London 1949— **18**
Alexander, Khandi 1957— **43**
Alexander, Margaret Walker 1915-1998 **22**
Alexander, Sadie Tanner Mossell 1898-1989 **22**
Alexander, Shaun 1977— **58**
Ali Mahdi Mohamed 1940— **5**
Ali, Ayaan Hirsi 1969— **58**
Ali, Hana Yasmeen 1976— **52**
Ali, Laila 1977— **27, 63**
Ali, Mohammed Naseehu 1971— **60**
Ali, Muhammad 1942— **2, 16, 52**
Allain, Stephanie 1959— **49**
Allen, Byron 1961— **3, 24**
Allen, Debbie 1950— **13, 42**
Allen, Ethel D. 1929-1981 **13**
Allen, Marcus 1960— **20**
Allen, Richard 1760-1831 **14**
Allen, Robert L. 1942— **38**
Allen, Samuel W. 1917— **38**
Allen, Tina 1955— **22**
Allen-Buillard, Melba 1960— **55**
Alston, Charles Henry 1907-1997 **33**
Amadi, Elechi 1934— **40**
Amaker, Harold Tommy, Jr. *See Amaker, Tommy*

Amaker, Norman Carey 1935-2000 **63**
Amaker, Tommy 1965— **62**
Amerie 1980— **52**
Ames, Wilmer 1950-1993 **27**
Amin, Idi 1925-2003 **42**
Amos, Emma 1938— **63**
Amos, John 1941— b8, **62**
Amos, Valerie 1954— **41**
Amos, Wally 1937— **9**
Anderson, Anthony 1970— **51**
Anderson, Carl 1945-2004 **48**
Anderson, Charles Edward 1919-1994 **37**
Anderson, Eddie "Rochester" 1905-1977 **30**
Anderson, Elmer 1941— **25**
Anderson, Ho Che 1969— **54**
Anderson, Jamal 1972— **22**
Anderson, Marian 1902— **2, 33**
Anderson, Michael P. 1959-2003 **40**
Anderson, Mike 1959— **63**
Anderson, Norman B. 1955— **45**
Anderson, Viv 1956— **58**
Anderson, William G(ilchrist), D.O. 1927— **57**
Andre 3000 *See Benjamin, Andre*
Andrews, Benny 1930-2006 **22, 59**
Andrews, Bert 1929-1993 **13**
Andrews, Mark *See Sisqo*
Andrews, Raymond 1934-1991 **4**
Angelou, Maya 1928— **1, 15**
Anna Marie *See Lincoln, Abbey*
Annan, Kofi Atta 1938— **15, 48**
Ansa, Tina McElroy 1949— **14**
Anthony, Carmelo 1984— **46**
Anthony, Michael 1930(?)— **29**
Anthony, Trey 1974— **63**
Anthony, Wendell 1950— **25**
Archer, Dennis (Wayne) 1942— **7, 36**
Archer, Michael D'Angelo *See D'Angelo*
Archer, Osceola *See Adams, Osceola Macarthy*
Archie-Hudson, Marguerite 1937— **44**
Arinze, Francis Cardinal 1932— **19**
Aristide, Jean-Bertrand 1953— **6, 45**
Arkadie, Kevin 1957— **17**
Armah, Ayi Kwei 1939— **49**
Armatrading, Joan 1950— **32**

Armstrong, (Daniel) Louis 1900-1971 **2**
Armstrong, Robb 1962— **15**
Armstrong, Vanessa Bell 1953— **24**
Arnez J, 1966(?)— **53**
Arnold, Monica *See Monica*
Arnold, Tichina 1971— **63**
Arnwine, Barbara 1951(?)— **28**
Arrington, Richard 1934— **24**
Arroyo, Martina 1936— **30**
Artest, Ron 1979— **52**
Arthur, Owen 1949— **33**
Asante, Molefi Kete 1942— **3**
Ashanti 1980— **37**
Ashe, Arthur Robert, Jr. 1943-1993 **1, 18**
Ashford, Emmett 1914-1980 **22**
Ashford, Evelyn 1957— **63**
Ashford, Nickolas 1942— **21**
Ashley, Maurice 1966— **15, 47**
Ashley-Ward, Amelia 1957— **23**
Atkins, Cholly 1930-2003 **40**
Atkins, David *See Sinbad*
Atkins, Erica 1972(?)— *See Mary Mary*
Atkins, Jeffrey *See Ja Rule*
Atkins, Juan 1962— **50**
Atkins, Russell 1926— **45**
Atkins, Tina 1975(?)— *See Mary Mary*
Atyam, Angelina 1946— **55**
Aubert, Alvin 1930— **41**
Auguste, (Marie Carmele) Rose-Anne 1963— **13**
Auguste, Arnold A. 1946— **47**
Auguste, Donna 1958— **29**
Augustine, Jean 1937— **53**
Austin, Gloria 1956— **63**
Austin, Jim 1951— **63**
Austin, Junius C. 1887-1968 **44**
Austin, Lovie 1887-1972 **40**
Austin, Patti 1948— **24**
Avant, Clarence 19(?)(?)— **19**
Awoonor, Kofi 1935— **37**
Awoonor-Williams, George *See Awoonor, Kofi*
Awoyinka, Adesiji *See Siji*
Ayers, Roy 1940— **16**
Azikiwe, Nnamdi 1904-1996 **13**
Ba, Mariama 1929-1981 **30**
Babangida, Ibrahim (Badamasi) 1941— **4**
Babatunde, Obba 19(?)(?)— **35**